Computer Graphics & Animation

Computer Graphics & Animation

M.C. TRIVEDI
N.N. JANI
K.I. LAKHTARIA
G.M. DAVE

JAICO PUBLISHING HOUSE
Ahmedabad Bangalore Bhopal Bhubaneswar Chennai
Delhi Hyderabad Kolkata Lucknow Mumbai

Published by Jaico Publishing House
A-2 Jash Chambers, 7-A Sir Phirozshah Mehta Road
Fort, Mumbai - 400 001
jaicopub@jaicobooks.com
www.jaicobooks.com

COMPUTER GRAPHICS & ANIMATION
ISBN 978-81-8495-010-6

First Jaico Impression: 2009
Fourth Jaico Impression: 2012

Printed by
Pashupati Printers
1/429/16, Gali No. 1, Friends Colony
Industrial Area, G. T. Road, Shahdara, Delhi - 95

Dedicated to my parents

Acknowledgements

A number of people have given invaluable comments on the manuscript at various stages in the writing of this book. In this regard, I owe a debt of gratitude to Prof B.S. Garg, Chancellor, J.R.N. Rajasthan Vidhyapeeth University, Udaipur & Prof Lokesh Bhatt, Vice-Chancellor, J.R.N. Rajasthan Vidhyapeeth University, Udaipur.

I am grateful to Dr. R.K. Bharadwaj, Director, I.M.S. Ghaziabad, Dr. Ashok Patel, Director, M.C.A. programme, North Gujrat University, Patan, Dr. Sanjay M. Shah, Director, S.V. Institute of Computer Studies Kadi, and Dr. Neeraj Bhargawa, Director, M.C.A. programme, M.D.S University, Ajmer for his encouragement at the very outset of this project. I am also thankful to Dr. S.S. Sarangedevot, Director (Computer Science & IT), J.R.N. Rajasthan Vidhyapeeth University, Udaipur, from whom I received excellent support in writing this book.

I am also grateful to Dr. N.N. Jani, Director, Kadi Sarva University, Gandhinagar, Mr. K.I. Lakhtaria and Mr. G. Dave, who assisted me in writing this book.

Contents

Preface

It is now clear that development of large software systems is an extremely complex activity where there are ample opportunities for errors to occur. Computer graphics attempts to provide methods to handle these complexities and enables us to produce reliable software systems with maximum productivity.

This book is aimed at students who have had no previous training in computer graphics, and is suitable for a one-semester course. It covers the syllabi taught in the B.Tech and M.C.A. courses in Gujrat Technical University, Gandhi Nagar, Rajasthan Technical University, Kota, J.R.N. Rajasthan Vidhyapeeth University, Udaipur, M.P. Technical & U.P. Technical University, Lucknow. It will also be useful for a project-based introductory course in computer graphics wherein both the students and the instructor can follow the chapters in the order given both in the lectures as well as in the project.

CHAPTER 1

Computer Graphics – An Overview

1.1 INTRODUCTION

Ancient man used drawings to communicate even before he learnt to talk, write or count. There is a popular saying "A picture is worth a thousand words". The era of computers has added one more saying "A computer is worth a million pictures".

Now, with the advances in computer hardware and software, graphics has come full circle and more and more people are teaching and learning graphics, and communicating and sharing their ideas through this medium. By graphics, we mean sketching, drawing, artwork or any such pictorial representation of an object/process that conveys information. Graphics includes engineering drawings of buildings, machines, bridges, dams etc; scientific drawings; x – y curves; network and process flow charts. Graphics has entered the fields of business, education, entertainment, virtual presence on the web and virtual environments.

Computer graphics is the field of visual computing. The most familiar class of computer graphics involves movies and video games. The use of graphics through simulation and virtual reality with animation has influenced our lives.

Computer graphics can be categorized as:

- Interactive Computer Graphics
- Passive Computer Graphics

In passive computer graphics there is no option for user interaction, e.g., movies and interactive computer graphics is used interactively by users, e.g. games.

1.2 APPLICATIONS

- Presentation Graphics
- Painting & Drawing
- Photo Editing
- Image Processing
- CAD
- Animation & Games
- Scientific Visualization
- E-learning
- Simulations
- VR Systems

Presentation Graphics

It is used to produce information for reports or to generate slides with projectors. The information is in the form of text, charts, graphs etc. It is commonly used to summarize financial, statistical and mathematical reports and economic data.

- Presentation components: Slides/pages (web)
- Presentation process: Slide show/navigation
- Software tools: MS Power Point

Painting & Drawing

Drawing or painting to create objects is carried out by changing the colour of pixels (tiny dots) in the domain of graphical objects.

- Software Tools: Page maker (Adobe), Publisher (MS)

Photo Editing

This uses software tools that allow altering and enhancing of images and controlling aspects of images.

- Tools: Photoshop (adobe), Corel Draw (coral), Fire works (Macromedia)

Image Processing

Nowadays, computers are used to create pictures. Image processing involves techniques to modify existing pictures, such as photographs and TV scans. There are two basic applications of image processing:

1) Improving picture quality.
2) Machine perception of visual information.

- Software Tool: Photoshop (Adobe)

CAD (Computer-Aided Design)

Various CAD methods are now commonly used in the design of buildings, automobiles, aircraft, watercrafts, textiles and many other products.

Designers use Computer Graphics for:

1) Mechanical design
   - M/C design (3D)
2) Civil design
   - Structural design
   - Architectural view
3) Electronics design
   - PCB design
4) Air craft design
   - Aero dynamic modelling & design
     - Design factors – Air pressure
       - Velocity
       - Weight

Animation & Games

Computer graphic methods are now commonly used to create animation pictures and various video games. Animation is the presentation of a succession of images at the rate of 30 or more per second, which causes the brain to perceive the movement as fluid and smooth.

- Software tool: Flash

Scientific Visualization

Scientific computations often involve many large numbers. It is difficult for the human brain to make sense out of this large volume of numbers obtained at the end of scientific computations. A scientific visualization technique that uses computer graphics allows one to interpret numerical data and make sense out of them quickly. Scientific visualization allows us to contemplate, explore and understand scientific phenomena much better.

- Software tool: MATLAB

1.3 ACTIVE AND PASSIVE DEVICES

It is important to first consider the difference between an active and a passive graphics device. An active graphics device allows the user to communicate with the computer graphically. It has the ability to reposition the cursor and read its new position. Devices include the alphanumeric keyboard, digitizer, light pen, joystick, trackball or mouse. A passive graphics device simply draws pictures under computer control. Examples are the dot matrix printer and an electrostatic plotter, pen and ink plotter, film recorder and storage tube refresh and raster CRT display.

1.4 INPUT DEVICES

The input device is one of the major components of computer-aided design. It is a mechanism for communication between the operator and the system. The input device converts the information into electronic signals and sends it to the computer system. The basic functions of an input device are:

1) To start the programme
2) To initiate certain commands
3) To enter data consisting of words and numbers
4) To insert and modify the image on the CRT screen.

Various devices are available for data input in graphics workstations.

1) Keyboard

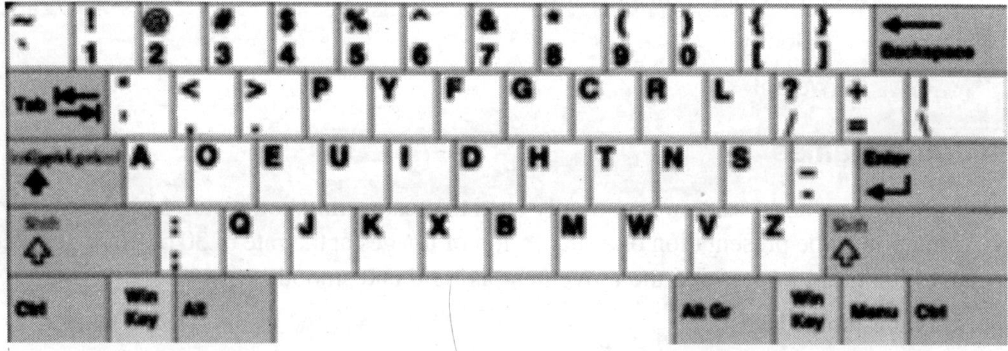

A keyboard is a peripheral, partially modelled after the typewriter keyboard. Keyboards are designed to input text and characters, as well as to operate a computer. Most of the keyboard keys produce non-graphical data as a label or number. Other keys such as function keys or control keys can produce actions when pressed, and other actions are made available by simultaneously pressing more than one action key. A multimedia keyboard offers special keys to access music, the web, and other frequently used programmes.

A keyboard is one of the primary methods of control in computer games. For instance, the arrow keys or a group of letters resembling the pattern of the arrow keys, can be used for movement of a game character. In many games, keys can be configured to the user's preferences.

2) Mouse

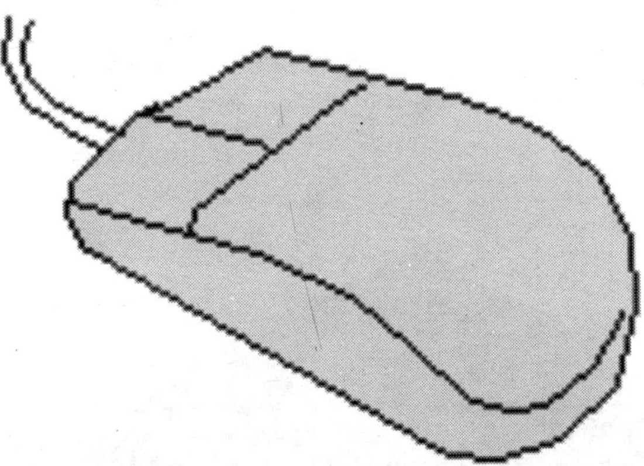

A mouse functions as a pointing device by detecting two-dimensional motion relative to its supporting surface. Physically, a mouse is a small hand–held box used to position the cursor on the screen. Wheels or rollers on the bottom of the mouse record the amount and direction of the movement. When the mouse is moved the cursor moves from its existing location. The mouse could be moved across your arm, and the screen cursor would move as well.

3) Graphics Tablet

A graphics tablet (digitizer) allows one to hand-draw images and graphics, similar to the way one draws images with a pencil and paper. These tablets may also be used to capture data of handwritten signatures.

A graphics tablet consists of a flat surface upon which the user may "draw" an image using an attached stylus, a pen-like drawing apparatus. The image generally does not appear on the tablet itself but, rather, is displayed on the computer monitor.

4) Trackball and Spaceball

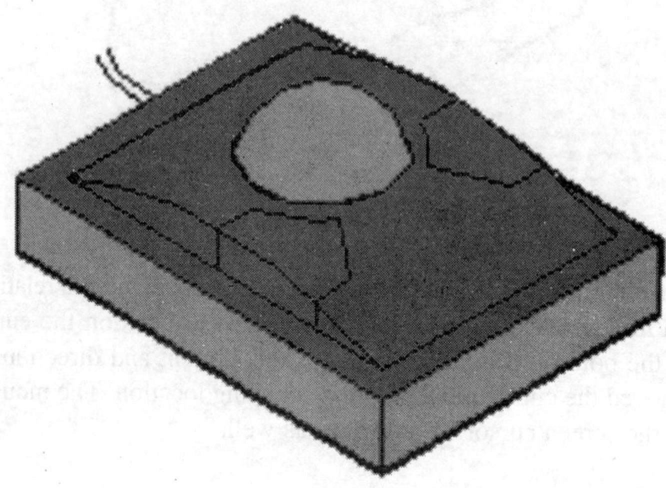

A trackball is a 2-D pointing device that resembles an upside-down mouse. Instead of rolling the mouse around the desktop, the user rotates the ball on the trackball with a thumb or finger. Trackballs are frequently used with Notebook Computers, which are often used where there is not enough desktop space to operate a mouse.

Large tracker balls are sometimes seen on computerized special-purpose workstations, such as the radar consoles in air-traffic control rooms or sonar equipment on a ship or submarine. Computer gamers have been able to successfully use trackballs in most modern computer games, including FPS, RPG, and RTS genres, with any slight loss of speed compensated for with an increase in precision.

Spaceball is an input device with *6 degrees of freedom* developed by 3DConnexion. Unlike trackball, spaceball does not actually move. The device is designed to ease navigation in 3D computer models, and is therefore primarily used by CAD and computer graphics professionals.

5) Touch Screen

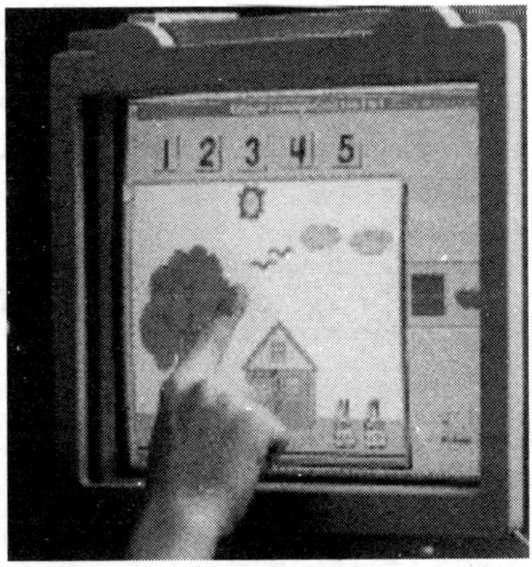

A display screen that is sensitive to the touch of a finger or stylus. Widely used on ATM machines, retail point-of-sale terminals, car navigation systems, medical monitors and industrial control panels, the touch screen offers several advantages. Touch screens also have assisted in recent changes in the design of personal digital assistant (PDA), satellite navigation and mobile phone devices, making these devices more usable. It is resistant to harsh environments, and on-screen buttons created by software enable an infinite number of options to be presented to the user without requiring a keyboard. They also accept hand printing, handwriting and graphics. All touch screens "digitize" the point of contact on screen into an X-Y coordinate.

6) Light Pen

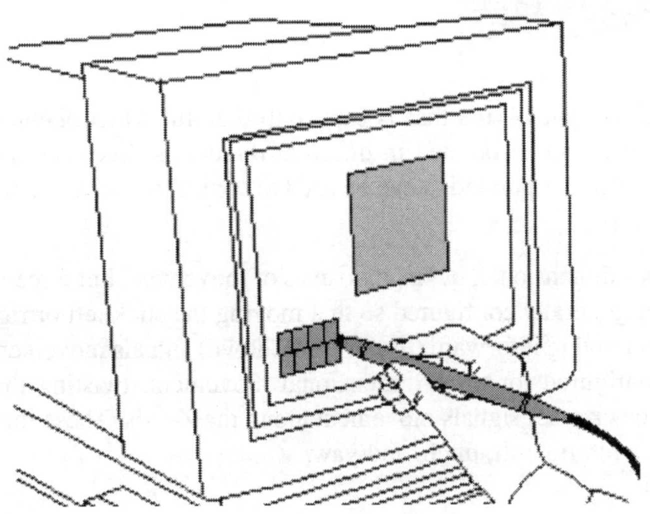

A light pen is an input device in the form of a light-sensitive wand used in conjunction with the computer's CRT monitor.

A light-sensitive stylus wired to a video terminal is used to draw pictures or select menu options. The user brings the pen to the desired point on the screen and presses the pen button to make contact. Screen pixels are constantly being refreshed. When the user presses the button, the pen senses light, and the pixel being illuminated at that instant identifies the screen location.

7) Joystick

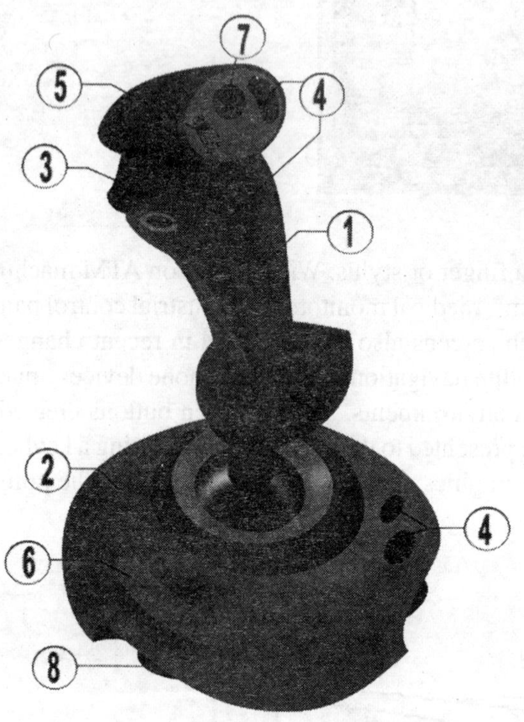

Joystick elements:

1. Stick
2. Base
3. Trigger
4. Extra buttons
5. Autofire switch
6. Throttle
7. Hat switch
8. Suction cup

A joystick is computer input device that is especially helpful when playing computer games. It consists of a handle that can be pointed in different directions. Because the computer can sense which direction the joystick is pointed, it can be used to control the movements of objects displayed on the computer screen.

Most joysticks are two-dimensional, having two axes of movement, but three-dimensional joysticks do exist. A joystick is generally configured so that moving the stick left or right signals movement along the X-axis, and moving it forward (up) or back (down) signals movement along the Y-axis. In joysticks that are configured for three-dimensional movement, twisting the stick left (counter-clockwise) or right (clockwise) signals movement along the Z-axis. These three axes - X Y and Z - are, in relation to an aircraft's roll, pitch, and yaw.

8) Data Glove

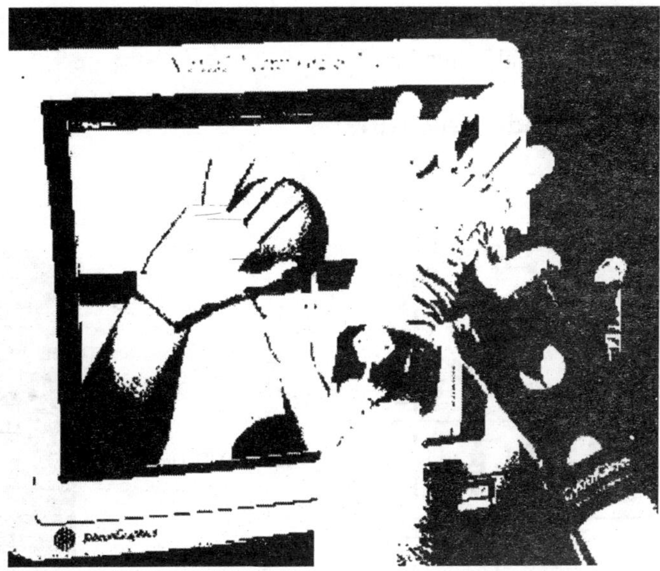

This is a glove used to report the position of a user's hand and fingers to a computer. For example in the above figure we can use it to grasp "virtual" object. The glove is constructed with a series of sensors that detect hand and finger motions. Input from the glove can be used to position or manipulate objects in a virtual scene.

9) Voice System

Speech recognition is the process of electronically converting a speech waveform (as the acoustic realization of a linguistic expression) into words (as a best-decoded sequence of linguistic units). It is used in some graphic workstations as an input device to accept voice command. The voice system input can be used to initial graphics operations or to enter data. These systems operate by matching an input against a predefined dictionary of words or phrases.

1.5 GRAPHICS PRIMITIVES

Elementary graphics building blocks are referred to as graphics primitives, such as a point, line or arc in two dimensions and a cylinder, cube and sphere in three dimensions. The main graphics primitive is a display device.

Display Devices: A display device is a device for presentation of information in visual form. For this, the information is acquired, stored or transmitted in various forms. When the input information is supplied as an electrical signal, the display is called an "electronic display". Electronic displays are available for presentation of visual and tactile information. Tactile electronic displays are usually intended for the blind or visually impaired; they use electro-mechanical parts to dynamically update a tactile image (usually of text) so that the image may be felt by the fingers.

Video Display Devices: Display devices present the output to the end user. Typically, a video monitor is a primary output device. The operation of monitors is based on CRT design; as well as some other technologies that are also available.

1.5.1 Refresh CRT (Cathode Ray Tube)

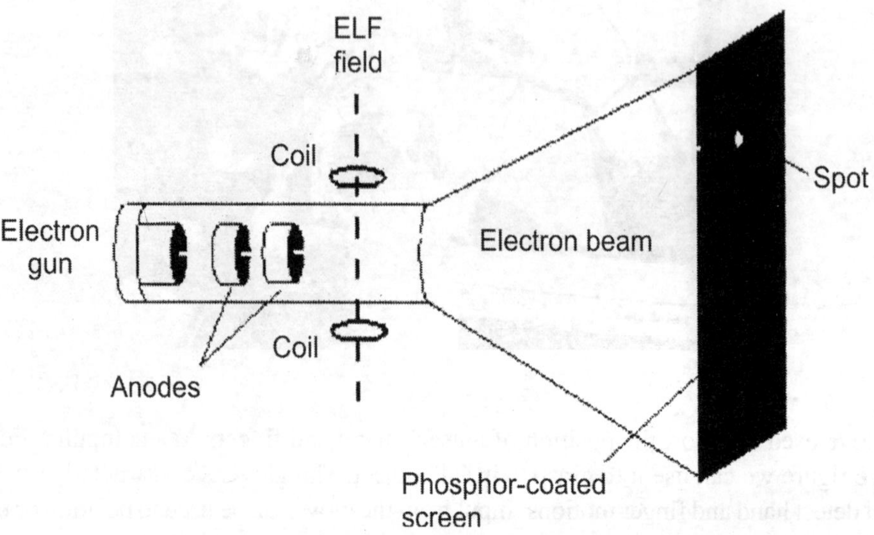

A cathode ray tube (CRT) is a specialized vacuum tube in which images are produced when an electron beam strikes a phosphorescent surface.

A cathode ray tube consists of several basic components, as shown in the above figure, and its operation is as given below:

1) The electron gun generates a narrow beam of electrons.
2) The anodes accelerate the electrons.
3) Deflecting coils produce an extremely low frequency electromagnetic field that allows for constant adjustment of the direction of the electron beam. There are two sets of deflecting coils: horizontal and vertical. (In the illustration, only one set of coils is shown for simplicity.)

The intensity of the beam can be varied. The electron beam produces a tiny, bright visible spot when it strikes the phosphor-coated screen. Picture information is given through the stream of electrons. The flow of these electrons is controlled by a display controller. Finally the controlled flow of electrons strikes the screen at display devices and produces scintillations on the screen of the display device and there by the image is formed.

The screen lights up at that spot for a fraction of a second. In order to see the image on the screen, a method is required to keep the spot lit for a longer period. There are two methods of doing this.

1) The tube is scanned repeatedly over the various points on the screen with a minimum repetition rate of 30 times per second, so that the human eye can perceive a steady picture without any flickering. Typically the scanning rate is kept between 30 and 60 times per second. This type of display is called a "Refresh" CRT, since the entire picture is refreshed during each scan.
2) The pattern of lighted spots in the picture is stored and kept lit till a change is required for another picture. This type of display requires a storage type CRT with an additional electron gun called a flood gun.

Scanning in refresh type video displays can be done in two ways: Raster Scan Display and Random Scan Display.

(a) Raster Scan Display

This is a technique for generating or recording the elements of a display image by means of a line-by-line sweep across the entire display space; for example, the generation of a picture of a television screen.

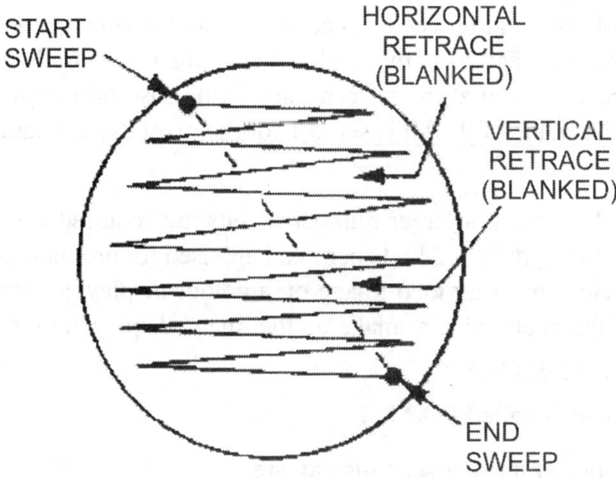

In a raster scan, the electron beam follows a fixed path. The beam starts at the upper left corner of the screen and moves horizontally to the right. This defines a scan line. During the scan the intensity of the beam is modulated according to the pattern of the desired image along the scan line. At the right edge of the screen, the screen is blanked and moved to the left edge and then positioned one unit below the previous starting point. This pattern of scanning is continued until the bottom corner on the right hand is reached. At this point one scan is completed and the beam is then repositioned at the upper left corner to start the next scan.

Each scan cycle is completed in about $^1/_{30}{}^{th}$ of a second which satisfies the need of persistence of vision thus creating the impression of continuous display and motion.

The three components for a raster scan display are:

- Frame buffer (bitmap)
- Display controller
- Display device

The frame buffer is the refresh storage area in digital memory, in which the attributes of all the pixels making up the image are stored in binary form. The display controller is the interface that transmits the contents of the frame buffer to the VDU memory in a form compatible with the display device maintaining the refresh rate. The display device converts the electrical signals into visible images on the screen.

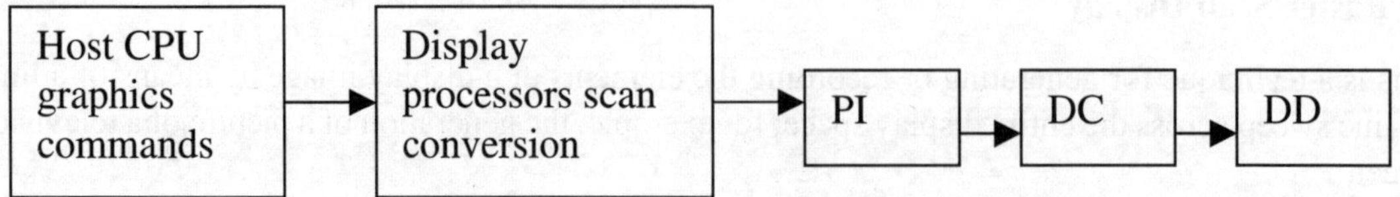

To produce any text or image on the screen, a raster is produced on the screen. The raster is a frame of a picture consisting of trace and retrace lines across the screen which is produced by moving the electron beam at a very high speed from the top left end of the screen to the bottom right corner of the screen. This raster is refreshed at the refresh rate. In the case of a monochrome VDU system there is one bit/pixel. The value of the bit is set to 1 for the pixel to glow and to 0 for the pixel not to glow.

In case of a colour VDU system, a larger number of bits are required for each pixel to provide information on colour and brightness. 24 bits per pixel are used for producing good quality. Though a pixel is the smallest element of a video image on a colour display, a pixel is made up of three different colours – red, green and blue to make up the image displayed on the screen.

- 1 bit/pixel is called BITMAP
- Multiple bits/pixel is called PIXMAP

Some of the characteristics of a raster scan display are:

i) Raster displays have less resolution.

ii) The lines produced are ziz-zag as the plotted values are discrete.

iii) A high degree of realism is achieved in a picture with the aid of advanced shading and hidden surface technique.

iv) Decreasing memory costs have made raster systems popular.

(b) Random Scan Display

In a random scan display the electron beam is directed only to the part of the screen where the picture is to be drawn. A random scan monitor draws one picture at a time therefore it is also known as a vector display. The refresh rate of a random scan system depends on the number of times it is to be displayed. Picture definition is stored in an area of memory called the refresh display file. For example, a pen plotter.

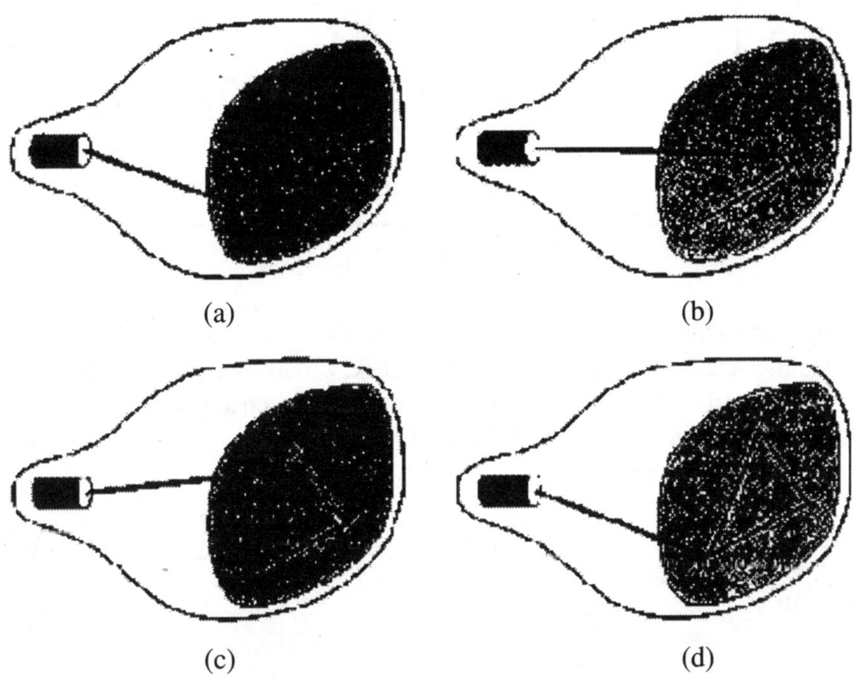

Some of the characteristics of a random scan display are:

i) Random displays have high resolutions since the picture definition is stored as a set of line drawing commands and not as a set of intensity values.

ii) Smooth lines are produced as the electron beam directly follows the line path.

iii) Realism is difficult to achieve.

iv) Random scan systems are generally costlier.

Colour CRT Methods

1) The first method is the beam penetration method. It has been used with a random scan monitor. In this, there are 2 layers of (R-Red, G-Green) phosphors inside the CRT screen. A low speed electron beam excites the red layer, a very high speed electron beam excites the green layer, an electron beam of intermediate speed excites both so we get yellow or orange.

2) The second method is the shadow-mask method. It has been used with a raster scan display. A shadow mask has three electron guns: red, green and blue (R, G, B).

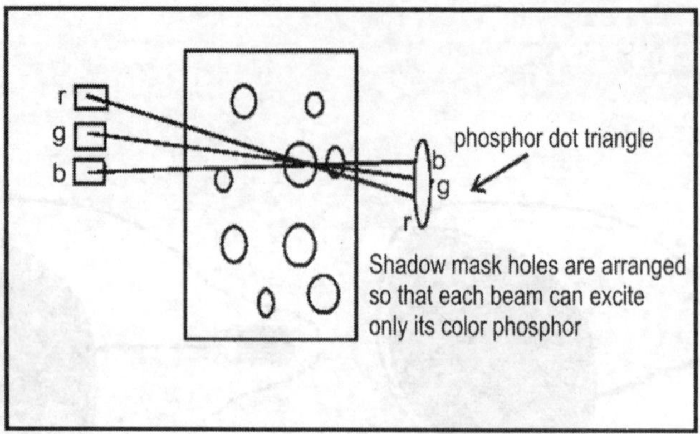

Fig. 1.1 : Delta-delta shadow mask

The above figure shows the delta-delta shadow mask method. The 3 beams of electrons from 3 guns are deflected and focused as a group on to a shadow mask, which contains a number of holes. When 3 beams pass through these holes, they activate a dot triangle, which appears as a small colour spot on the screen. We can obtain various colours by varying the intensity levels of the three beams.

Example:

R	G	B	colour
0	0	0	black
0	0	1	blue
0	1	0	green
0	1	1	cyan
1	0	0	red
1	0	1	magenta
1	1	0	yellow
1	1	1	white

Important parameters of the CRT are:

(a) Pixel: A pixel may be defined as the smallest size object or colour spot that can be displayed and addressed on a monitor. Any image that is displayed on the monitor is made up of thousands of such small pixels (also known as picture elements. The closely spaced pixels divide the image area into a compact and uniform two-dimensional grid of pixel lines and columns. Each pixel has a particular colour and brightness value. Though the size of a pixel depends mostly on the size of the electron beam within the CRT, they are too fine and close to each other to be perceptible by the human eye. The finer the pixels the more the number of pixels displayable on a monitor-screen. However it should be remembered that the number of pixels in an image is fixed by the program that creates the image and not by the hardware that displays it.

(b) Resolution: This is the number of points that can be plotted in the x and y direction.

Typical resolutions are:

320 x 200
640 x 480
800 x 600
1024 x 768
1280 x 1024

Examples

i) Compute the size of a 640 x 480 image in inches at 240 pixels per inch.

   Sol: 640/240 by 480/240 or 2.67 by 2 inches.

ii) Compute the resolution per inch of a 2 x 2 inch image that has 512 x 512 pixels.

   Sol: 512/2 or 256 pixels per inch.

(c) Aspect ratio: Aspect ratio is the ratio of the width of image to the height of image. To draw any image on the screen, AR plays an important role.

Example, if an image has a height of 2 inches and an aspect ratio of 1.5, what is its width?

Aspect ratio = width\height

Width = 1.5 x height = 1.5 x 2 = 3 inches

For example, consider a VDU with AR = 4/3, we want to draw a circle on the screen. In the case of a circle the value in both the horizontal and vertical directions should be the same. Normally the number of pixels in the horizontal and vertical directions is different, so if the same value of the radius is drawn in both the horizontal and vertical directions – then the circle will appear as ellipse. To draw a true circle, the radius has to be adjusted in the horizontal and vertical directions.

(d) Persistence: It is defined as the time it takes for the emitted light from the screen to decay to $1/10^{th}$ of its original intensity.

Advantages of CRT Monitors

- Less expensive - Although the prices of LCD monitors have decreased, comparable CRT displays still cost less.
- Better colour representation - CRT displays have historically represented colours and different gradations of colour more accurately than LCD displays. However, LCD displays are gaining ground in this area, especially with higher-end models that include colour-calibration technology.

- More responsive - Historically, CRT monitors have had fewer problems with ghosting and blurring because they redrew the screen image faster than LCD monitors. Again, LCD manufacturers are improving on this with displays that have faster response times than they did in the past.
- Multiple resolutions - If you need to change your display's resolution for different applications, you are better off with a CRT monitor because LCD monitors do not handle multiple resolutions as well.
- More rugged - Although they are bigger and heavier than LCD displays, CRT displays are also less fragile and harder to damage.

1.5.2 LCD Monitors

Liquid crystal display technology works by blocking light. Specifically, an LCD is made of two pieces of polarized glass (also called substrate) that contain a liquid crystal material between them. A backlight creates light that passes through the first substrate. At the same time, electrical currents cause the liquid crystal molecules to align to allow varying levels of light to pass through to the second substrate and create the colours and images that you see.

Active and Passive Matrix Displays

Most LCD displays use active matrix technology. A thin film transistor (TFT) arranges tiny transistors and capacitors in a matrix on the glass of the display. To address a particular pixel, the proper row is switched on, and then a charge is sent down the correct column. Since all the other rows that the column intersects are turned off, only the capacitor at the designated pixel receives a charge. The capacitor is able to hold the charge until the next refresh cycle.

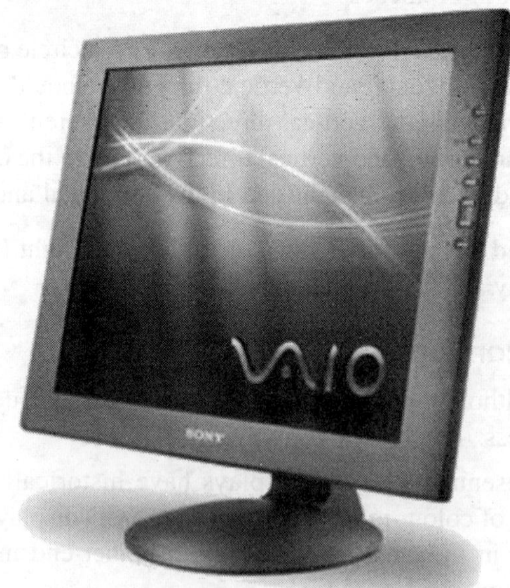

Fig. 1.2 : Sony flat-panel display (Photo courtesy : Sony)

The other type of LCD technology is passive matrix. This type of LCD display uses a grid of conductive metal to charge each pixel. Although they are less expensive to produce, passive matrix monitors are rarely used today due to the technology's slow response time and imprecise voltage control compared to active matrix technology.

LCD Features and Attributes

To evaluate the specifications of LCD monitors, there are a few more things you need to know.

Native Resolution

Unlike CRT monitors, LCD monitors display information well only at the resolution they are designed for, which is known as the native resolution. Digital displays address each individual pixel using a fixed matrix of horizontal and vertical dots. If you change the resolution settings, the LCD scales the image and the quality suffers. Native resolutions are typically:

- 17 inch = 1024 x 768
- 19 inch = 1280 x 1024
- 20 inch = 1600 x 1200

Viewing Angle

When you look at an LCD monitor from an angle, the image can appear dimmer or even disappear. Colours can also be misrepresented. To compensate for this problem, makers of LCD monitors have designed wider viewing angles. (Do not confuse this with a wide screen display, which means the display is physically wider.) Manufacturers give a measure of viewing angle in degrees (a greater number of degrees is better). In general, look for between 120 and 170 degrees. Because manufacturers measure viewing angles differently, the best way to evaluate a screen is to test the display yourself. Check the angle from the top and bottom as well as the sides, bearing in mind how you will typically use the display.

Brightness or Luminance

This is a measurement of the amount of light the LCD monitor produces. It is given in nits or one candela per square meter (cd/m^2). One nit is equal to one cd/m^2. Typical brightness ratings range from 250 to 350 cd/m^2 for monitors that perform general-purpose tasks. For showing movies, a brighter luminance rating such as 500 cd/m^2 is desirable.

Contrast Ratio

The contrast ratio rates the degree of difference of an LCD monitor's ability to produce bright whites and dark blacks. The figure is usually expressed as a ratio, for example, 500:1. Typically, contrast ratios range from 450:1 to 600:1, and they can be rated as high as 1000:1. Ratios more than 600:1, however, provide little improvement over lower ratios.

Response Rate

The response rate indicates how fast the monitor's pixels can change colours. The faster this occurs the better as it reduces the ghosting effect when an image moves, leaving a faint trail in such applications as videos or games.

Adjustability

Unlike CRT monitors, LCD monitors have much more flexibility for positioning the screen the way you want it. LCD monitors can swivel, tilt up and down, and even rotate from landscape (with the horizontal plane longer than the vertical plane) to portrait mode (with the vertical plane longer than the horizontal plane). In addition, because they are lightweight and thin, most LCD monitors have built-in brackets for wall or arm mounting.

Besides the basic features, some LCD monitors have other conveniences such as integrated speakers, built-in universal serial bus (USB) ports and anti-theft locks.

Advantages of LCD Monitors

- Require less power - Power consumption varies greatly with different technologies. CRT displays are somewhat power-hungry, at about 100 watts for a typical 19-inch display. The average is about 45 watts for a 19-inch LCD display. LCDs also produce less heat.
- Smaller and weigh less - An LCD monitor is significantly thinner and lighter than a CRT monitor, typically weighing less than half as much. In addition, you can mount an LCD on an arm or a wall, which also takes up less desktop space.
- More adjustable - LCD displays are much more adjustable than CRT displays. With LCDs, you can adjust the tilt, height, swivel and orientation from the horizontal to the vertical mode. As noted previously, you can also mount them on the wall or on an arm.
- Less eye strain - Because LCD displays turn each pixel off individually, they do not produce a flicker like CRT displays do. In addition, LCD displays do a better job of displaying text compared with CRT displays.

1.5.3 Plasma Display

The plasma video display was co-invented in 1964 at the University of Illinois at Urbana-Champaign by Donald Bitzer, H. Gene Slottow and a graduate student Robert Willson for the PLATO Computer System. The original monochrome (orange, green, yellow) video display panels were very popular in the early 1970s because they were rugged and needed neither memory nor circuitry to refresh the images. A long period of sales decline occurred in the late 1970s as semiconductor memory made CRT displays cheaper than plasma displays.

A plasma display panel (PDP) is a type of flat panel display now commonly used for large TV displays (typically above 37 inches or 940 mm). Many tiny cells located between two panels of glass hold an inert mixture of noble gases (neon and xenon). The gas in the cells is electrically turned into plasma, which then excites phosphors so that they emit light. Plasma displays are commonly confused with LCDs, another lightweight, flat screen display but using very different technology.

1.6 INPUT TECHNIQUES

Input techniques are used to enter something into a system or are expended in its operation to achieve output. The main input techniques are:

1) Positioning techniques
2) Pointing and selection
3) Inking and pointing
4) Online character recognition

1.6.1 Positioning Techniques

Positioning is the most important input technique, it is sometimes known as locating. The user indicates a position on the screen with an input device and this position is used to insert a symbol or to define the end point of a line. Positioning operations can benefit in a number of ways from the use of feedback. There are various examples of positioning feedback, some of which are given below:

- Positioning constraints
- Scales & guidelines
- Rubber-band techniques

- Dragging
- Dimensioning techniques
- Graphical potentiometers

1.6.2 Pointing and Selection

Graphical input devices play a very important role in allowing the user to point to information on the screen. In many applications pointing rather than positioning is the basis for interaction. The user may have no need to add more information to the picture and may be interested solely in studying and asking questions about the information already displayed. The major functions of pointing and selection are as follows:

- The use of selection points
- Defining a boundary rectangle
- Multiple selections
- Menu selection

1.6.3 Inking and Pointing

If we sample the position of a graphical input device at regular intervals and display a dot at each sampled position, a trail of the movements of the device will be displayed (see fig. 1.3). This technique, which closely simulates the effects of drawing on paper, is called inking.

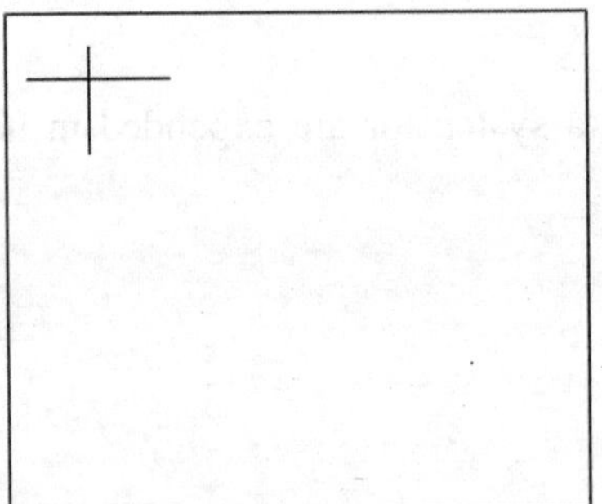

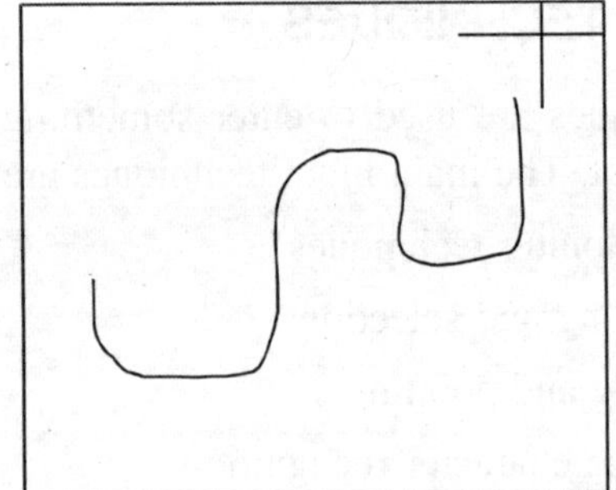

Fig. 1.3

A raster display incorporating a random-access frame buffer can be treated as a pointing surface for interaction purposes. As the user moves the cursor around, a trace of its path can be left on the screen. The users can build up freehand drawings of surprisingly good quality. It is possible to provide a range of tools for pointing on a raster display. These tools take the form of brushes that lay down trails of different thickness and colours.

1.6.4 Online Character Recognition

Character recognition requires fairly substantial computing resources. On-line handwriting recognition is a very important technique for convenient human computer interface. Pen-based input has a lot of advantages. First of all, it helps novice users, old people and housewives to conveniently use a computer. It also makes a small size portable computer (PDA, handheld PC, palm PC, etc.) possible because therc is no need for a keyboard or keypad. We had worked on a 'Notepad Computer Project' from 1992 to 1995 along with six companies and a few universities. As a result, we have on-line Korean characters (Hangul), numeral and English alphabet recognizers. After this exercise we tried to improve the speed, memory size and recognition rate of the recognizers. From 1996 to 1997, we ported our recognizer to small size RISC OS with ETRI and recently, we succeeded in poring it to handheld PC with MS windows CE 2.0. It now appears to be near-to-market quality. Nowadays we are focusing on English recognition.

1.7 MATHEMATICS FOR COMPUTER GRAPHICS

Points and Vectors

A point is a position specified with coordinate values in some reference frame, so that the distance from the origin depends on the choice of the reference frame. Point coordinates are given by the values of the ordered pair (x, y). A vector, on the other hand, is defined as the difference between two point positions. Thus, for a two-dimensional vector, we have

$$\begin{aligned} \mathbf{V} &= \mathbf{P}_2 - \mathbf{P}_1 \\ &= (x_2 - x_1, y_2 - y_1) \\ &= (V_x, V_y) \end{aligned}$$

where the Cartesian *components* (or Cartesian *elements)* V_x and V_y are the projections of V onto the x and y-axes. We can describe a vector as a *directed* line *segment* that has two fundamental properties: magnitude and direction.

Point Representation

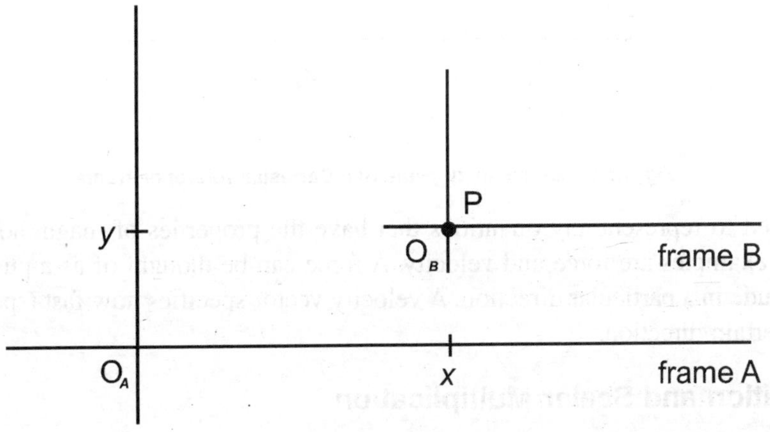

Fig. 1.4 : Position of point P with respect to two different Cartesian reference frames

Vector Representation

Definition: A vector is a line segment that has two fundamental properties:

- Magnitude
- Direction

  If V (V_x, V_y) be a vector then the

  Magnitude of a vector is

$$|V| = \sqrt{V_x^{\,2} + V_y^{\,2}}$$

Direction of a vector in terms of angular displacement from the x-axis is

$$\alpha = \tan^{-1}\left(\frac{V_y}{V_x}\right)$$

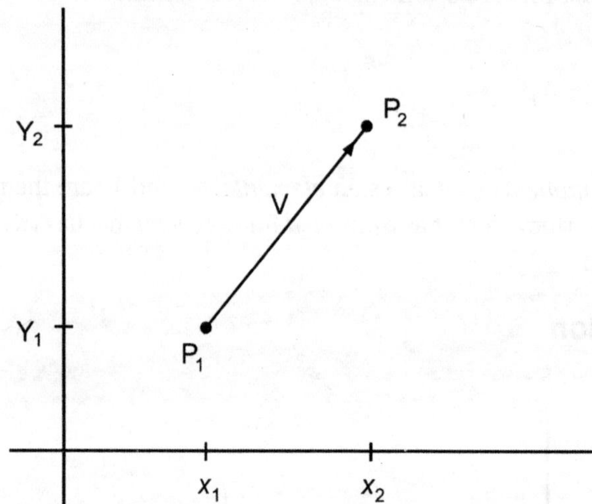

Fig. 1.5 : Vector V in xy plane of a Cartesian reference frame

Vectors are used to represent any quantities that have the properties of magnitude and direction. Two common examples are force and velocity. A force can be thought of as a push or a pull of a certain magnitude in a particular direction. A velocity vector specifies how fast (speed) an object is moving in a certain direction.

Vector Addition and Scalar Multiplication

Vectors are mathematical quantities used to represent concepts such as force or velocity which have both a magnitude and a direction.

The fig. 1.6 below shows vector v with initial point A and terminal point B.

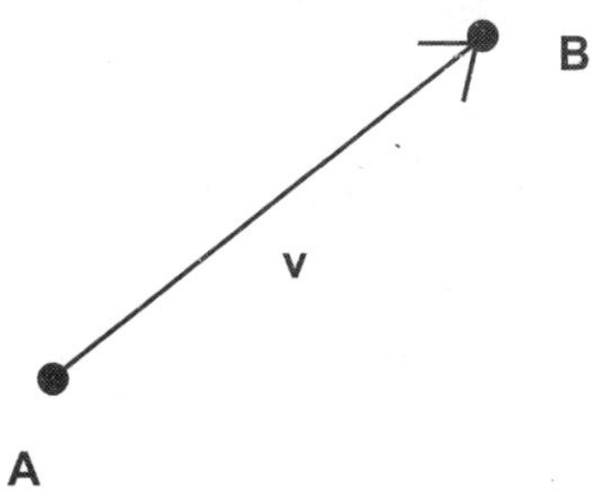

Fig. 1.6

Components of a Vector

The component form of a vector v with initial point A(a1,a2) and terminal point B(b1,b2) is given by

$$v = < b1 - a1 , b2 - a2 >$$

If a vector is given by v = < v1 , v2 > , its magnitude || v || is given by

$$\| v \| = SQRT(v1^2 + v2^2)$$

Example 1 : Find the components and the magnitude of vector v with initial point A(2,3) and terminal point B(4,5).

Solution to example 1:

Use above definition to find vector v

v = < v1 , v2 > = < b1 - a1 , b2 - a2 >

= < 4 - 2 , 5 - 3 > = < 2 , 2 >

and its magnitude || v ||

$\| v \| = SQRT(v1^2 + v2^2)$

$= SQRT(2^2 + 2^2) = SQRT(8) = 2\ SQRT(2)$

Scalar Multiplication of a Vector

The scalar multiplication of vector v = < v1 , v2 > by a real number k is the vector kv given by

k v = < k v1 , k v2 >

Addition of two Vectors: By definition, the sum of two vectors is obtained by adding corresponding components.

The addition of two vectors v(v1 , v2) and u (u1 , u2) gives vector v + u = < v1 + u1 , v2 + u2>

Example 2: Vectors v and u are given by their components as follows

v = < -2 , 3> and u = < 4 , 6>

Find each of the following vectors.

1 : v + 2u

2 : u - 4v

Solution to example 2:

First carry out the scalar mutliplication 2 u then the addition

1 : v + 2u = <-2 , 3> + 2 <4 , 6> = <-2 , 3> + <8 , 12>

= <6 , 15>

2 : u - 4v = <4 , 6> + (- 4) <-2 , 3> = <4 , 6> + <8 , -12>

= <12 , -6>

Example 3: v and u are vectors given by

v = < 1 , -2> and u = < u1 , u2>

Find components u1 and u2 of the vector u so that v + 3u = 0.

Solution to example 3:

We first obtain v + 3u in terms of u1 and u2

v + 3u = <1 , -2> + 3 <u1 , u2>

= <1 , -2> + <3 u1 , 3 u2>

= <1 + 3 u1 , -2 + 3 u2>

For the above vector to be equal to vector 0, its two components have to be equal to 0, hence

1 + 3u1 = 0 and -2 + 3u2 = 0

Solve the first equation for u1 and the second equation for u2

u1 = -1/3 and u2 = 2/3

1.8 SUMMARY

- Ancient man used drawings to communicate even before he learnt to talk, write or count. There is a popular saying "A picture is worth a thousand words". The era of computers added one more saying "A computer is worth a million pictures".
- Computer graphics is the field of visual computing. The most familiar class of computer

graphics involves movies and video games. The use of graphics through simulation and virtual reality with animation has influenced our lives.

- An active graphics device allows the user to communicate with the computer graphically. An active graphics device has the ability to reposition the cursor and read its new position. Devices include alphanumeric keyboards, digitizers, light pens, joy sticks, track balls or mouse.
- A passive graphics device simply draws pictures under computer control. Examples are dot matrix printers and an electrostatic plotter, pen and ink plotters, film recorder and storage tube refresh and raster CRT displays.
- The input device is one of the major components of computer aided design it consists of a mechanism for communication between the operator and the system. The input device converts the information into electronic signals and sends it to the computer system.
- Display devices present the output to the end user. Typically, the video monitor is a primary output device. The operation of monitors is based on CRT design, and other technologies that are also available.
- A technique for generating or recording the elements of a display image by means of a line-by-line sweep across the entire display space; for example, the generation of a picture on a television screen.
- A frame buffer is the refresh storage area in digital memory, in which attributes of all pixels making up the image are stored in binary form.
- Display controller is the interface that transmits the contents of the frame buffer to VDU memory in a form compatible with the display device maintaining the refresh rate. A display device converts the electrical signals into visible images on the screen.
- In a random scan display the electron beam is directed only to that part of the screen where the picture is to be drawn. Random scan monitors draw one picture at a time therefore they are also known as vector displays.
- Aspect ratio is the ratio of the width of the image to its height. AR plays an important role in drawing any image on the screen.
- Persistence is defined as the time for the emitted light from the screen to decay to $1/10^{th}$ of its original intensity.

1.9 REVIEW QUESTIONS

1. Discuss the role of computer graphics and differentiate between Interactive Computer Graphics and Passive Computer Graphics.
2. Discuss the application of computer graphics.
3. Discuss active and passive computer graphics devices.
4. Write the functions of input devices.
5. Explain the role of display devices and how it is achieved.
6. Discuss the functioning of a cathode ray tube in detail.

7. Discuss the liquid crystal display and differentiate it from a plasma display.
8. Consider three different raster systems with resolutions of 640 by 480, 1280 by 1024 and 2560 by 2048. What size frame buffer (in bytes) is needed for each of these systems to store 12 bits per pixel? How much storage is required for each system if 24 bits per pixel are to be stored?
9. Suppose an RGB raster system is to be designed using an 8-inch by 10-inch screen with a resolution of 100 pixels per inch in each direction. If we want to store 6 bits per pixel in the frame buffer, how much storage (in bytes) do we need for the frame buffer?
10. How long would it take to load a 640 by 480 frame buffer with 12 bits per pixel, if 10^5 bits can be transferred per second? How long would it take to load a 24-bit per pixel frame buffer with a resolution of 1280 by 1024 using this same transfer rate?
11. Suppose we have a computer with 32 bits per word and a transfer rate of 1 mip (one million instructions per second). How long would it take to fill the frame buffer of a 300-dpi (dot per inch) laser printer with a page size of 8.5 inches by 11 inches?
12. Consider two raster systems with resolutions of 640 by 480 and 1280 by 1024. How many pixels could be accessed per second in each of these systems by a display controller that refreshes the screen at a rate of 60 frames per second? What is the access time per pixel in each system?
13. Suppose we have a video monitor with a display area that measures 12 inches across and is 9.6 inches high, if the resolution is 1280 by 1024 and the aspect ratio is 1, what is the diameter of each screen point?
14. How much time is spent scanning across each row of pixels during refresh on a raster system with a resolution of 1280 by 1024 and a refresh rate of 60 frames per second?
15. Consider a non-interlaced raster monitor with a resolution of *n* by *m* (*m* scan lines and *n* pixels per scan line), a refresh rate of *r* frames per second, a horizontal retrace time of t_{horz}, and a vertical retrace time of t_{vert}. What is the fraction of the total refresh time per frame spent in retrace of the electron beam?
16. What is the fraction of the total refresh time per frame spent in retrace of the electron beam for a non-interlaced raster system with a resolution of 1280 by 1024, a refresh rate of 60 Hz, a horizontal retrace time of 5 microseconds, and a vertical retrace time of 500 microseconds?
17. Assuming that a certain full-colour (24-bit per pixel) RGB raster system has a 512 by 512 frame buffer, how many distinct colour choices (intensity levels) would we have available? How many different colours could we display?
18. Given vectors v = <-3 , 2> and u = <-2 , 0>, find the following vectors.

    - v + 2u , v - (1/2)u
19. Vectors v and u are given by v = <4 , 1> and u = <u1 , u2>,

    find components u1 and u2 so that 2 v - 3 u = 0 .

CHAPTER 2

Graphics Functions & Drawing Algorithms

2.1 BUILT IN FUNCTIONS PRESENT IN A GRAPHICS HEADER FILE

Name of the built in function and the corresponding syntax	***The purpose of using the function***
arc (x, y stangle, endangle, radius);	To draw any arc this function is used where x and y represent the radius, strangle is the starting angle in radians, end angle is thc end angle in radians and radius is the proposed radius of the curve.
bar (left, top, right, bottom);	This function is used to draw a bar chart. Here the left, top, right and bottom are the co-ordinates of the bar.
bar3d (left, top, right, bottom, depth, topflag);	This function is used to draw a bar chart in 3 dimensional form. Here the left, top, right and bottom are the co-ordinates of the bar. The depth indicates the bar chart depth and topflag indicates the style for the top.
Circle (x, y, radius);	This function is used to draw a circle where (x, y) indicates the centre co-ordinate and the 'radius' indicates the radius of the circle.'
cleardevice();	It is used to clear the drawn device.
clearviewport();	It is used to clear the current viewport.

closegraph();	It is used to close the graph
detectgraph (*graphdriver, *graphmode);	This function is used to find the current graphics driver and the graphics mode used.
drawpoly (numpos, const *polypos);	This function is used to draw any polygon where numpos is the number of points and polypos points to a sequence of x, y coordinates.
elipse (x, y, stangle, endangle, xradiusm, yradius);	This function is used to draw any ellipse where x, y represent the centre co-ordinate, stangle is the starting angle in radians, endangle is the end angle in radians and xradius and yradius represent the radius in the x and y directions.
Fillellipse (0x. y, radius, yradius);	This function is used to draw any filled ellipse where x, y represent the centre co-ordinates, xradius and yradius, represent the radius in the x and in y directions.
Fillpoly (numpos, const *polypos);	This function is used to draw any filled polygon where numpos is the number of points and polypos points to a sequence of x, y coordinates.
Floodfill (x, y, border);	This function is used to paint any closed body where x, y are the co-ordinates of any internal point and border is the border colour value.
Obtainarccoords (struct arccoordstype *arccordds);	Returns the arc coordinates and the stangle and endangle of the drawn arc.
Obtainaspectratio(*xasp, *yasp);	Returns the aspect ratio of current mode where y and x factor is 10000 i.e. pixels are square
Obtainbakcolour();	Background colour can be picked up using this function.
Obtaincolour();	Foreground colour can be picked up using this function.
Obtaindefaultpalette();	The default palette used can be picked up using this function.
Obtaindrivername();	The driver name can be picked up using this function.
Obtainfillpattern (char *pattern);	The paint filling pattern can be selected and can be picked up using this function

Obtainfillsettings (struct filsettingstype *fillinfo);	Paint filling settings.
Obtaingraphmode();	Returns the current graphics mode.
Obtainimage (left, top, right, bottom, *bitmpa);	Stores the image from left, top to right bottom coordinate in the allocated space pointed by the bitmap.
Obtainlinesetting (struct linesettingstype *lineinfo);	Returns the current line style, line pattern and thickness to the structure pointer lineinfo (structure defined in graphics.h) default value is style=0, upattern=0 and thickness=1
Obtainmaxcolour();	Returns the maximum colour number out of 16 palette.
Obtainmaxmode();	Returns maximum mode supported by the driver.
Obtainmaxx();	Returns the maximum pixels in the x direction of the current mode.
Obtainmaxy();	Returns the maximum pixels in the y direction of the current mode.
Obtainmodername (mode_number);	Accepts a mode number and returns a name of the corresponding mode number.
Obtainmoderange (graphicdriver, *lomode, *himode)	Returns a graph drivers low mode and high mode which is supported by the driver.
Obtainpixel(x,y);	Returns the colour (0-15) of the specified pixel at the x, y coordinates.
Obtainpalettesize();	Returns the palette size of the current mode.
Obtaintextsettings (struct textsettingstype *texttypeinfo);	Returns the text settings such as font, direction, charsize, horizontal and vertical orientations into the structure defined in graphics.h
Obtainviewsetings (struct viewporttype *viewport)	Returns the current viewport settings i.e. left, top and right, bottom coordinate along with the viewpoint clip status
Obtainx();	Returns the current x coordinate position.
Obtainy();	Returns the current y coordinate position.
Graphdefaults();	Reset all the graphics settings to their default values.

Grapherrormsg (errorcode);	Returns an error code related to a graph error.
Graphfreemem (void far * ptr, unsigned size); Graphobtainmem(unsigned graphresult());	Returns a code equivalent to the graph results.
Imagesize (left, top, right, bottom)	Returns the image size from left, top coordinate to right, bottom coordinate.
Initgraph (*graphdriver, *graphmode, pathtodriver);	Sets the graphics mode and loads the graphics driver where graphdriver is the name of the graphics driver which will be detected and returns the mode number in graphmode, pathtodriver points to the path where all .bgi files (graphics driver) are stored.
Installuserdriver (const char *name huge (*detecte()); installuserfont (const char *name);	Installs user defined fonts where the font segment is pointed by name pointer.
Line (x1, y1, x2, y2);	Draws a line from x1, y1, to x2, y2
Linerel (dx, dy);	Draws a line from current position to a distance dx, dy, relative to the current position.
Lineto (x, y);	Draws the line from current position to the x, y coordinate.
Moverel (dx, dy);	Moves the positions relative to the current position in dx and dy directions.
Moveto (x,y)	Moves the position to the x and y coordinates from the current positions.
Outtext (const char *textstring)	Prints the text at the current position
Outtextxy (x,y, const char *textstring);	Prints the text pointed by textstring from the x, y coordinates
Pieslice (x, y, stangle, endangle, radius);	Draws a pie slice from the starting angle to ending angle centred at x, y with a radius.
Putimag (left, top, const *bitmap, op);	Displays the image on the screen from the left, top coordinate where the bitmap points to the image. Op parameter is used to see how the displayed picture will be drawn on to the screen.
Putpixel (x, y, colour);	Plots the pixel at x, y coordinate with specified colour.

Rectangle (left, top, right, bottom); bottom.	Draws a rectangle from left, top to right
Restorecrtmode();	Loads all the registers with the values used in textr mode when returning from graphics mode.
Sector (X, Y, StAngle, EndAngle, XRadius, YRadius);	Draws an elliptical sector from StAngle to EndAngle with Xradius for the horizontal radius and Yradius for the vertical radius and the sector is solid fill with the colour.
Setactivepage (page);	Sets a page to be activated for output if the page is supported by the system.
Setallpalette (const struct palettetpe * palette);	Sets all 16 palettes with the specified colours, the colour values are stored into a structure pointed by the palette (structure defined in graphics.h).
Setaspectratio (xasp, yasp)	Changes the default aspect ratio with the user specified ratio where xasp is the x aspect ratio and yasp is the y aspect ratio.
Setbkcolour (colour);	Sets the current background colour with one of the palette colours where colour is the palette number.
Setcolour (colour);	Sets the foreground colour where colour is the colour number range from (0 – 15).
Setfillpattern (cosnt char *upattern, colour)	Sets the foreground colour where colour is the colour number range from 0 – 15.
Setfillstyle (pattern, colour)	Sets the fill style with pattern and colour number where pattern, ranges from 0 - 12 indicated solid or hatch fill, this specified filling is possible when call floodfill().
Setgraphbufsize (unsigned, bufsize); Setgraphmode (mode);	Sets the current mode with a specified mode number.
Setlinestyle (linestyle, unsigned upattern, thickness);	Sets the line style pattern and width where linstyle ranges from 0 - 4 specifying solid, centre or dotted linr upsyyrtn specifies the pattern of line i.e. slash or backslash fill or solid ill, thickness specifies the line is normal or thick width.
Setpalette (colournum,colour)	Sets a palette with the specified colour where colournum is the palette.

Setgbpalette (colournum,red,green,blue)_	Sets the palette (0 - 15) specified with the colournum with the red, green and blue values for the required colour.
Settextjustify (horitz,vert)	Sets the text alignment specified by horiz and vert parameter where horiz and vert specifies left, centre, right, bottom or top text,default is left and top text.
Settextstyle (font,direction,charsize)	Sets the text style with font range from 0 - 4 i.e. gothic, triplex, sansserif etc. and direction(0,1) and the character size ranges from 0 – 7.
Setusercharsize (multx,divx,multy,divvy)	Sets the user defined fonts to change character width and height.
Setviewport (left,top,right,bottom,clip)	Sets a view port from left-top to right-bottom clip specify whether the drawing are clipped to the viewport or not.
Setvisualpage (page)	Sets a page specified with the page number and all the output is directed to the page.number of page should be supported by the current graphics mode.
Setwritemode (mode) Textheight (const char *textstring)	Returns the height of string pointed by textstring in pixels.
Textwidth (const char *textstring)	Returns the width of string pointed by textstring in pixels.

2.2 GRAPHICS DRIVERS

Graphics drivers are software, which drive the graphics card to draw the graphics objects properly. Without using the proper graphics driver file, no graphics object can be drawn on the screen. Normally, initgraph loads a graphics driver by allocating memory for the driver (through graphobtainmem), then loading the appropriate. BGI file from disk.

- Graphdriver is an integer that specifies the graphics driver to be used. You can mention the graphdriver value using a constant of the graphics_drivers enumeration type.
- Graphmode is an integer that specifies the initial graphics mode. However, if you are not sure or if you do not know the exact specification of the graphics driver file as previously mentioned, you can mention '*graphdriver=DETECT'. If this type of syntax is used, then initgraph sets *graphmode to the highest possible resolution available for the detected driver automatically. You can obviously use the value of *graphmode as discussed in the graphics_modes enumeration type if you are sure about the file.

- Pathtodriver specifies the default path where initgraph looks for graphics drivers first. The extension of the graphics driver files will be BGI if the driver files are not available at that location, it will try to find the same from the current directory. If we use NULL as the value of pathtodriver, the driver files must be present in the current directory. This is also the path settextstyle searches for the stroked character font files (*.CHR).

Program

```
#include <graphics.h>
#include<stdlib.h>
#include<stdio.h>
#include<conio.h>
{
                                            /*Request auto detection*/
Int gdriver, detectgraph·(&gdriver, & gmode); gmode, errorcode;
                                            /*Initialize graphics mode*/
                                            /* Read result of initialization*/

errorcode = graphresult();
if (errorcode !=grOk)                 /* an error occurred */
{
printf("Graphics error: %s\n", grapherrormsg(errorcode));
printf("Press any key to halt:");
obtainch();
exit(1);                              /*return with error code*/
}
Line(0,  0, obtainmaxx()), obtainmaxy());     /* Draw a line*/
                                            /* Clean up*/
obtainch();
closegraph();
}
```

Using the language C, the required functions are setpixel() and putpixel() having the syntax:

setpixel (x, y); and

putpixel (x, y, colour);

Where x and y represent the co-ordinates of the point to be drawn on the screen and 'colour' is the required colour to be used to draw the point.

Therefore, in a program if we write:

```
setpixel (100, 200);
```

It will draw a point at the co-ordinates x = 100 and y = 200 with the colour white.

Similarly,

```
putpixel (100, 200, 3);
```

will draw a point on the co-ordinate x = 100 and y = 200 with the colour number 3, i.e. with the colour number 3 of the used colour palette.

2.3 ALGORITHMS

2.3.1 Line Drawing

There are different methods that can be used to draw any straight line. We will discuss these algorithms one by one.

It is important to note that the points can only be drawn at the integer co-ordinate values. So if we use the function:

```
Putpixel (50.4,100.8, 2);
```

then the point will be drawn on the rounded off integer value of the given co-ordinate, i.e. at the value (50, 101), for this reason a straight line may be seen on the screen as a zig-zag line as shown below:

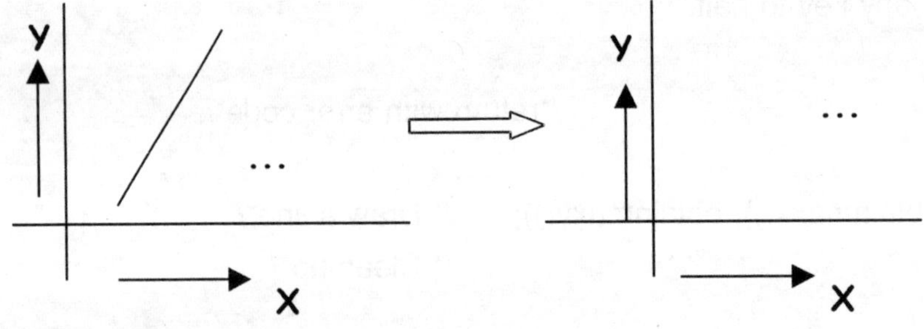

Required lines **As will be displayed on the screen**

So, to draw more accurate lines, we have to choose console systems having a better resolution.

Line Drawing Algorithms

There are different algorithms available using which we can draw different types of straight lines. The different methods are given below.

Direct method

This is the easiest and most straight forward approach amongst all the existing methods. We know that any straight line can be represented using the relation:

$y = mx + c$ (2.1)

Where 'm' represents the slope of the line and 'c' represents the intercept of the line on y-axis as shown in the figure below:

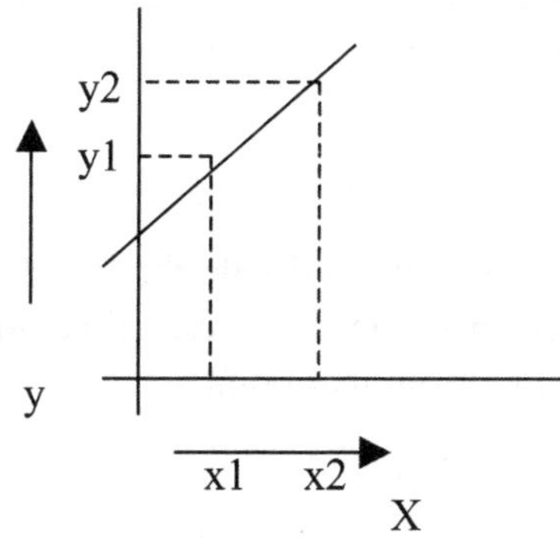

Assume that in the line, there are two points present, having the co-ordinates (x_1, y_1) and (x_2, y_2) respectively. These two points may also be the two end points of the line. So, from these two co-ordinates we can find the value of the slope and the intercept as:

$m = (y_2 - y_1)/(x_2 - x_1)$ (2.2)

and $c = y_1 - m_1 x_1$ (2.3)

We can now set the set of co-ordinates to draw the line using the equations (2.2) and (2.3).

Starting from the co-ordinate (x_1, y_1) and moving towards the end co-ordinate (x_2, y_2), we can find small incremental values of x and y as:

$dy = m.dx$ (2.4)

The algorithm for this method will be as shown below:

Step-1: Accept the two end point co-ordinates (x_1, y_1) and (x_2, y_2) from the user.

Step-2: Compute $m = (y_2 - y_1)/(x_2 - x_1)$ and $c = y_1 - m.x_1$

Step-3: Assume any incremental value of $x(dx)$ [for smaller values of dx, the line will be smoother]

Step-4: Compute the corresponding incremental value by using the relationship $dy = m.dx$ of equation (2.4)

Step-5: Compute next co-ordinate of the line as: $x = x_1 + dx$ and $y = y_1 + dy$ and draw the point at the co-ordinate (x,y)

Step-6: Check if $|x_2 - x| <$ error limit and $|y_2 - y| <$ error limit. If it is true then go to step 5 otherwise, compute $x_1 = x$ and $y_1 = y$ and go to step 5.

Step-7: Stop the process.

2.3.1.1 DDA Algorithm

This method is an improvement on the previous method. Here an attempt is made to reduce the floating-point arithmetic to some extent.

In this method, the calculation starts from equation (2.4) i.e. $dy = m.dx$

This equation will be utilized when an interval of dx is assumed in order to find the corresponding interval of dy. But, if we assume the increment of 'y' as 'dy' and calculate the value of x, we have to change equation (2.4) to:

$$dx = dy/m \qquad (2.5)$$

Here the logic is as follows: First we have to divide the length of the line by segments of equal length having an integral value, either in the x or y direction, and calculate the other value to the nearest rounded integer draw the line from that point.

There are certain possible conditions as given below:

1) If the slope is less than or equal to 1

Here we will assume the incremental value of x (dx) as 1 (i.e. the next x value) and compute the next value of y using the relation:

$$y' = y \pm m$$

Here, y is the previous value in the y direction and y' is the new running value of the co-ordinate. The '+' sign is used to indicate that the line is to be drawn from left to right direction and the '-' sign for the reverse direction.

2) If the slope is positive and greater than 1

In this condition we have to increment the value of $y(dy)$ by 1 and find the corresponding value of x using the relation:

$$x' = x \pm 1/m$$

Where, x is the previous value in the x direction and x' is the new co-ordinate value in the x direction.

Here, the term 1/m will be taken as '+' for the left to right movement of the line whereas, it will be taken as '-' for a line passing from right to left.

Similarly, for a line with a negative slope, dx and/or dy should be taken as -1 instead of +1 for obvious reasons.

Algorithm

Step-1: Accept start point (x_1,y_1) and end point (x_2,y_2) from the user.

Step-2: Compute $x_x = x_2 - x_1$ and $y_y = y_2 - y_1$

Step-3: Set the running co-ordinates (x, y) to the starting value (x_1, y_1).

Step-4: Check if $x_x > y_y$ then set the step value to x_x else set the step value to y_y

Step-5: Compute the incremental values in the x and y directions as:

$$dx = x_x/\text{step value}$$

$$\text{and } dy = y_y/\text{step value}$$

Step-6: Draw the point at the co-ordinate (x, y)

Step-7: Compute the next co-ordinate as $dx = x_x/\text{step value}$ and $dy = y_y/\text{step value}$

Step-8: Draw the point at the co-ordinate (x, y)

Step-9: Compute next co-ordinate as $x = x + dx$ and $y = y + dy$

Step-10: If the number of iterations is greater than the step values go to step 11 else go to step 6.

Step-11: Stop the process.

Program

```
/*
________________________________________

DDA line drawing algorithm
________________________________________

*/
# include <graphics.h>
# include <math.h>
# include <conio.h>
# include <iostream.h>
void DDALine(int x1,int y1,int x2,int y2,int iColor);
void main()
{
        int gDriver=DETECT,gMode;

        int x1,x2,y1,y2,iColour;

        initgraph(&gDriver,&gMode,"c:\\tc\\bgi");
        cleardevice();
        cout<<endl<<"Enter x1  : ";
        cin>>x1;
```

```
        cout<<"Enter y1  : ";
        cin>>y1;
        cout<<endl<<"Enter x2  : ";
        cin>>x2;
        cout<<"Enter y2  : ";
        cin>>y2;
        cout<<endl<<"Enter COLOR  : ";
        cin>>iColour;
        cleardevice();
        DDALine(x1,y1,x2,y2,iColor);

        obtainch();
}
void DDALine(int x1,int y1,int x2,int y2,int iColor)
{
        float dX,dY,iSteps;
        float xInc,yInc,iCount,x,y;

        dX = x1 - x2;
        dY = y1 - y2;

        if (fabs(dX) > fabs(dY))
        {
                iSteps = fabs(dX);
        }
        else
        {
                iSteps = fabs(dY);
        }
        xInc = dX/iSteps;
        yInc = dY/iSteps;

        x = x1;
        y = y1;
```

```
        circle(x,y,1);

        for (iCount=1; iCount<=iSteps; iCount++)
        {
                putpixel(floor(x),floor(y),iColor);
                x -= xInc;
                y -= yInc;
        }
        circle(x,y,1);
        return;
}
```

2.3.1.2 Bresenham's Algorithm for Line Drawing

A more accurate and efficient algorithm to draw a line is given by Bresenham where floating-point arithmetic is avoided to a great extent and only the incremental integer calculations are carried out.

In this method the first objective is to choose position of the closest pixel to the line for its path of integer value. This is shown in the figure given below.

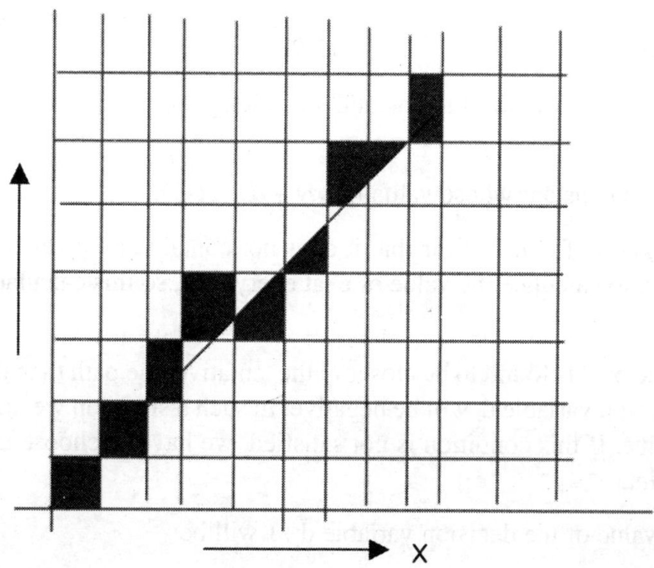

Here the closest pixel path is found out first for each point of the line at each sample step. For example, suppose we have to draw a point on the line at the co-ordinates (25, 30.4), then we first have to determine whether the co-ordinates (25, 30) or (25, 31) are closer to that point and the closest pixel is illuminated to draw the line. All the pixels are drawn in this manner, but the selection procedure will be different for positive and negative slopes.

1) For a positive slope less than unity

In this case the sample rate is taken for the co-ordinates with intervals having the values of the x-axis. Thus for each increment in the value of x, the corresponding y value is to be calculated and from this, the closest value of y is traced out. After that, the point is illuminated.

So, for any co-ordinate (x_i, y_i), we have to find the next position of $(x_i + 1)$ with the addition of the incremental value of dx. Using the equation of the straight line we have to determine the next position of y i.e. $(y_i + 1)$. But only that value of y will be accepted which is closest to $(y_i + 1)$. From equation 2.1 we can find the next probable value of y as: $y = m(x_{i+1} + 1) + c$

So, the difference between y_1 and y, and y and y_{i+1} will be:

$$dy_1 = y - y_1 = m(x_i + 1) + cy_i \qquad (2.6)$$

$$dy_2 = (y_i + 1) - y = y_i + 1 - m(x_i + 1) - c \qquad (2.7)$$

Where dy_1 and dy_2 are the difference parameters. The difference between these two values will be:

$$dy_1 - dy_2 = 2m(x_i + 1) - 2y_i + 2c - 1 \qquad (2.8)$$

In order to continue the calculation using integers only, we have to introduce a new variable d_i for the ith step of the calculations as:

$$d_i = dx(dy_1 - dy_2)$$

$$= 2dyx_i - 2dx.y_i + c' \qquad (2.9)$$

As we have chosen a small position incremental step along the x axis, i.e. $x_i + 1 > x_{i,}$ the sign of $dy_1 - dy_2$ depends on dx.

Here the value of c′ is a constant whose value is $2dy + dx$ (2c-1).

Looking at the expression of c′ it is clear that it does not contain any pixel co-ordinate value and thus it is not necessary to calculate the value of c′ at every step, so this calculation will not be kept inside the loop.

If the pixel at the value of y_i is found to be closer to the tentative line path than the pixel at the value of $y_i + 1$, then the decision variable d_i will be negative. In such a situation we have to draw the point at the lower pixel value. If this condition is not satisfied, we have to choose the next higher pixel value to draw the point.

In the next step, the value of the decision variable d_i+1 will be:

$$d_i + 1 = 2dy\alpha x_i + 1 - 2dx\alpha y_{i+1} + c'$$

Subtracting equation (2.8) from equation (2.9) we obtain:

$$d_{i+1} - d_i = 2dy\ (x_{i+1} - x_i) - 2dx(y_{i+1} - y_i) \qquad (2.10)$$

Algorithm

Step-1: Accept the co ordinate of the two end points (x_1, y_1) and (x_2, y_2) and draw the first point at co-ordinate (x_1, y_1)

Step-2: Compute dx, dy, $2dy$ and $2dy - 2dx$ using the relations: $dx = x_2 - x_1$ and $dy = y_2 - y_1$.

Step-3: Compute the initial value of the decision variable d_1 as: $2dy - dx$.

Step-4: Assume $x_i = x_1$ and $d_i = d_1$.

Step-5: Check if $d_i < 0$ then draw a point at the pixel (x_{i+1}, y_{i+1}) and if $d_i + 1 = 2dy$ go to step 7.

Step-6: Draw a point at the position (x_{i+1}, y_{i+1}) and compute $d_{i+1} = d_i + 2dy - 2dx$.

Step-7: Compute $x_i = x_i + dx$. If, $x_i < x_2$, go to step 5.

Step-8: Stop the process.

Program

```
// Program to draw bresenham line


#include<stdio.h>
#include<conio.h>
#include<graphics.h>
void linebres(int,int,int,int);


void main()
{
        int gd=DETECT,gm;
        int x1,y1,x2,y2;
        printf("Enter the value of x1:");
        scanf("\n %d",&x1);
        printf("Enter the value of y1:");
        scanf("\n %d",&y1);
        printf("Enter the value of x2:");
        scanf("\n %d",&x1);
        printf("Enter the value of y2:");
        scanf("\n %d",&y2);
        initgraph(&gd,&gm,"c:\\tc\\bgi");
```

```
        linebres(x1,y1,x2,y2);
        obtainch();
        closegraph();
}
void linebres(int xa,int ya,int xb,int yb)
{
        int dx=abs(xb-xa);
        int dy=abs(yb-ya);
        int p=2*dy-dx;

        int x,y,xe;
        if(xa>xb)
        {
                x=xb;
                y=yb;
                xe=xa;
        }
        else
        {
                x=xa;
                y=ya;
                xe=xb;
        }
        putpixel(x,y,15);
        if(xa ==xb)
        {
                if(yb > ya)
                {
                        for( ;y<=yb;y++)
                                putpixel(x,y,15);
                }
                else
                {
                        y=yb;
```

```
                    for( ;y<=ya;y++)
                            putpixel(x,y,15);
            }
    }
    else
    {
            while(x < xe)
            {
                    x++;
                    if(p< 0)
                            p=p+2*dy;
                    else
                    {
                            y++;
                            p = abs(p+2*(dy-dx));
                     }
                     putpixel(x,y,15);
                    }
            }
    }
```

2.3.2 Drawing a Circle

It is a common fact that in graphics applications and drawing systems, drawing circles, circular arcs or elliptical shapes is very necessary.

The basic equation of a circle is:

$$x^2 + y^2 = r^2 \qquad (2.11)$$

Where the centre of circle lies at the origin and 'r' is the radius of the circle.

If the centre co-ordinate of the circle is not at the origin, i.e. at the co-ordinate (0,0) the equation will change to:

$$(x - x_c)^2 + (y - y_c)^2 = r^2$$

Where (x_c, y_c) is the centre co-ordinate of the circle. So to draw a circle using this relationship, we can change it to the form:

$$(y - y_c)^2 = r^2 - (x - x_c)^2$$

or, $y - y_c = \pm \sqrt{r^2 - (x - x_c)^2}$

or, $y = y_c \pm \sqrt{r^2 - (x - x_c)^2}$

If you look carefully at the circle drawn on the screen by executing the program you will find that the spacing between the positions of the plotted pixels is not uniform. This problem can be reduced to some extent by interchanging the values of x and y at each position, but this is not easy.

Another major problem of this method is that it involves an enormous amount of floating point arithmetic, so that the circle will be drawn slowly.

A better method of drawing a circle is by equally spaced pixels along the boundary of the circle. But this will require Polar co-ordinates.

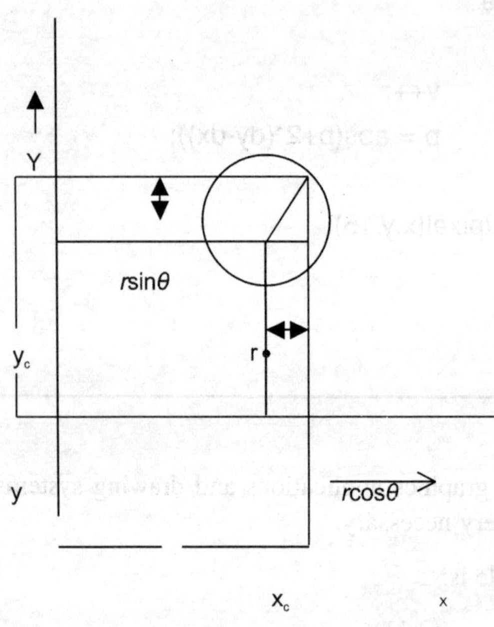

To draw any point (x, y) along the boundary of the circle, we can write x and y in Polar co-ordinates as:

$\boldsymbol{x = x_c + r\cos\theta}$ (2.12)

and $\boldsymbol{y = y_c + r\sin\theta}$ (2.13)

and using these two equations we can draw a circle using the following algorithm.

Step-1: Accept (x, y) and r.

Step-2: Assume the initial value of $\theta = 0$ radians.

Step-3: Compute (x, y) using the relations from the equations $x = x_c + r\cos\theta$ and $y = y_c + r\sin\theta$ and draw a point at that co-ordinate.

Step-4: Update the value of θ with a predefined step value

Step-5: Check if $\theta \leq 2\pi$ go to step 3 otherwise go to step 6

Step-6: Stop the process.

Here we should set the 'step value' to obtain continuous points along the periphery of the circle as far as possible, but in this case the number of floating point calculations will be increased. So a compromise should be made between the two. Normally, in this case a step size of $1/r$ is recommended to obtain almost equally spaced pixels along the border of the line.

However, the problem of floating point arithmetic will still remain in this system.

A point to be kept in mind is that the quality of the pictures produced depends on the graphics system and adapter used in the computer.

A program is written using this algorithm where a default step value is assumed as $1/r$, though it can be changed by the user when the program is executed.

2.3.2.1 Bresenham's Algorithm to draw a Circle

As circle is a perfectly symmetric figure, so we can draw an arc in one quadrant of the coordinate system and the full circle in the other three quadrants can be drawn by drawing identical arcs.

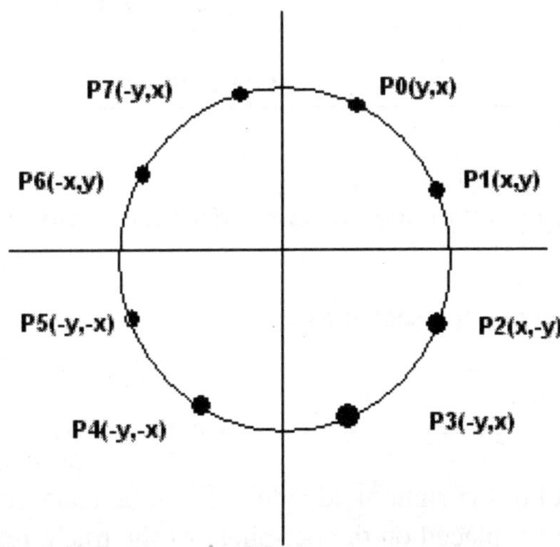

If we have the co-ordinates of one point on the circumference of the circle, the co-ordinates of the other seven points can be obtained as follows:

Original: $P_1(x, y)$

Computed: $P_2(x, -y)$, $P_3(y, -x)$, $P_4(-y, -x)$

$P_5(-x, -y)$, $P_6(-x, y)$, $P_7(-y, -x)$ and $P_8(y, x)$

If the origin is shifted to the co-ordinate (x_c, y_c), we can add x_c to x and y_c to y to obtain the respective co-ordinates.

This method indicates that, if we can draw one-eighth of a circle using the proper computations, we can draw co-ordinates as obtained above.

To draw a circle, we have to manipulate a non-linear equation given as:

$(x - x_c)^2 + (y - y_c)^2 = r^2$

or, $y = y_c + \sqrt{r^2 - (x - x_c)^2}$ (2.14)

but to draw the circle efficiently and at faster speed we have to avoid floating point arithmetic and trigonometric calculations as far as possible.

Bresenham's algorithm allows us to do this, by using integer form of arithmetic only. Using this method, a part of a circle, between the angles 0 to 45° is generated and the other seven segments are obtained by the reflection images of the same.

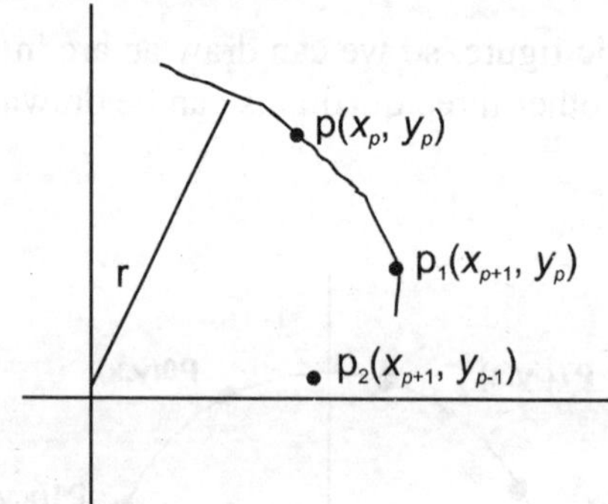

We have to choose the closest point on the true circle from these two points P_1 and P_2 as shown in the figure above.

The equation of the circle can be represented as:

$x^2 + y^2 = r^2$

or, $x^2 + y^2 - r^2 = 0$ (2.15)

but for both the points p_1 and p_2 the right hand side will not be equal to 0 as these two points are neighbouring points and are not placed on the periphery of the true circle. Suppose:

$d_1 = (x_p + 1)^2 + y_p^{\,2} - r^2$ for the point P_1

and $d_2 = (x_p + 1)^2 + (y_p - 1)^2 - r^2$ for the point P_2

where d_1 and d_2 are the distances from the true circle. It should be noted that the sign of d_1 and d_2 will not be the same. One will be greater than 0 and the other will be less than 0.

The sum of these distances can be expressed as:

$d_p = d_1 + d_2$

$= (x_p + 1)^2 + y_p^{\ 2} - r^2 + (x_p + 1)^2 + (y_p - 1)^2 - r^2$

$= 2(x_p + 1)^2 + y_p^{\ 2} + (y_p - 1)^2 - 2r^2$

So, when d_p becomes less than 0, we can write $|d_1| < |d_2|$ and thus p_1 will be the closest point to the true circle otherwise p_2 should be chosen as the closest point.

In this way we can set a decision variable d_{p+1} for the next step of computation as:

$d_{p+1} = 2(x_{p+1}+1)^2 + y_{p+1}^{\ 2} + (y_{p+1}-1)^2 - 2r^2$

so $d_{p+1} - d_p = 2(x_{p+1}+1)^2 + y_{p+1}^{\ 2} + (y_{p+1}-1)^2 - 2(x_p+1)^2 - y_p^{\ 2} - (y_p-1)^2$

Now replacing x_{p+1} by x_p+1 we can write

$d_{p+1} = d_p + 4x_p + 2(y^2_{p+1} - y_p)^2 - 2(y_{p+1} - y_{p)} + 6$

So, if previously p_1 was the chosen point (i.e. if $d_p < 0$, then $y_p+1 = y_p$ and thus

$d_{p+1} = d_p + 4x_p + 6$

But, if p_2 was chosen previously (i.e. if, d_p => 0), then

$y_p+1 = y_p - 1$ and we can write

$d_p+1 = d_p + 4(x_p - y_p) + 10$

We can summarise these as:

$\boldsymbol{d_p+1 = d_p + 4x_p + 6}$ **if** $\boldsymbol{d_p < 0}$ (2.16)

and = $\boldsymbol{dp + 4(x_p - y_p) + 10}$ **if** $\boldsymbol{d_p \geq = 0}$ (2.17)

To obtain the starting value of d_p we put (0, r) as the starting pixel co-ordinate,

So, $d_p = 2(0 + 1)^2 + r^2 + (r - 1)^2 - 2r^2$

$= 3 - 2r$

This would be our starting parameter of the decision variable.

Now we can write the algorithm of the same with a view to starting the drawing with the coordinate (0,0) and the initial value d as 3-2r and draw the pixel. After this we have to calculate the new value of the decision variable d and find the new value of y to draw the next point. After obtaining the proper value of y, we have to increment the value of x.

Algorithm

Step-1: Accept the value of the radius r

Step-2: Initialize $x = 0$, $y = r$ and $d = 3 - 2r$

Step-3: Draw the pixel at the co-ordinate (x, y)

Step-4: Check, if $d < 0$ then compute the new value of d as: $d + 4x + 6$:
Go to step 6

Step-5: Compute $d = d + 4(x - y) + 10$ and decrease the value of y by 1, i.e.
$y = y - 1$

Step-6: Increment the value of x by 1, i.e. $x = x + 1$

Step-7: Check, if the condition $x \leq y$ is satisfied, go to step 3

Step-8: Stop the process

2.3.2.2 Midpoint Circle Algorithm

This method is very similar to Bresenham's algorithm, but simpler and eliminates the floating point calculations.

Here a function having two variables x and y is considered to draw a circle and as:

$$f(x, y) = x^2 + y^2 - r^2 \qquad (2.18)$$

where the origin of the circle is considered at the origin and the radius is accepted as r.

Using this logic, any arbitrary point having the co-ordinates (x, y) is assumed and we check if:

- $f(x, y) < 0$ - then the assumed value of the co-ordinates must be inside the area of the circle.
- $f(x, y) > 0$ - then the assumed value of the co-ordinates must be outside the area of the circle.
- $f(x, y) = 0$ -then the assumed value of the co-ordinates must be on the periphery of the circle.

This feature is shown in the following figure

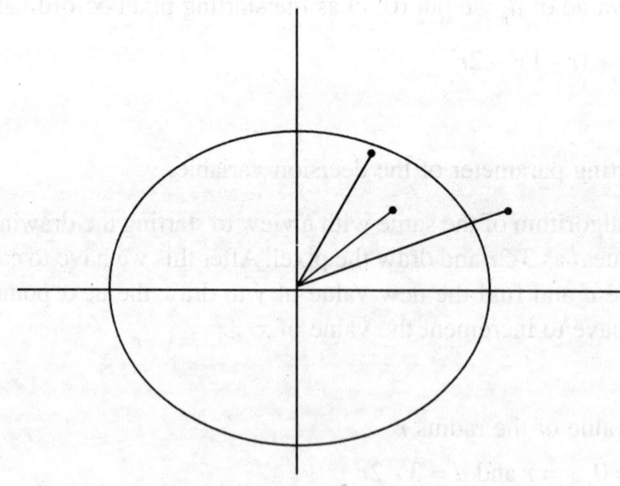

In general, the above points can be written as: A point is already drawn at the co-ordinates (x_p, y_p). The next possible values of the two co-ordinates (similar to Bresenham's algorithm and as per the above figure) will be:

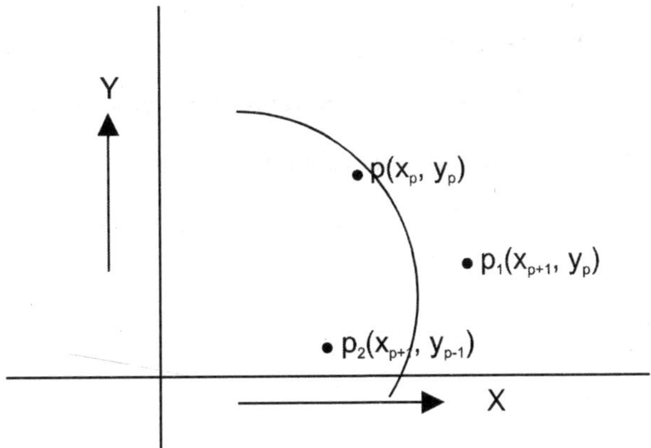

At point $p_1(x_p + 1, y_p)$

At point $p_2(x_p + 1, y_{p-1})$

Now consider a point which is in the middle of positions p_1 and p_2. Thus, the new assumed mid point co-ordinates will be:

$p' = (x_p + 1, y_p - 1/2)$

Now, substituting these co-ordinates in $f(x,y)$ we obtain the decision parameter d_p as:

$$d_p = f(x_p + 1, y_p - 1/2)s$$
$$= (x_p + 1)^2 + (y_p - 1/2)^2 - r^2$$

As we have already seen, if d_p becomes negative, the midpoint is definitely inside the area of the circle and thus the point p_2 will definitely be the closest point from the true circle and will be accepted. But, if the value of the decision parameter d_p becomes positive, we have to accept the point p_1, as this will be the closest point in this case.

Similarly for the next step, the decision parameter d_{p+1} can be expressed as:

$$d_{p+1} = (x_{p+1} + 1)^2 + (y_{p+1} - 1/2)^2 - r^2$$

but as we have incremented the value of the x co-ordinate by +1, we can write:

$$x_{p+1} = x_p + 1$$

so, $d_{p+1} = (x_p + 2)^2 + (y_{p+1} - 1/2)^2 - r^2$

or $d_{p+1} - d_p = (x_p + 2)^2 + (y_{p+1} - 1/2)^2 - r^2 - \{(x_p + 1)^2 + (y_p - 1/2)^2 - r^2\}$

$$= \{(x_p + 2)^2 - \{(x_p + 1)^2\} + \{(y_{p+1} - 1/2)^2 - (y_p - 1/2)^2\}$$

$$= \{x_p^2 + 4x_p + 4 - x_p^2 - 2x_p - 1\} + \{y^2_{p+1} + ¼ - y^2_p + y_p - 1/4\}$$

$$= (2x_p + 3) + (x^2_{p+1} - y^2_p) - (y_{p+1} - y_p)$$

$$= \{2(x_{p+1}) + 1\} + (y^2_{p+1} - y^2_p) - (y_{p+1} - y_p) \quad (2.19)$$

$$d_{p+1} = d_p + 2(x_{p+1}) + 1 + (y^2_{p+1} - y^2_p) - (y_{p+1} - y_p) \quad (2.20)$$

If the point p_1 is chosen as shown in the previous figure, we can write: $y_{p+1} = y_p$

But if the point p_2 is chosen, then we have the relation: $y_{p+1} = y_{p-1}$

Thus substituting these values in the above expression (2.20) we can write:

$$d_{p+1} = d_p + 2(x_p + 1) + 1$$

$$= d_p + 2x_p + 3 \quad \text{if } d_p \text{ is negative}$$

And

$$d_{p+1} = d_p + 2(x_p + 1) - 2(y_p - 1)$$

$$= d_p + 2(x_p - y_p) + 5 \quad \text{if } d_p \text{ is positive or zero}$$

To begin the iteration we have to accept the initial value to start with. Here the co-ordinate (0, *r*) is accepted as the starting co-ordinate to obtain the initial value of d_p.

Substituting the value of the co-ordinate (0, *r*) in the expression for d_p we obtain:

$$d_p = (0 + 1)^2 + (r - 1/2)^2 - r^2$$

$$= 1 + r^2 - r + 1/4 - r^2$$

$$= 5/4 - r$$

Using this logic and expression we can write the following algorithm:

Algorithm

Step-1: Accept the value *r*

Step-2: Assume $x = 0$, $y = r$ and compute $d_p = 1 - r$

Step-3: Draw the point at the co-ordinate (*x*, *y*). For the centre co-ordinate (x_c, y_c), draw the point at $(x + x_c, y + y_c)$ and also draw the same for the other octants.

Step-4: Check, if $d_p < 0$, compute the next value of d_p using the relation $d_p = d_p + 2x + 3$ and go to step 6

Step-5: Compute $d_p = d_p + 2(x - y) + 5$, decrease the value of the next y to $y = y - 1$

Step-6: Increment the value of *x* by 1 i.e. $x = x + 1$

Step-7: Check if $x \le y$, go to step 3

Step-8: Stop the process

Program:

```
/*
________________________________
Midpoint Circle Drawing
________________________________
*/
# include <iostream.h>
# include <conio.h>
# include <graphics.h>
# include <math.h>
void Circle(int,int,int);
void oncirclepoint(int,int,int,int);
void main()
{
        int gDriver=DETECT, gMode;
        initgraph(&gDriver,&gMode,"c:\\tc\\bgi");

        int Radius, xC, yC;
        cout<< endl << "Enter Centre point coordInates...";
        cout<<endl<<"  Xc    : ";
        cin>>xC;
        cout<<endl<<"  Yc    : ";
        cin>>yC;
        cout<<endl<<"Radius  : ";
        cin>>Radius;
        cleardevice();
        Circle(Radius,xC,yC);
        obtainch();
        return;
}
void Circle(int Radius,int xC,int yC)
{
        int P;
```

```
        int x,y;
   //   void oncirclepoint(int x,int y);
        P = 1 - Radius;
        x = 0;
        y = Radius;
        oncirclepoint(x,y,xC,yC);
        while (x<=y)
        {
                x++;
                if (P<0)
                {
                        P += 2 * x + 1;
                }
                else
                {
                        P += 2 * (x - y) + 1;
                        y—;
                }
                oncirclepoint(x,y,xC,yC);
        }

}
void oncirclepoint(int x,int y,int xC,int yC)
{
        putpixel(xC + x,yC + y,1);
        putpixel(xC + x,yC - y,1);
        putpixel(xC - x,yC + y,1);
        putpixel(xC - x,yC - y,1);
        putpixel(xC + y,yC + x,1);
        putpixel(xC - y,yC + x,1);
        putpixel(xC + y,yC - x,1);
        putpixel(xC - y,yC - x,1);
}
```

2.3.3 Drawing an Ellipse

We call a circular closed boundary as a circle if the diameter along both the horizontal and vertical directions remains the same. If they are different, it is called an ellipse.

An ellipse can be defined as a closed surface area having two focus points (focii) and the sum of the distances from these two focus points to all the points on the periphery is equal. This is shown in the figure below:

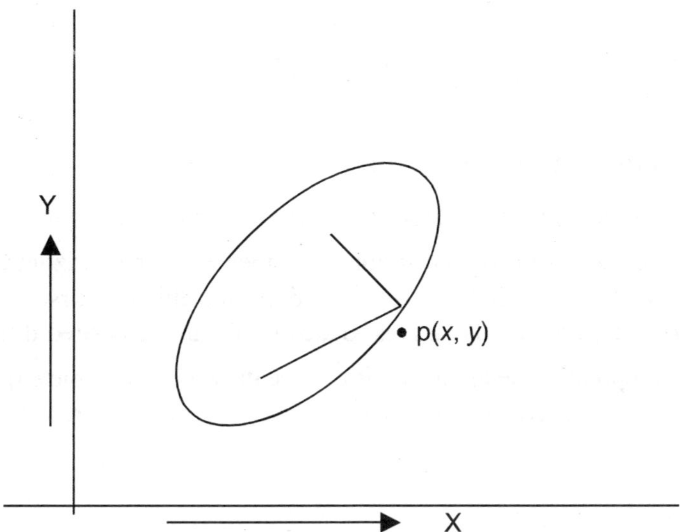

Here it is assumed that the two focus points are F_1 and F_2 and p is any point on the periphery of the ellipse having the co-ordinate (x, y). d_1 and d_2 are the respective distances of the two points from p.

We can write the relationship as:

$$\boldsymbol{d_1 + d_2 = \text{constant}} \qquad (2.21)$$

But, d_1 and d_2 can be expressed as:

$$\boldsymbol{d_1} = \sqrt{(x-x_1)^2+(y-y_1)^2} \qquad (2.22)$$

$$\text{and } d_2 = \sqrt{(x-x_2)^2+(y-y_2)^2}$$

Where the co-ordinates of the two focus points are assumed to be (x_1, y_1) and (x_2, y_2) respectively.

From equations (2.21) and (2.22), we can write:

$$\sqrt{(x-x_1)^2+(y-y_1)^2} + \sqrt{(x-x_2)^2+(y-y_2)^2} = \boldsymbol{K} \qquad (2.23)$$

where K is a constant.

Using the above equation, a general algorithm can be developed to form an ellipse as:

Algorithm

Step-1: Accept the co-ordinates of the two focus points, i.e. (x_1, y_1) and (x_2, y_2)

Step-2: Accept any co-ordinate (x, y) on the ellipse and draw a point at that co-ordinate.

Step-3: Substituting the above values, compute the value of K.

Step-4: Increment the value of x by 1 and find the new co-ordinate of the ellipse and draw the point there.

Step-5: Repeat Step 4 for the entire possible range of x.

Step-6: Stop the process.

Midpoint Algorithm for Drawing an Ellipse

The midpoint algorithm, as used in the case of a circle, is applied here with two reservations:

- The ellipse is drawn in standard position, i.e. either along the horizontal or vertical axes. To draw an ellipse other than in these two directions, the ellipse is first developed along either of the above axes and then the axis is rotated to obtain the desired direction.
- Unlike the mid point circle algorithm it is to be drawn in a complete quadrant and then the image is to be copied as a mirror image to the other three quadrants.

Re-arranging equation (2.23), we obtain:

$$((x - x_c)/a)^2 + ((y - y_c)/b)^2 = 1$$

Where 'a' is the radius of the ellipse along the major axis (semi major axis) and 'b' is the radius of ellipse along the minor axis.

Using the polar co-ordinate system we can write the expressions for the x and y co-ordinates as:

$$x = x_c + r_1 \cos\theta \qquad (2.24)$$

$$y = y_c + r_2 \sin\theta \qquad (2.25)$$

Using the (x, y) co-ordinates we can draw the segment of the ellipse in the first quadrant by verifying the values of x. Then we can obtain segments in the other quadrants by creating the mirror image of it.

By swapping x, y and r_1, r_2 we can also draw a vertical ellipse using the same technique.

Using this method we can draw any ellipse at any position. In this case, the ellipse is first drawn using the standard x and y axes and then the image is rotated by the desired angle to draw the required image.

Midpoint Algorithm for Drawing an Ellipse

The midpoint algorithm, as used in case of circle, is applied here with two reservations:

- The ellipse is drawn in the standard position, i.e. either along the horizontal or vertical axes. To draw an ellipse in any other direction, the ellipse is first developed along the horizontal or vertical axes and its axis is rotated to obtain the desired position.

- Unlike the midpoint circle algorithm the segment of the ellipse is drawn in a complete quadrant and this image copied as a mirror image in the other 3 quadrants.

Using equation (2.23), and re-arranging the terms we obtain:

$$((x - x_c)/a)^2 + ((y - y_c)/b)^2 = 1$$

Assuming x_c and y_c as (0, 0) for the time being we can write:

$$\mathbf{x^2/a^2 + y^2/b^2 = 1} \qquad (2.26)$$

Multiplying both sides by a^2b^2 gives:

$x^2b^2 + y^2a^2 = a^2b^2$

As a mathematical function the equation for an ellipse can be written as:

$$\boldsymbol{f(x, y) = x^2b^2 + y^2a^2 - a^2b^2} \qquad (2.27)$$

For any assumed co-ordinate (x', y'):

- If $f(x', y')$ becomes less than 0, then the assumed co-ordinate (x', y') must be inside the area of the ellipse.
- If $f(x', y')$ becomes 0, then the assumed c-ordinate must be on the boundary of the ellipse.
- If $f(x', y')$ becomes greater than 0, then the assumed co-ordinate (x', y') must be outside the area of the ellipse.

To start with we have to clearly identify the differences present between a circle and an ellipse. At the time of drawing a circle we have drawn a point on (x_p, y_p); the next tentative co-ordinate will be either p_1 having the co-ordinates (x_p, y_p) and $(x_p + 1, y_p - 1)$ for one octant of the circle. However, in the case of an ellipse, it can be understood from the following figure that for the point p having the co-ordinate (x_p, y_p), the next probable co-ordinates are $(x_p + 1, y_p)$ and $(x_p + 1, y_p - 1)$.

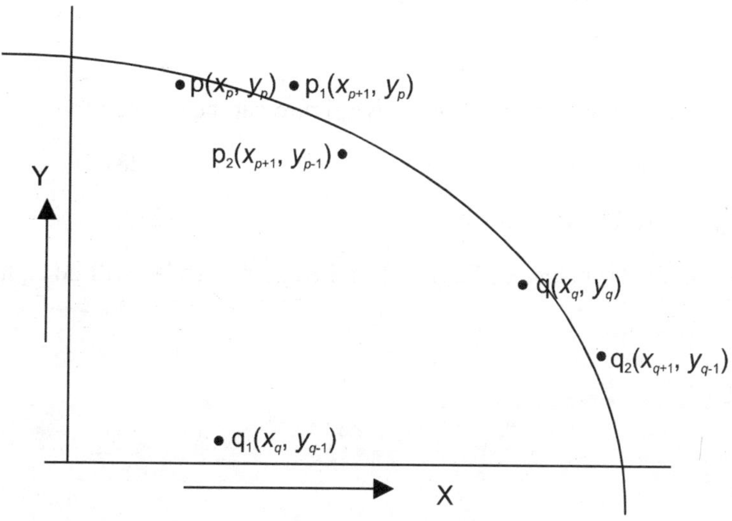

For the point q that is drawn, having the co-ordinates (x_q, y_q), the next probable point to be drawn will be either q_1 or q_2 having the co-ordinates (x_q, y_{q-1}) and (x_{q+1}, y_{q-1}) respectively. So, in this area, the mode of calculation will be different from that in the upper side as seen for the previous point p.

Thus in this case we have to keep track to determine the form of calculation that should be followed to trace the ellipse.

To check this, we have to keep track of the slope of the periphery of the ellipse in the first quadrant from an angle from 90° to 0°.

To do this, we have to divide the ellipse into two regions, viz. Region 1 and Region 2 as shown in the figure below to find a point K where the slope becomes – 1. In Region 1 it will be less than 1 and in Region 2 it will be greater than 1.

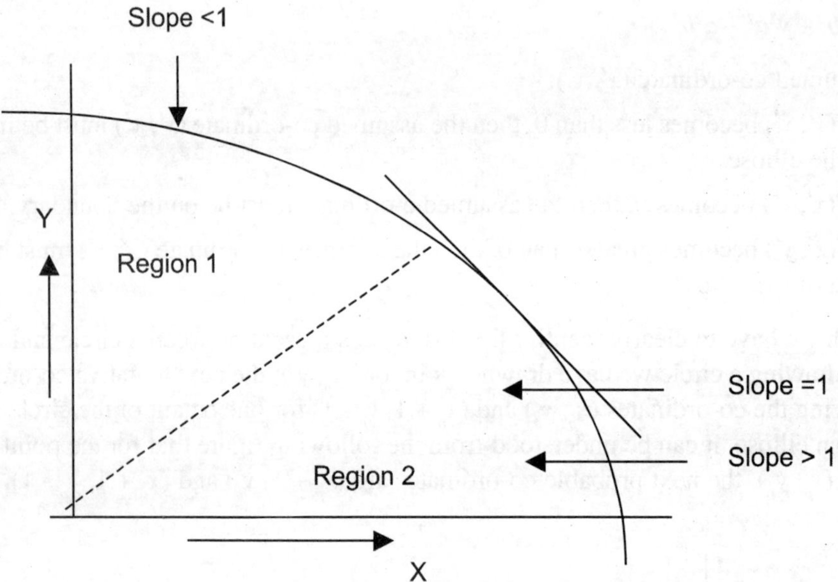

Now the slope of the curve as shown in the above figure can be defined by:

$$f(x, y) = x^2b^2 + y^2a^2 - a^2b^2 \qquad (2.28)$$

$$d_y/d_x = -2b^2x/2a^2y = -b^2x/a^2y \qquad (2.29)$$

At the point *K*, i.e. at the boundary of Region 1 and Region 2, *dy/dx* will be equal to

- 1, therefore,

$d_y/d_x = -b^2x/a^2y$

$= -1$

$b^2x = a^2y$

In order to identify in which area we are at the present time, we have to check as follows:

- If $b^2x > a^2y$ Then we will be in Region 2 and if
- $b^2x \leq a^2y$ Then we will be in Region 1.

In Region 1

Assuming that the first point to be drawn is (0, b) i.e. at the intersection of the y axis in positive direction and the path of the ellipse. Let us also assume that we have already obtained the last point 'p' on the ellipse's periphery at the co-ordinate (x_p, y_p). As we are now in Region 1, we have to select the next point either at p_1 with the co-ordinate (x_{p+1}, y_p) or at the point p_2 having the co-ordinate (x_{p+1}, y_{p-1}). The mid point of the two points p_1 and p_2 will have the co-ordinate (x_{p+1}, $y_{p-1/2}$).

Thus, the decision parameter d_p at this point will be:

$$d_p = f(x_{p+1}, y_{p-1/2})$$
$$= b^2(x_{p+1})^2 + a^2(y_{p-1/2})^2 - a^2b^2$$

Using the same concept it can be seen that, if d_p becomes less than 0, then the mid point will be inside the area and so the point p_1 is to be selected. But if it is not less than 0, i.e. if it becomes 0 or is positive, the mid point will definitely lie outside the ellipse and thus we have to select the point p_2. Similarly, for the next step, the decision parameter will be:

$$d_p = f(x_{p+1}, y_{p-1/2})$$
$$= b^2(x_{p+1})^2 + a^2(y_{p\ 1/2})^2 - a^2b$$

But as $x_{p+1} = x_p+1$, substituting we obtain,

$$d_{p+1} - d_p = b^2[(x_{p+1}+1)^2 - x_p+1]p$$

Using the same concept it can be seen that, if d_p becomes less than 0, then the mid point will be inside the area and so the point p_1 is to be selected. If it is not less than 0, i.e. if it becomes 0 or positive, the mid point will definitely lie outside the ellipse and thus we have to select the point p_2. Similarly, for the next step, the decision parameter will be:

$$d_p+1 = f(x_{p+1} + 1, y_{p+1} - 1/2)$$
$$= b^2(x_{p+1} + 1)^2 + a^2(y_{p+1} - 1/2)^2 - a^2b^2$$

But as $x_{p+1} = x_p+1$, substituting we obtain,

$$d_{p+1} - d_p = b^2[(x_{p+1} + 1)^2 - x_{p+1}] + a^2[(y_{p+1} - 1/2)^2 - (y_p-1/2)^2]$$

So, $d_{p+1} = d_p + 2b^2x_{p+1} + b^2 + a^2\ [(y_{p+1}-1/2)2]$

If for the previous point, point p_1 is chosen which means d_p is negative, we have $y_{p+1} = y_p$. Similarly, if the point p_2 is chosen which means d_p is greater than or equal to 0, we have $y_{p+1} = y_p-1$. Thus for the present value of the decision parameter d_p, the next value can be calculated as:

$$d_{p+1} = d_p + 2b^2x_{p+1} + b^2 \quad \text{if } d_p < 0$$

and $d_{p+1} = d_p + 2b^2x_{p+1} + b^2 - 2a^2y_{p+1}$ if $d_p \geq 0$

The starting co-ordinate for the iteration is $(0,b)$, substituting this value in to the expression we obtain:

$d_{p1} = b^2 + a^2(b - 1/2)^2 - a^2b^2$

$= \mathbf{b^2 - a^2b + a^2/4}$ (2.30)

In Region 2

In this region we can develop the same set of equations as shown below:

Suppose in Region 2, the last point drawn 'q' has the co-ordinates (x_q, y_q), then the next probable point will be either q_1 at the co-ordinate (x_q, y_{q-1}) or at q_2 at the co-ordinate (x_q+1, y_q-1). The midpoint of these two points will be $(x_q + 1/2, y_q - 1)$. So, the decision parameter at this point will be:

$d_q = f(x_q+1, y_q-1)$

$= \mathbf{b^2(x_q + 1/2)^2 + a^2(y_q-1)^2 - a^2b^2}$ (2.31)

Again, using the same logic we can say that if d_q is less than 0, the midpoint will be inside the ellipse and hence the point q_2 will be chosen. Similarly if d_q is 0 or greater than 0, it will be outside or on the curve itself, and in this case the point q_1 is to be chosen.

Again for the next point, the value of the decision parameter will be:

$d_{q+1} = f(x_{q+1} + 1/2, y_{q+1} - 1)$

$= \mathbf{b^2(x_{q+1} + 1/2)^2 + a^2(y_{q+1} - 1)^2 - a^2b^2}$ (2.32)

Now, as $y_{q+1} = y_q - 1$, we can write:

$d_{q+1} - d_q = [b^2(x_{q+1} + 1/2)^2 - (x_q + 1/2)^2] + a^2[(y_{q+1} - 1)^2 - y^2_{q+1}]$

so, $\mathbf{d_{q+1} = d_q + [b^2(x_{q+1} + 1/2)^2 - (x_q + 1/2)^2] - 2a^2y_{q+1} + a^2}$ (2.33)

In the same way we can write:

$d_{q+1} = d_q + 2b^2x_{q+1} - 2a^2y_{q+1} + a^2$ if $d_q < 0$

and $d_{q+1} = d_{q1} - 2a^2y_{q+1} + a^2$ if $d_q \geq 0$

Using the same technique, we can find the starting value of the decision parameter using the last co-ordinate of Region 1. Assume it to be (x_k, y_k), then,

$d_{q1} = f(x_k + 1/2, y_k - 1)$

$= \mathbf{b^2(x_k + 1/2)^2 + a^2(y_k - 1)^2 - a^2b^2}$ (2.34)

Thus we have obtained the relationships of the two defined regions, namely Region 1 and Region 2.

To obtain the complete segment of the ellipse for the first quadrant we have to sum up all these relationships. We start the drawing from the co-ordinate $(0, b)$ using the relationship obtained for

Region 1 and will keep track of the slope of the curve. This step will be repeated using the same relationships until and unless the slope becomes -1. After this we use the equations and relationships for Region 2.

After obtaining the complete segment for the first quadrant, the mirror image can be obtained for other quadrants.

Initially it was assumed for the centre co-ordinate was (0, 0). For any other centre co-ordinate (x_c, y_c), the generated co-ordinate of the point will be ($x + x_c$, $y + y_c$). Now let us write the algorithm.

Algorithm

Step-1: Accept the centre co-ordinate (x_c, y_c) and the length of the semi major axis a and b.

Step-2: Compute the first point co-ordinate (x_0, y_0) as (0, b) and draw the point.

Step-3: Compute the initial value of the decision parameter $dp_1 = b^2 - a^2b + a^2/4$
Assume $dp = d_p+1$. Obtain the next assumed co-ordinate (x_p+1, y_p) for the origin (0,0).

Step-4: Compute and compare the decision parameter using the relationships:

$d_{p+1} = d_p + 2b^2x_{p+1} + b^2$ if $d_p < 0$ and

and $d_{p+1} = d_p + 2b^2x_{p+1} + b^2 - 2a^2y_{p+1}$ if $d_p \geq 0$

Step-5: Compute the slope, if the condition $b^2x \geq a^2y$ is satisfied, repeat from Step 4.

Step-6: This will be the starting point of Region 2. Compute the initial value of the decision parameter as $d_{q1} = b^2(x_k + 1/2)^2 + a^2(y_k - 1)^2 - a^2b^2$. Assume $d_q = d_{q1}$

Step-7: Now compute the next decision parameter d_q+1 using the relationships:

$d_{q+1} = d_q + 2b^2x_{q+1} - 2a^2y_{q+1} + a^2$ if $d_q < 0$

and $d_{q+1} = d_{q1} - 2a^2y_{q+1} + a^2$ if $d_q \geq 0$

Step-8: Increment the value of x and repeat from Step 7 up to the value $x = a$.

Step-9: Stop the process.

This algorithm will draw the ellipse segment for the first quadrant only. Plot the mirror image of the ellipse by drawing the co-ordinates (x, $-y$) ($-x$, y) and ($-x$, $-y$) respectively.

This algorithm is for an ellipse having its centre at the origin (0, 0). For any given origin (x_c, y_c), each point is to be shifted by ($x + x_c$, $y + y_c$) respectively.

Program:

```
// Program to draw ellipse
#include<stdio.h>
#include<conio.h>
#include<graphics.h>
void EllipseMidpoint(int,int,int,int);
void EllipsePlotPoint(int,int,int,int);
```

```
void main()
{
        int gd=DETECT,gm;
        int x1,rx,y1,ry;
        initgraph(&gd,&gm,"c:\\tc\\bgi");
        printf("\nEnter the value of centre Point");
        printf(" \nx1=:");
        scanf("%d",&x1);
        printf("\n y1=");
        scanf("%d",&y1);
        printf("\n Enter the value radiuses :");
        printf(" \n rx=");
        scanf("%d",&rx);
        printf("\n ry=");
        scanf("%d",&ry);
        cleardevice();
        EllipseMidpoint(x1,y1,rx,ry);
   //   EllipseMidpoint(50,100,5,50);
        obtainch();
        closegraph();
}
void EllipseMidpoint(int xc,int yc,int Rx,int Ry)
{
        int Rx2=Rx*Rx;
        int Ry2=Ry*Ry;
        int twoRx2=2*Rx2;
        int twoRy2=2*Ry2;
        int p;
        int x=0;
        int y=Ry,px=0,py=twoRx2*y;

        EllipsePlotPoint(xc,yc,x,y);
        p=ceil(Ry2-(Rx2*Ry)+(0.25*Rx2));
```

```
	while(px<py)
	{
		x++;
		px+=twoRy2;
		if(p<0)
			p+=Ry2+px;
		else
		{
			y—;
			py-=twoRx2;
			p+=Ry2+px-py;
		}
	EllipsePlotPoint(xc,yc,x,y);
	}
	p=ceil(Ry2*(x+0.5)*(x+0.5)+Rx2*(y-1)*(y-1)-Rx2*Ry2);
	while(y>0)
	{
		y—;
		py-=twoRx2;
		if(p>0)
			p+=Rx2-py;
		else
		{
			x++;
			px+=twoRy2;
			p+=Rx2-py+px;
		}
	EllipsePlotPoint(xc,yc,x,y);
	}
}
void EllipsePlotPoint(int xc,int yc,int x,int y)
{
	putpixel(xc+x,yc+y,15);
```

```
        putpixel(xc-x,yc+y,15);
        putpixel(xc+x,yc-y,15);
        putpixel(xc-x,yc-y,15);
}
```

2.4 FILLING WITH COLOURS

We start the discussion on filling a closed body with a colour. Of course we can fill a closed surface by using a set of different colours or with a pattern or style of colours.

We can only paint a body when the area closes in on itself, otherwise it is like trying to keep some paint in a pot with a hole in it. In the latter case the colour will leak out of the pot. Similarly if we try to paint an image that does not close in on itself the colour will spread all over the screen.

There are two approaches to painting a closed body.

- By determining the overlap intervals of the scan lines through a given area.
- By starting the painting at a given interior position and painting outwards from this point up to the specified boundary conditions.

Normally the first method is used in the case of painting squares, rectangles, circles and other simply shaped bodies whereas the second method is used in more complex figures.

2.4.1 The Scan Line Filling Method

In this method the points of intersection of the scan lines and the boundary of the body are first located. As in real life situations, scan lines in the monitors always remain parallel to the horizontal base line, we will consider all the scan lines parallel to the x-axis. For any image, the number of intersection points will always be even if the scan lines pass through it. But, if the scan lines pass through any of the vertex points, the number of intersection points will be odd, (see figure below).

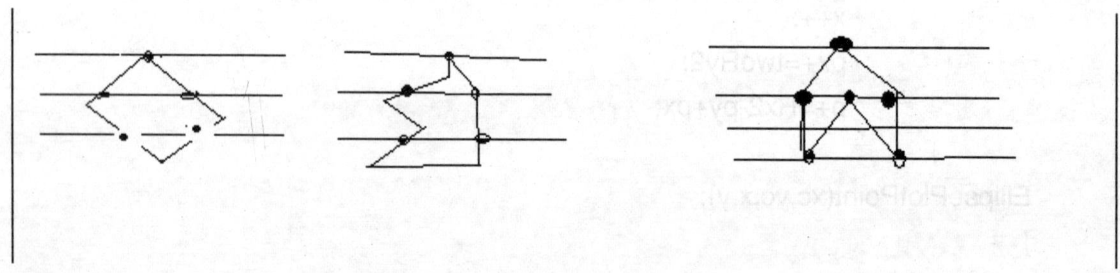

When painting an image, a colour raster line is passed uniformly from the uppermost surface to the lowermost line. This raster line should not be visible until it crosses the boundary surface of the body for the first time. After that the pixels are to be illuminated until the raster line crosses the boundary again on the opposite side.

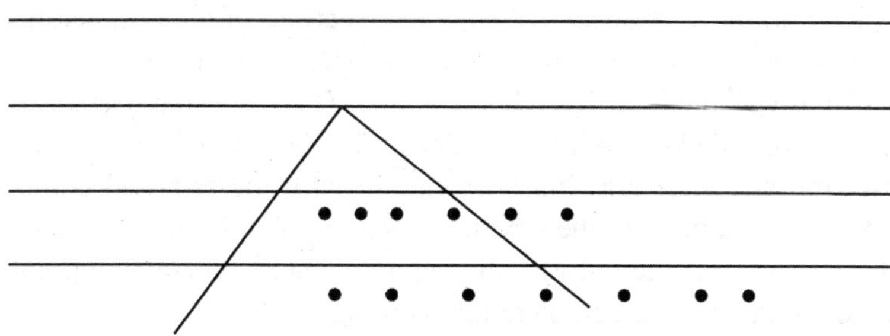

The first crossing of the scan line will cause a switch to turn on to start painting with a colour whereas, the second point of crossing will cause the switch to turn off the colour. Thus, the switch must be kept in the off state by default.

In the case of the scan line crossing the vertex, we have to check whether the two edges emanating from it extend to the same side of the scan line or to different sides. If it extends to the same side of the scan line, the scan line definitely does not cross an edge but in the second case it does.

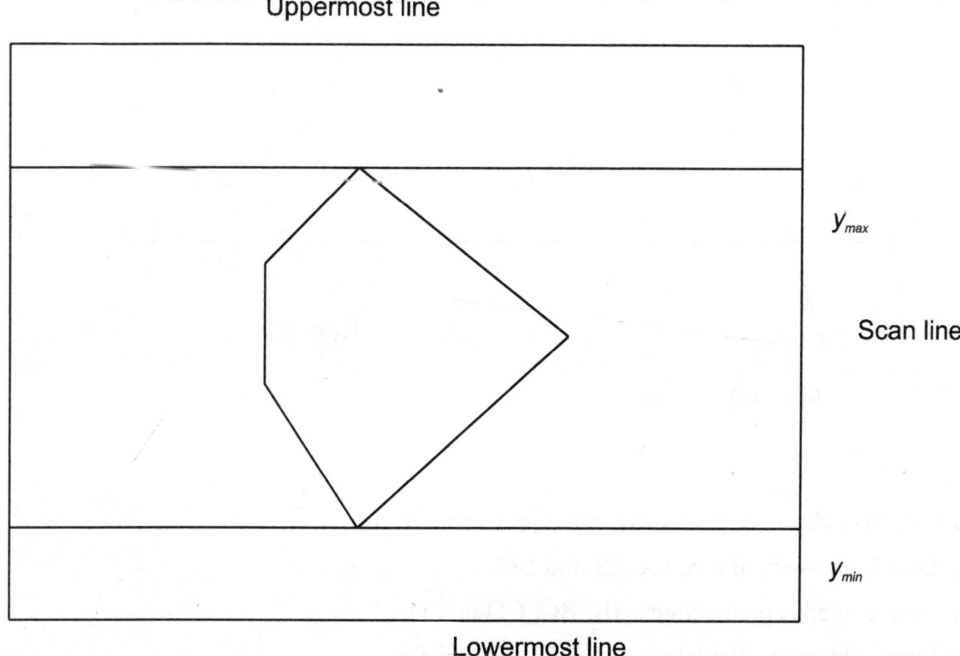

We can still improve the process by minimizing the time. We do not need to pass the scan line from the upper most horizontal line to the lowermost line. If we can find the maximum and minimum value of the y co-ordinate, we can pass the scan line from the line at y_{max} to that at y_{min} or vice-versa. This will save time.

In the same way, we do not need to check for edge intersections at the leftmost pixel and continue to test through the complete area of scanning. We can simply compute, in advance, all the points at which the boundary lines will intersect with this scan line. The co-ordinate values of pixels may not be integers, but they are rounded off to integer values. Finally to fill the polygon, we will move to the leftmost intersection and start drawing horizontally with the required colour up to the next intersection point, then we again go to the next intersection point, if any, on the same line, without drawing a line, after that we will again draw a line up to the next intersection point. This process is to be continued up to the last line to complete the painting.

Now using this technique let us start painting a figure. In the figure given below, the vertices are marked as A, B, C, D and E. Assume for simplicity, that there are only four scan lines present marked as 1, 2, 3, and 4 respectively.

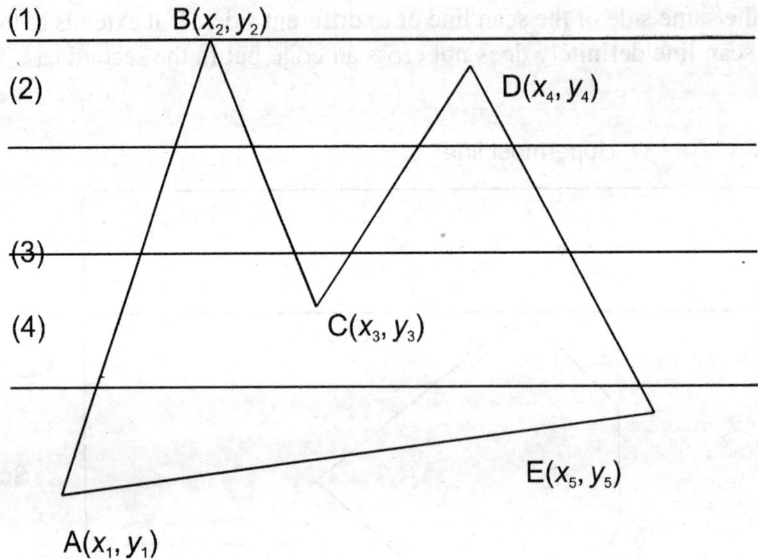

Below we see how the scan lines cross the edges of the figure.

Scan Line 1 intersects the edges AB and BC.

Scan Line 2 intersects the edges AB, BC, CD and DE.

Scan Line 3 intersects the edges AB, BC, CD and DE.

Scan Line 4 intersects the edges AB and DE.

We can keep these values along with their corresponding y_{min}, y_{max} and x co-ordinate values of the vertex at $y = y_{min}$

We will also trace the inverse of the slope (1/m) for all the edges as shown below:

Edge	y_{min}	y_{max}	*x* co-ordinate of the vertex with $y = y_{min}$	Inverse of the slope
AB	y_1	y_2	x_1	$1/m_1$
BC	y_3	y_2	x_3	$1/m_2$
CD	y_3	y_4	x_3	$1/m_3$
DE	y_5	y_4	x_5	$1/m_4$
EA	y_1	$y_{5\text{-}1}$	x_1	$1/m_5$

Observe that in the above table the value of y_{max} at the edge EA is written as $y_{5\text{-}1}$ and not y_5 like the others. The reason for this is that when a scan line intersects a vertex which is jointed by two monotonically increasing or decreasing edges, obtaining two intersection points at the vertex would give incorrect results. To avoid this problem we take only one intersection point at the vertex. However, if the vertex is a local minimum or maximum such as the point 'C', no special treatment would be necessary. In this case, the two intersection points can be treated as a common member point to produce a pair of points for the filling operation.

Sorting the table with respect to y_{min} in ascending order, gives:

Edge	y_{min}	y_{max}	x co-ordinate of the vertex with $y = y_{min}$	Inverse of the slope
AB	y_1	y_2	x_1	$1/m_1$
EA	y_1	$y_{5\text{-}1}$	x_1	$1/m_5$
DE	y_5	y_4	x_5	$1/m_4$
BC	y_3	y_2	x_3	$1/m_2$
CD	y_3	y_4	x_3	$1/m_3$

From the above we observe that edges AB and EA are at the top of the list which indicates that both edges have been organized from the lowest vertex point having the co-ordinate (x_1, y_1). The corresponding values of their slopes are m_1 and m_5 respectively.

As we have already discussed the scan lines should be active from the minimum value of y of the figure that is to be painted. In the above example, the scan should start from $y_{min} = y_1$ which is already stored in the list. The other point of intersection between the edges and successive scan lines can be found out by the method of incrementation.

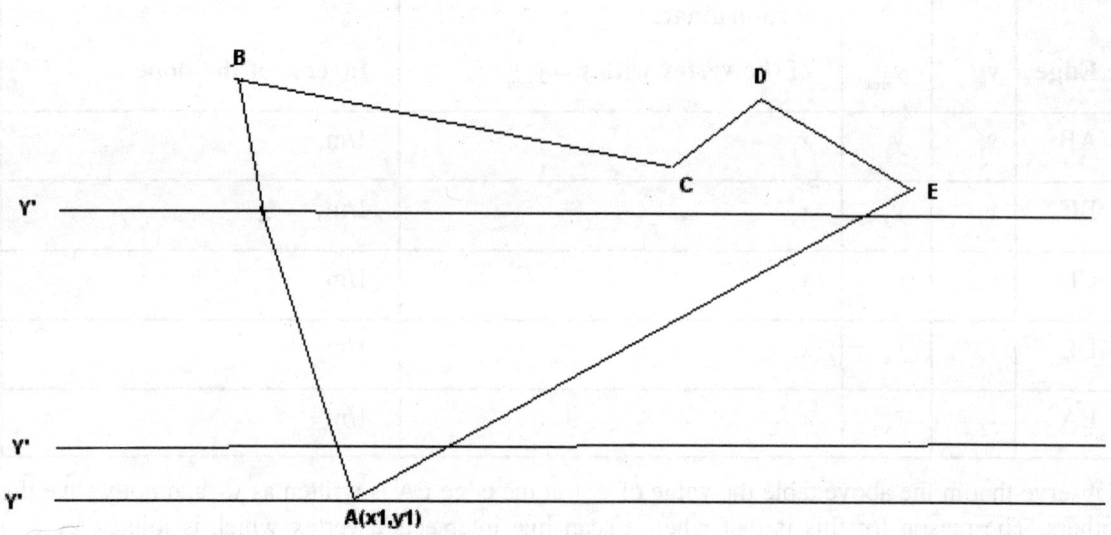

Incrementation is applied in the following way. Suppose that a point having the co-ordiante (*x*, *y*) lies on a line of slope 'm'. The next point will be (*x*+1/m, *y*+1) because m = *dy*/*dx*. Thus, if the increment value of *y*(*dy*) is +1, *dx* will be 1/m.

When the first scan line touches the edges BA & AE at *y* = *y*', the next point of intersection of the edge AE with the next scan line at *y* = *y*' will have the co-ordinates (x_1+1/m_5, *y*+1), as the slope here is m_5 and *dy* = 1.

In this way the scan line will be moved in the upward direction, when it reaches y_{max}, the particular section from the list will be discarded. For example, when the scan line is at $y = y^k$ then it will reach the value of y_{max} at the edge AE (i.e. $y = y^5$-1), and the edge AE will have to be de-activated from the list. The scan will be continued in this way.

Algorithm

Step-1: Note the starting and end co-ordinates of the edges of the body.

Step-2: Find the highest (y_{max}) and lowest (y_{min}) values present along the y-axis of each edge.

Step-3: Start the scan line, parallel to the x-axis from the value of y_{min} in the list and find the point of intersection with the edges of the body.

Step-4: Sort the corresponding values of the y co-ordinate in ascending order and determine the rightmost cutting edge point.

Step-5: Check if y_{max} ≥ scan value for an edge, if so include that edge. When the condition y_{max} < scan value is satisfied, no more comparisons will be needed as the values of the y coordinate will have already been sorted.

Step-6: Update the value of y and continue the tasks from step 3 and step 5 as long as y is less than or equal to y_{max}.

To study the algorithm let us take another example and prepare the table.

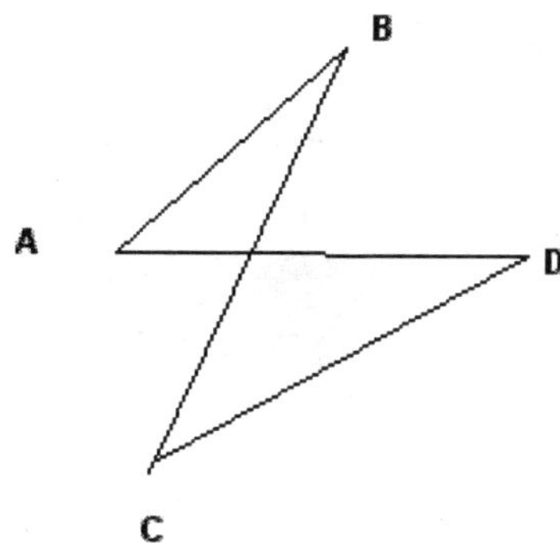

Assume that the co-ordinates of vertices are:

A = (50, 100), B = (150, 150), C = (45, 40), D = (180, 60)

The table of values will be as follows:

Edge	y_{max} **(in ascending order)**	y_{max}	d_x **= 1/m**	x **(when** $Y = y_{min}$**)**	**Next** x $x = x + d_x$
CD	40	60	-6.75	45	38
BC	40	150	0.954	45	46
AB	100	150	-2	50	48

2.4.2 The Boundary Fill System

Another method of a colour fill algorithm is the boundary fill method. Here the area in any closed loop can be painted starting from a point, inside the body.

If the boundary of the body is in a single colour, then this algorithm proceeds outward, pixel-by-pixel, until the boundary colour is not reached. The user may also choose the same border colour of the body so that a region of solid colour can be seen.

In this method, a pixel co-ordinate (x, y) is accepted from the user which is placed inside the body.

The boundary colour that exists is also entered. The painting starts with the neighbouring coordinates of (*x*, *y*) if it does not already exist in the boundary colour.

The neighbouring pixel can be traced out using two methods: (i) Four connected method and (ii) eight connected method. In the four-connected method, the pixels to be painted in the upper, lower, left and right direction as shown below:

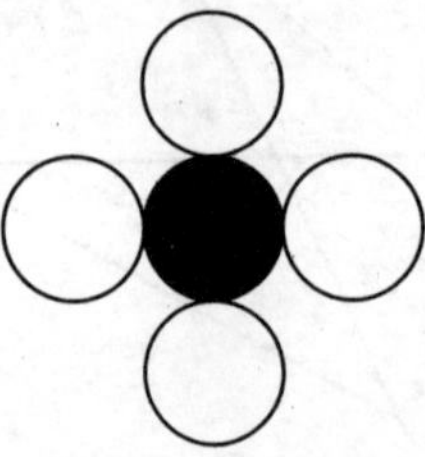

In the eight connected method, the four diagonal pixels are also considered and this is shown below. Using the second method, we can fill the body with colour more correctly and accurately.

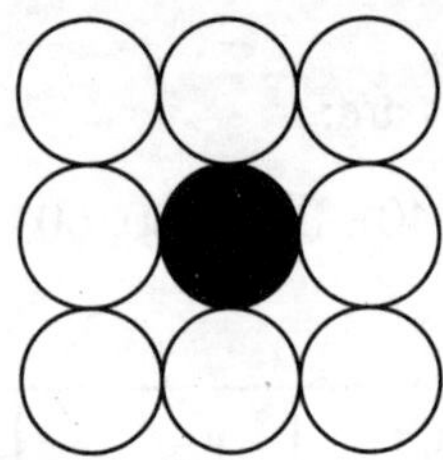

An algorithm of this logic is given below:

Step-1: Read the co-ordinate (*x*, *y*).

Step-2: Read the fill colour and boundary colour.

Step-3: Check, if the current co-ordinate (*x*, *y*) lies on the boundary and if the current colour is the same as the fill colour, go to step 9.

Step-4: Paint the current pixel (*x*, *y*) with fill colour.

Step-5: Go to step 2 with (*x* + 1, *y*) co-ordinate.

Step-6: Go to step 2 with (*x* - 1, *y*) co-ordinate.

Step-7: Go to step 2 with (*x*, *y* + 1) co-ordinate.

Step-8: Go to step 2 with (*x*, *y* - 1) co-ordinate.

Step-9: Stop the process.

In the above algorithm, we use the 4-connected approach.

Program

```
// Program to boundary fill with 4 neighbourhood points
```

```
#include<stdio.h>
#include<conio.h>
#include<graphics.h>
#include<math.h>
void boundaryfill4(int x,int y,int fillcolour,int boundarycolor)
{
        int current;
        current=obtainpixel(x,y);
        if((current!=fillcolor)&&(current!=boundarycolor))
        {
                putpixel(x,y,fillcolor);
                delay(10);
                boundaryfill4(x+1,y,fillcolor,boundarycolor);
                boundaryfill4(x-1,y,fillcolor,boundarycolor);
                boundaryfill4(x,y+1,fillcolor,boundarycolor);
                boundaryfill4(x,y-1,fillcolor,boundarycolor);
        }
}
void main()
{
        int gd=DETECT,gm;
        int x,y,fill;
        initgraph(&gd,&gm,"C:\\tc\\bgi");

        printf("\n Enter x:");
        scanf("%d",&x);
        printf("\n Enter y:");
        scanf("%d",&y);
        printf("\n Enter fillcolor:");
        scanf("%d",&fill);
        cleardevice();
        circle(x,y,15);
        boundaryfill4(x,y,fill,15);
```

```
        obtainch();
        closegraph();
}
```

2.4.3 The Flood Fill System

Flood fill is a small variant on a boundary fill. It replaces *old* pixels with the *fill* colour. A basic computer graphics task is the flood-fill task. The purpose of flood-fill is to fill an arbitrary bounded space on the screen with a given colour (we will be using black). For example, it is a flood-fill algorithm that allows colourization of old black and white movies. Another way that we can fill an area that is not defined within a single colour is with the help of a flood fill algorithm.

To run a flood-fill algorithm, you need a grid of pixels (which are simply dots on the screen) each of which can be either on or off, and a location within that grid at which to start filling. The pixel at the start location should be off. The flood-fill algorithm sets the start location to on, along with all of its horizontal and vertical neighbours that are off, and all of their horizontal and vertical neighbours that are off, *etc.* This 'flooding' stops when a pixel that is already on is reached. You can think of the pixels that are initially on as walls, and of the start location as a hose pumping out water. The water fills as much area as it can, but it is stopped by the walls.

Program

```
// Program to flood fill the object
#include<stdio.h>
#include<conio.h>
#include<graphics.h>
#include<math.h>
void flood_fill4(int x,int y,int fill,int oldcolor)
{
        if(obtainpixel(x,y)==oldcolor)
        {
                putpixel(x,y,fill);
                delay(10);
                flood_fill4(x+1,y,fill,oldcolor);
                flood_fill4(x-1,y,fill,oldcolor);
                flood_fill4(x,y+1,fill,oldcolor);
                flood_fill4(x,y-1,fill,oldcolor);

        }
}
```

```
void main()
{
        int x,y,fill;
        int gd=DETECT,gm;
        initgraph(&gd,&gm,"C:\\tc\\bgi");
        printf("\n Enter x:");
        scanf("%d",&x);
        printf("\n Enter y:");
        scanf("%d",&y);
        printf("\n Enter Fillcolor:");
        scanf("%d",&fill);
        cleardevice();
        circle(x,y,15);
        flood_fill4(x,y,fill,0);
        obtainch();
        closegraph();
}
```

2.5 SUMMARY

- Graphics drivers are software, which drives the graphics card to draw the graphics objects properly. Without using the proper graphics driver file, no graphics object can be drawn on the screen.
- Graphdriver is an integer that specifies the graphics driver to be used. You can mention the graphdriver a value using a constant of the graphics_drivers enumeration type.
- A more accurate and efficient method of line drawing algorithm is given by Bresenham where the floating-point arithmetic is avoided to a great extent and only the incremental integer calculations are carried out.
- A better method of drawing a circle is by drawing equally spaced pixels along the boundary of the circle. But this will require the co-ordinates to be in the Polar form.
- As circle is a perfectly symmetric figure, we can draw a circle by drawing an arc in one quadrant of the coordinate system and the remaining arcs in the other three quadrants can be drawn by drawing the images of this arc.
- By using Bresenham's algorithm for drawing a circle, we can avoid the floating-point arithmetic and trigonometric calculations as this algorithm uses integer arithmetic only. Using this method, a part of a circle, between the angles 0 and 45° is generated and the other seven segments are obtained by the reflection images of the same.

- In boundary fill algorithms, if the boundary of the body exists in a single colour, then this algorithm proceeds outward, pixel by pixel, until the boundary colour is not reached. The user may also choose the same border colour of the body so that a solid colour region can be seen.
- To run a flood-fill algorithm, you need a grid of pixels (which are simply dots on the screen) each of which can be either on or off, and a location within that grid at which to start filling.

2.6 REVIEW QUESTIONS

1. Discuss the various functions used in graphics.
2. Discuss line drawing algorithms and differentiate DDA algorithms with Bresenham's line algorithm.
3. Write algorithms for DDA line drawing and implement the algorithm in C language.
4. Write algorithms for Bresenham's line drawing and implement the algorithm in C language.
5. Write algorithms for mid-point circle and implement them in C language.
6. Write algorithms for mid-point ellipse and implement them in C language.
7. Discuss the concepts of filling and inside tests.
8. Write short notes on the following:
   a. Flood fill algorithm
   b. Boundary-fill algorithm
   c. Scan-line polygon fill algorithm

CHAPTER 3

Viewing Transformation and Clipping

3.1 INTRODUCTION

When we define an image in a world coordinate system, then in order to display that image we must somehow map the image to the physical output device. This is a two-stage process. For 3 dimensional images we must first project down to 2 dimensions, since our display device is 2 dimensional. Next, we must map the 2D representation to the physical device. This section deals with the second part of this process, i.e. the 2D World Device Coordinates (WDC) to 2D Physical Device Coordinates (PDC). We will first discuss the concept of a window on the world (WDC), and then a viewport in Normalized Device Coordinates (NDC), and finally the mapping WDC to NDC to PDC.

Window

When we model an image in World Device Coordinates (WDC) we are not interested in the entire world but only a portion of it. Therefore we define the portion of interest which is a polygonal area specified in world coordinates, called the "window".

Example: To plot x vs. cos(x) for x between 0.0 and 2Pi. Now cos x will be between -1.0 and +1.0. So we want the window as shown alongside.

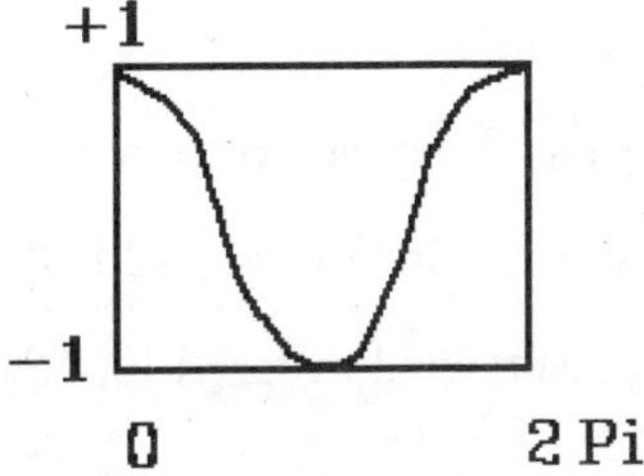

The command to set a window is Set_window2(xw_{min}, xw_{max}, yw_{min}, yw_{max}). For the above plot we use the following command:

Set_window2(0, 6.28, -1.0, +1.0)

We can use the window to change the apparent size and/or location of objects in the image. Changing the window affects all the objects in the image. These effects are called "zooming" and "panning".

Zooming

Assume you are drawing a house:

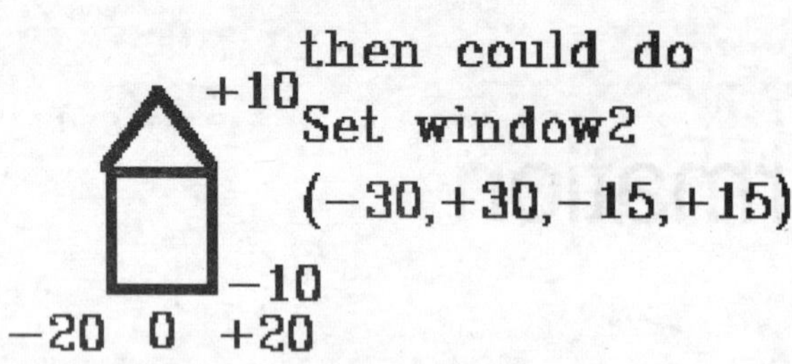

If you increase the window size, the house appears smaller, i.e., you have zoomed out:

Set_window(-60, +60, -30, +30)

<–"Zoom" out

If you decrease the window size the house appears larger, i.e., you have zoomed in:

Set_window(-21, +21, -11, +11)

Thus we can change the apparent size of an image, in this case a house, by changing the window size.

Panning

What about the position of the image?

A. Set_window(-40, +20,-15,+15)

B. Set_window(-20,+40,-15,+15)

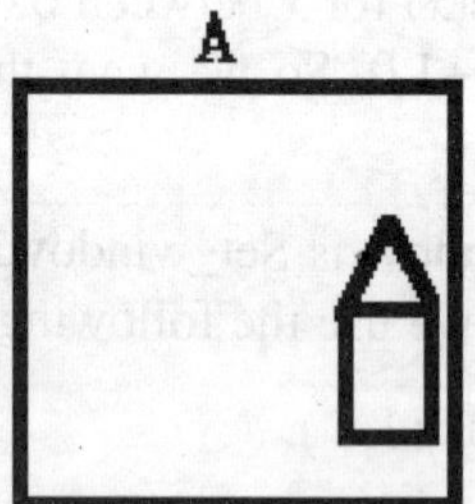

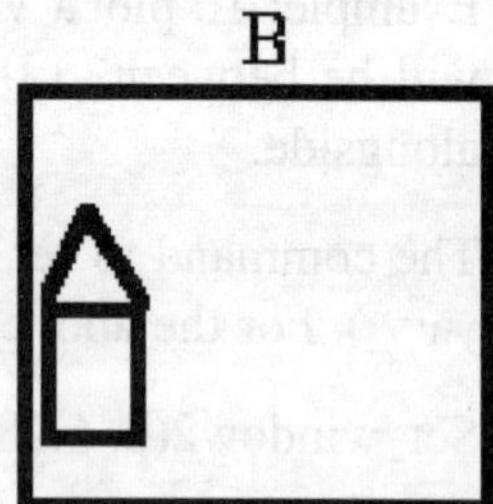

Moving all objects in the scene by changing the window is called "panning".

3.2 2D VIEWPORT TO PHYSICAL DEVICE TRANSFORMATION

3.2.1 2D Viewing Transformation: Viewport

The user may want to create images on different parts of the screen so we define a viewport in Normalized Device Coordinates (NDC). Using NDC also allows for output device independence. Later we will map from NDC to PDC.

Normalized Device Coordinates: Let the entire display surface have coordinate values:

$0.0 <= x, y <= 1.0$

Command: Set_viewport2(xv_{min},xv_{max}, yv_{min}, yv_{max})

Examples

To draw in the bottom half of the screen: Set_viewport2(0.0, 1.0, 0.0, 0.5)

To draw in the upper right hand corner: Set_viewport2(0.5, 1.0, 0.5, 1.0)

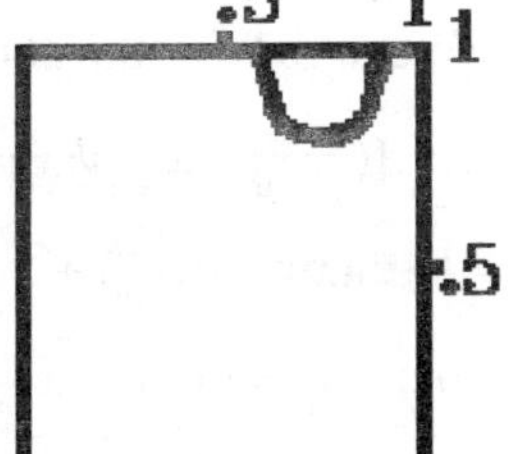

One can display multiple images in different viewports:

Set_window(-30, +30, -15, +15);

Set_viewport(0.0, 0.5, 0.0, 0.5); — lower left

Draw_house;

Set_viewport(0.5, 1.0, 0.0, 0.5); — lower right

Draw_house;

Set_viewport(0.0, 0.5, 0.5, 1.0); — upper left

Draw_house;

Set_viewport(0.5, 1.0, 0.5, 1.0); — upper right

Draw_house;

This gives the images shown alongside:

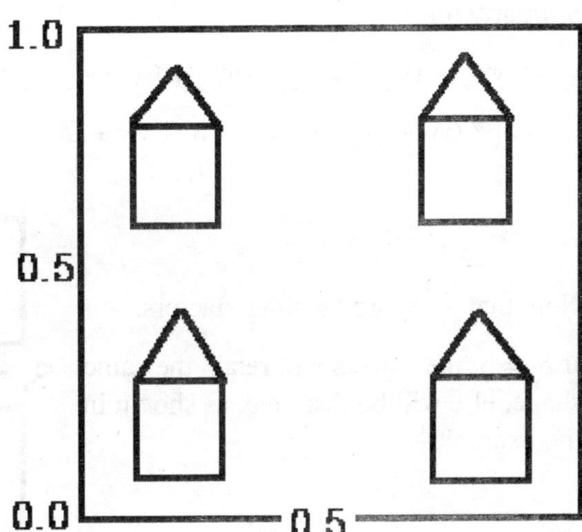

3.2.2 2D Window To Viewport Transformation

To map a point from WDC to NDC, as shown below:

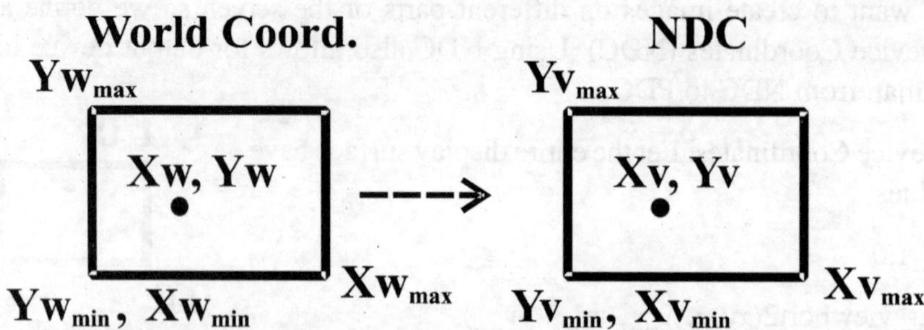

We can see from the above that to maintain relative position we must have the following relationship:

$$\frac{xw - xw_{min}}{xw_{max} - xw_{min}} = \frac{xv - xv_{min}}{xv_{max} - xv_{min}}$$

$$\frac{yw - yw_{min}}{yw_{max} - yw_{min}} = \frac{yv - yv_{min}}{yv_{max} - yv_{min}}$$

We can rewrite the above as:

$xv = [(xv_{max} - xv_{min})/(xw_{max} - xw_{min})] * (xw - xw_{min}) + xv_{min}$

$= S_x * (xw - xw_{min}) + xv_{min} = S_x * xw + C_x$

where $S_x = (xv_{max} - xv_{min})/(xw_{max} - xw_{min})$

$C_x = S_x * (- xw_{min}) + xv_{min}$

Similarly for y

$y_v = [(yv_{max} - yv_{min})/(yw_{max} - yw_{min})] * (yw - yw_{min}) + yv_{min}$

$= S_y * (yw - yw_{min}) + yv_{min} = S_y * yw + C_y$

Note that S_x, S_y are "scaling" factors.

If $S_x = S_y$ the objects will retain the same shape, else will be distorted, as shown in the example.

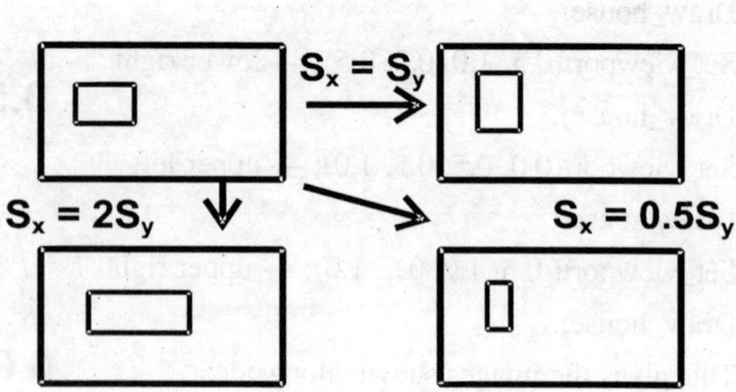

3.2.3 2D Viewport to Physical Device Transformation

To transform to Physical Device Coordinates (PDC), we have to multiply the Normalized Device Coordinates (NDC) by the resolution in pixels.

$x_p = xv * x_{num}$

$y_p = yv * y_{num}$

Note: Remember the aspect ratio problem, e.g., for CGA mode 6 (640 x 200) => 2.4 horizontal pixels = 1 vertical pixel.

Therefore: 200 vertical pixels = 480 horizontal pixels, so

y_{num} = 199 {0 => 199}

x_{num} = 479 {0 => 479}

Also we have to take into account the fact that (0, 0) is in the upper left corner, rather than the lower left corner, so the actual equation used is:

$x_p = xv * x_{num}$

$y_p = y_{num} - yv * y_{num}$

As a check if

xv = 0.0 => xp = 0 (left)

xv = 1.0 => xp = 479 (right)

yv = 0.0 => yp = 199 - 0 = 199 (bottom)

yv = 1.0 => yp = 199 - 199 = 0 (top)

3.3 CLIPPING

Clipping refers to the removal of a part of a scene. Internal clipping removes parts of a picture outside a given region; external clipping removes parts inside a region.

In other words we can say that clipping (clipping algorithm) is a procedure that identifies those portions of a picture that are either inside or outside a specified region of a space. The region against which an object is to be clipped is called the clip window or clip rectangle.

Applications of clippings are:

1) Extracting part of a defined scene for viewing.
2) Identifying visible surfaces in 3-D views.
3) Antialiasing line segments or object boundaries.
4) Displaying a multi window environment.
5) Creating objects using solid-modelling procedures.

Primitive methods available for a clipping algorithm are given below:

- Point clipping
- Line clipping
- Polygon clipping.

Curve clipping and text clipping are also possible.

3.3.1 Point Clipping

If the x coordinate boundaries of the clipping rectangle are x_{min} and x_{max}, and the y coordinate boundaries are y_{min} and y_{max}, then the following inequalities must be satisfied for a point at (x, y) to lie inside the clipping rectangle:

$$x_{min} < x < x_{max}$$

and $y_{min} < y < y_{max}$

If any of the four inequalities do not hold, the point is outside the clipping rectangle.

Program

```
// Program to clip the point
#include<stdio.h>
#include<conio.h>
#include<math.h>
#include<graphics.h>
struct point
{
        int x,y;
};
   // clipwindow(wmin,wmax);
  void clipwindow(struct point wmin,struct point wmax)
        {
                rectangle(wmin.x,wmin.y,wmax.x,wmax.y);
        }


void main()
{
```

```
        struct point wmin,wmax;
        int a,b;
        int gd=DETECT,gm;
        initgraph(&gd,&gm,"C:\\tc\\bgi");
        printf("\n Enter Co-ordinates Of Clip Window");
        printf("\n Enter Wmin.x");
        scanf("%d",&wmin.x);
        printf("\n Enter Wmin.y");
        scanf("%d",&wmin.y);
        printf("\n Enter Wmax.x");
        scanf("%d",&wmax.x);
        printf("\n Enter Wmax.y");
        scanf("%d",&wmax.y);
        clrscr();
                clipwindow(wmin,wmax);


//      rectangle(wmin.x,wmin.y,wmax.x,wmax.y);
        printf("\n Enter Point with two x & y coordinate Position:");
        scanf("%d %d",&a,&b);

        if(wmin.x<=a<=wmax.x && wmin.y<=b<=wmax.y)
        {
                putpixel(a,b,1);
        }
        else
                printf("\n Point is outside the window Rectangale");

        //      clipwindow(wmin,wmax);
                getch();
                closegraph();
}
```

3.3.2 Line Clipping

This section treats clipping of lines against rectangles. Although there are specialized algorithms for rectangle and polygon clipping, it is important to note that other graphic primitives can be clipped by repeated application of the line clipper.

To clip a line, we need to consider only its endpoints, not its infinite number of interior points. If both endpoints of a line lie inside the clip rectangle, the entire line lies inside the clip rectangle and can be trivially accepted. If one endpoint lies inside and one outside, the line intersects the clip rectangle and we must compute the intersection point. If both endpoints are outside the clip rectangle, the line may or may not intersect the clip rectangle and we need to perform further calculations to determine whether there are any intersections.

Simple example of line clipping

This is a simple example of line clipping: The display window is the canvas and also the default clipping rectangle, thus all line segments inside the canvas are drawn.

Before clipping

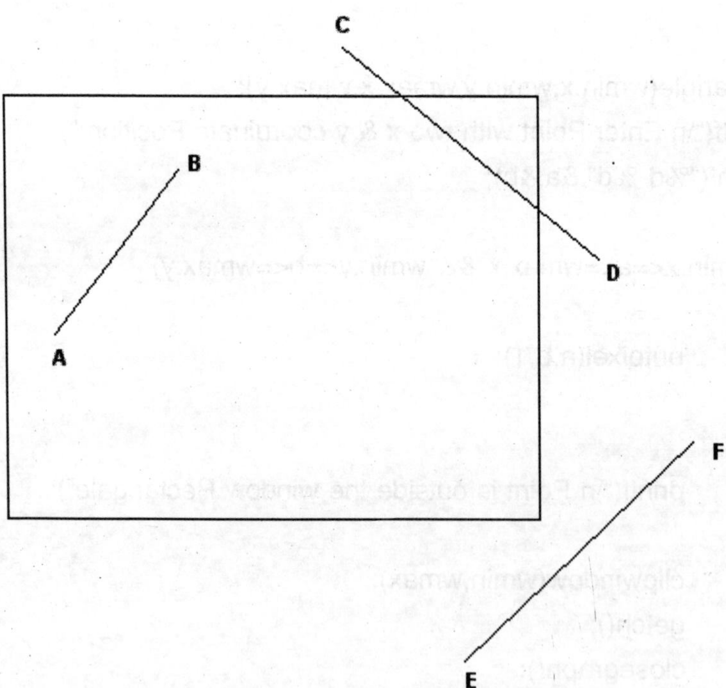

After clipping

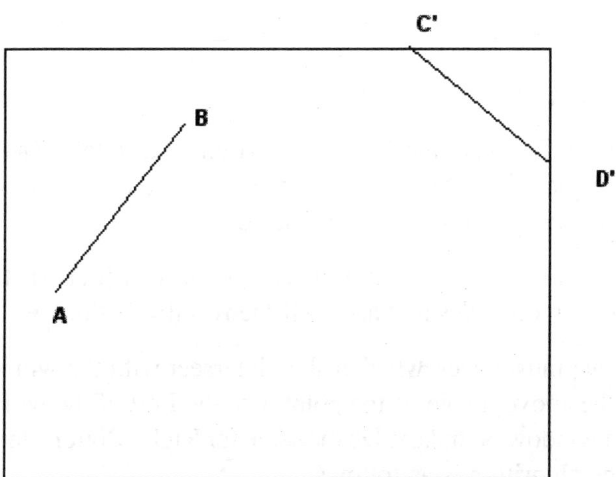

Sutherland-Cohen line clipping

Every line endpoint is assigned a 4 bit region code. The appropriate bit is set depending on the location of the endpoint with respect to that window component as shown below:

Endpoint Left of window:

Then set bit 1

Endpoint Right of window:

Then set bit 2

Endpoint Below window:

Then set bit 3

Endpoint Above window:

Then set bit 4

1001	1000	1010
0001	0000	0010
0101	0100	0110

Example:

P1 -> 0001, P 2 -> 1000

P3 -> 0001, P4 -> 0100

P5 -> 0000, P6 -> 0010

P7 -> 0001, P8 -> 0001

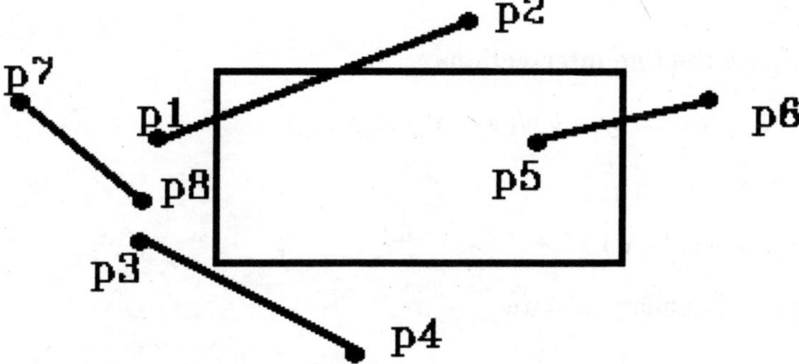

One can determine the bit code by testing the endpoints with the window as follows:

If x is less than xw_{min} then set bit 1

If x is greater than xw_{max} then set bit 2

If y is less than yw_{min} then set bit 3

If y is greater than yw_{max} then set bit 4

Note: We can use 4 element Boolean matrix and set C[Left] = true/false (1/0). If both endpoints = 0000 (in window) then display line. If both endpoints have a bit set in same position (P7, P8) then the line is completely outside the window and is rejected.

Thus one can do logical AND of region codes and reject if the result is -0000 and can do logical OR of region codes and accept if the result = 0000.

For the rest of the lines we must check whether they intersect with the window. They may still be outside, e.g. P3 - P4 in the above image. If the point is to the Left of the window then compute the intersection with the Left window boundary. Do the same for Right, Bottom and Top. Then recompute region code retest. So the algorithm is as follows:

1) Compute region code for endpoints
2) Check for trivial accept or reject
3) If step 2 is unsuccessful then compute window intersections in order: Left, Right, Bottom, Top (only do 1)
4) Repeat steps 1, 2, 3 until complete.

Example

I. 1) P_1 = 0001 2) no 3) $P_1 = P_1'$

P_2 = 1000

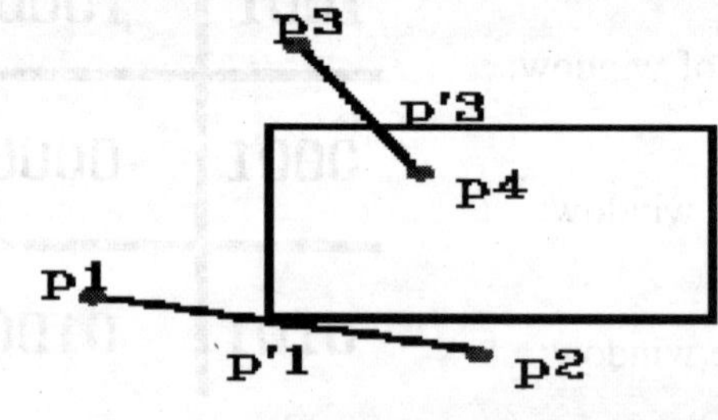

II. 1) P_1'= 0000 2) no 3) $P_2 = P_2'$

P_2 = 1000

III. 1) P_1' = 0000 2) Yes - accept & display

P_2' = 0000

To compute the line intersections

for P'_1: $m = dy/dx = (y_1 - y'_1)/(x_1 - x'_1)$ $P_1(x_1, y_1)$

$P_1'(x_1', y_1')$

or $y_1' = y_1 + m(x_1' - x_1)$

but for Left boundary $x_1' = xw_{min}$

for Right boundary $x_1' = xw_{max}$

Similarly for Top/Bottom, e.g. P_3'

$x_3' = x_3 + (y_3' - y_3)/m$

for Top $y_3' = yw_{max}$ for Bottom $y_3' = yw_{min}$

Algorithm

The more efficient Cohen-Sutherland Algorithm performs initial tests on a line to determine whether intersection calculations can be avoided.

Steps for Cohen-Sutherland algorithm

1) End-points pairs are checked for trivial acceptance or trivial rejected using the outcode.
2) If not trivial-acceptance or trivial-rejected, divided into two segments at a clip edge.
3) Iteratively clipped by testing trivial-acceptance or trivial-rejected, and divided into two segments until completely inside or trivial-rejected.

Pseudo-code of Cohen-Sutherland algorithm

Trivial acceptance/reject test

To perform trivial accept and reject tests, we extend the edges of the clip rectangle to divide the plane of the clip rectangle into nine regions. Each region is assigned a 4-bit code determined by where the region lies with respect to the outside halfplanes of the clip-rectangle edges. Each bit in the outcode is set to either 1 (true) or 0 (false); the 4 bits in the code correspond to the following conditions:

- Bit 1 : outside halfplane of top edge, above top edge $y > y_{max}$
- Bit 2 : outside halfplane of bottom edge, below bottom edge $y < y_{min}$
- Bit 3 : outside halfplane of right edge, to the right of right edge $x > x_{max}$
- Bit 4 : outside halfplane of left edge, to the left of left edge $x < x_{min}$

Program

```
/*******************************************************************************************
This program demonstrates line clipping using the Cohen-Sutherland algorithm. The
rectangle is defined to be the virtual viewport and the clipping is done with respect to that
rectangle.
*******************************************************************************************/

#include<conio.h>
#include<stdio.h>
#include<graphics.h>
```

```
typedef unsigned int outcode;

void
CohenSutherLandLineClipAndDraw(double,double,double,double,double,double,double,double,int);

/* Prototype for the encoding the Bit - codes for the endpoints of the line*/
outcode compOutcode(double ,double,double,double,double,double);

/*Enumerated datatype for the left,right,top and above boundaries against
which the clipping is to be done */

enum{
        TOP = 0x1,
        BOTTOM = 0x2,
        LEFT = 0x4,
        RIGHT = 0x8
    };

void main()
{
                int gdriver = DETECT,gmode;
        initgraph(&gdriver,&gmode,"c:\\tc\\bgi");

        cleardevice();
        setcolor(BLUE);
        /*Line to be clipped */
        Printf("\n Before clipping :");
        line(100,20,500,450);

        setcolor(YELLOW);
        /*The rectangle as the virtual viewport*/
        rectangle(120,120,400,400);
        setcolor(BLUE);
```

```
        getch();

CohenSutherLandLineClipAndDraw(100,20,500,450,120,400,120,400,BLACK);
        printf("\n After clipping:");
        getch();
}


void CohenSutherLandLineClipAndDraw(double x0,double y0,double x1,double y1,double
xmin,double xmax,double ymin,double ymax,int color)
{

outcode outcode0,outcode1,outcodeOut;
int accept = 0,done = 0;
int x,y;

outcode0 = compOutcode(x0,y0,xmin,xmax,ymin,ymax);
outcode1 = compOutcode(x1,y1,xmin,xmax,ymin,ymax);

        do
        {
                if(!(outcode0 | outcode1))
                {
                        accept = 1;
                        done = 1;
                }
                else if(outcode0 & outcode1)
                {
                        done = 1;
                }
                else
                {
                        //outcodeOut = outcode0 ? outcode0 : outcode1;
                        if(outcode0 != 0)
```

```
        outcodeOut = outcode0;
    else
        outcodeOut = outcode1;

    if(outcodeOut & TOP)
    {
        x = x0 + (x1-x0) * (ymax - y0)/(y1-y0);
        y = ymax;
    }
    else if(outcodeOut & BOTTOM)
    {
        x = x0 + (x1-x0) * (ymin - y0)/(y1-y0);
        y = ymin;
    }
    else if(outcodeOut & RIGHT)
    {
        y = y0 + (y1-y0) * (xmax - x0)/(x1-x0);
        x = xmax;
    }
    else
    {
        y = y0 + (y1-y0) * (xmin - x0)/(x1-x0);
        x = xmin;
    }

    if(outcodeOut == outcode0)
    {
        x0 = x;
        y0 = y;
        outcode0 = compOutcode(x0,y0,xmin,xmax,ymin,ymax);
    }
    else
    {
```

```
                    x1 = x;
                    y1 = y;
                    outcode1 = compOutcode(x1,y1,xmin,xmax,ymin,ymax);
                }

            }
        }while(done == 0);

        if(accept == 1)
        {
            cleardevice();
            line(x0,y0,x1,y1);
            setcolor(YELLOW);
            rectangle(120,120,400,400);
        }
}


outcode compOutcode(double x,double y,double xmin,double xmax,double ymin,double
ymax)
{
        outcode code=0;

        if(y>ymax)
            code = code | TOP;
        else if(y<ymin)
            code = code | BOTTOM;
        if(x>xmax)
            code = code | RIGHT;
        else if(x<xmin)
            code = code | LEFT;

        return code;
}
```

3.3.3 Polygon Clipping

Polygon clipping differs from line clipping in several respects.

1) The input to the clipper is a polygon, which for simplicity we will view as a list of $n \geq 3$ vertices $(v_0, v_1, \ldots, v_{n-1})$
2) The output from the clipper is one or more polygons.
3) The clipping process may generate vertices that do not lie on any of the edges of the original polygon.
4) Complex polygons (that is, non-convex polygons) may lead to strange artefacts.

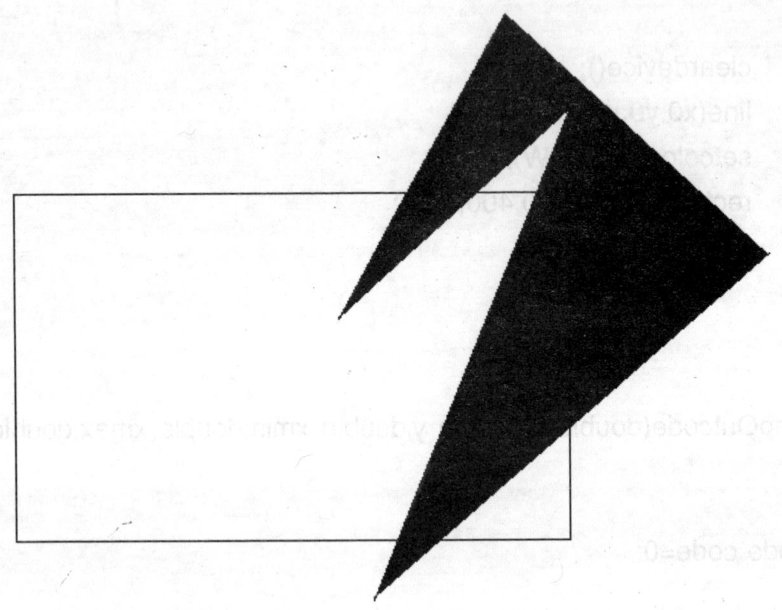

Before Clipping

After Clipping

Sutherland-Hodgman polygon clipping

Since polygons are basic primitives, algorithms have been developed for clipping them directly. The Sutherland-Hodgman algorithm is a polygon clipper. It was a basic component in James Clark's "Geometry Engine," which was the precursor to the first "Silicon Graphics" machines. This algorithm clips any *subject polygon* (convex or concave) against any *convex clipping window*, but we will usually pretend the clipping window is an upright rectangle.

Given a *subject* polygon with an ordered sequence of vertices:

$v_1, v_2, \ldots\ldots, v_{n-1}, n \geq 3,$

the Sutherland-Hodgman algorithm compares each subject polygon edge against a single clip window edge, saving the vertices on the inside of the edge and the intersection points when the edges are crossed. The clipper is then re-entered with this intermediate polygon and another clip window edge.

Given a clip window edge and a subject polygon edge, there are four cases to consider:

1) The subject polygon edge goes from outside one clip window edge to outside the other clip window edge. In this case we output nothing.
2) The subject polygon edge goes from outside one clip window edge to inside the other clip window edge. In this case we save intersection and inside vertex.
3) The subject polygon edge goes from inside one clip window edge to outside the other clip window edge. In this case we save intersection point.
4) The subject polygon edge goes from inside one clip window edge to inside the other clip window edge. In this case we save second inside point (the first was saved previously).

To complete the description, we need to consider the first vertex of the subject polygon and its last edge. If the first vertex is inside the current edge we save it to the list of vertices in the intermediate polygon, otherwise we drop it. For the last edge, note that if nothing has yet been saved in the intermediate polygon, the entire subject must not be visible in the clip window, so we can quit. Otherwise, if the last subject edge crosses clip window edge, the intersection point must be appended to the intermediate polygon.

First clip window edge:

Starting with the original triangle (subject polygon), we set the intermediate polygon to null and find:

1) Start vertex: p_0 is outside the edge, so is not saved in the intermediate polygon vertex list.
2) Subject edge p_0p_1 crosses the clip edge and so the intersection i_{01} is saved in the intermediate list (i_{01}).
3) p_1 is inside the edge, so it is saved in the intermediate list. (i_{01}, P_1)
4) Subject edge p_1p_2 does not cross the clip edge and so no intersection is computed.
5) p_2 is inside the edge, so it is saved in the intermediate list. (i_{01}, P_1, P_2)

6) Last edge p_2p_0: We have output some data, so we will continue.

   (a) Subject edge p_2p_0 does cross the clip edge and so the intersection i_{01} is saved in the intermediate list. (i_{01}, p_1, p_2, i_{20})

Second clip window edge:

1) Start vertex: i_{01} is inside the edge, so is saved in the intermediate polygon vertex list - intermediate list (i_{01}).
2) Subject edge $i_{01}p_1$ crosses the clip edge and so the intersection i_{011} is saved in the intermediate list.
3) (i_{01}, i_{011}). p_1 is outside the edge, so it is not saved.
4) Subject edge p_1p_2 does cross the clip edge and so the intersection i_{12} is saved in the intermediate list. (i_{01}, i_{011}, i_{012})
5) p_2 is inside the edge, so it is saved in the intermediate list. (i_{01}, i_{011}, i_{012}, p_2)
6) Subject edge p_2i_{20} does not cross the clip edge and so no intersection is computed.
7) i_{20} is inside the edge, so it is saved in the intermediate list (i_{01}, i_{011}, i_{012}, p_2, i_{20})
8) Last edge $i_{20}i_{01}$: We have output some data, so we will continue.

   a) Subject edge $i_{20}i_{01}$ does not cross the clip edge and so no intersection is saved.

3.4 SUMMARY

- When we model an image in World Device Coordinates (WDC) we are not interested in the entire world but only a portion of it. Therefore we define the portion of interest which is a polygonal area specified in world coordinates, called the "window".
- Clipping refers to the removal of part of a scene. Internal clipping removes parts of a picture outside a given region; external clipping removes parts inside a region.
- In other words a clipping algorithm is a procedure that identifies those portions of a picture that are either inside or outside a specified region of space. The region against which an object is to clip is called clip window or clip rectangle.
- To clip a line, we need to consider only its endpoints, not the infinite number of interior points. If both endpoints of a line lie inside the clip rectangle, the entire line lies inside the clip rectangle and can be trivially accepted.

3.5 REVIEW QUESTIONS

1. Write a procedure to implement the view port.
2. Write routines to implement the setViewRepresentacion3 and setViewIndex functions.
3. Write a procedure to transform the vertices of a polyhedron to projection coordinates using a parallel projection with a specified projection vector.
4. Write a procedure to obtain different parallel-projection views of a polyhedron by first applying a specified rotation.
5. Write a procedure to perform a one-point perspective projection of an object.

6. Write a procedure to perform a two-point perspective projection of an object.
7. Develop a routine to perform a three-point perspective projection of an object.
8. Write a routine to convert a perspective projection frustum to a regular parallelepiped.
9. Extend the Sutherland-Hodgman polygon-clipping algorithm to clip three-dimensional planes against a regular parallelepiped.
10. Devise an algorithm to clip objects in a scene against a defined frustum. Compare the operations needed in this algorithm to those needed in an algorithm that clips against a regular parallelepiped.
11. Modify the two-dimensional Liang-Barsky line-clipping algorithm to clip three-dimensional lines against a specified regular parallelepiped.
12. Modify the two-dimensional Liang-Barsky line-clipping algorithm to clip a given polyhedron against a specified regular parallelepiped.
13. Set up an algorithm for clipping a polyhedron against a parallelepiped.
14. Write a routine to perform clipping in homogeneous coordinates.
15. Using any clipping procedure and orthographic parallel projections, write a program to perform a complete viewing transformation from world coordinates to device coordinates.
16. Using any clipping procedure, write a program to perform a complete viewing transformation from world coordinates to device coordinates for any specified parallel projection vector.

CHAPTER 4

3D Graphics

4.1 INTRODUCTION TO 3D GRAPHICS

3D computer graphics are graphics that use a three dimensional representation of geometric data. A picture having height, width and depth is three dimensional (or 3D). A picture that has height and width but no depth is two dimensional (or 2D).

3D animation is a process where characters or objects are created as moving images. Rather than traditional flat or 2D characters, these 3D animation images give the impression of being able to move around and they can be observed from all angles, just as in real life.

3D animation technology is relatively new and if done by hand it would take thousands of hours to complete one short section of moving film. The use of computers and software has simplified and accelerated the 3D animation process. As a result, the number of 3D animators as well as the use of 3D animation technology has increased.

Computer graphics generates and displays 3D objects in 2-dimensional space like a computer screen. For this purpose 2-dimensional x-axis and y-axis graphics properties like position, colour and brightness along with an additional 3-D pixel that adds depth, indicating where the point lies on an imaginary z-axis, are used. When many 3-D pixels are combined, each with its own depth value, the result is a three-dimensional surface, which is called a texture.

3D graphics also supports multiple objects interacting with one another. 3D graphics can be applied in a variety of cases, such as:

- Presenting basic geometric shapes (circle, triangle, square)
- Presenting 3D text
- Applying a 3D effect to existing 2D objects (shadow, lighting)

- Presenting special created objects (design)
- Integrating more than one 3D object
- Integrating a 3D object with a 2D object
- Presenting an object in animation form (cartoon, video game, product demo)

For example, video games, 3D films and animation pictures are the most common way to see 3D objects.

To create 3D graphics, we divide the procedure in to three main phases.

1) 3D Modelling

This describes the process of forming the shape of an object.

2) Layout and animation

This describes the *motion* and *placement* of objects within a scene.

3) 3D rendering

This produces an image of an object.

The main aim of 3D is to make an object seem real. Among the most important of these are shapes, surface textures, lighting, perspective, depth of field and anti-aliasing.

Examples of 3-D images

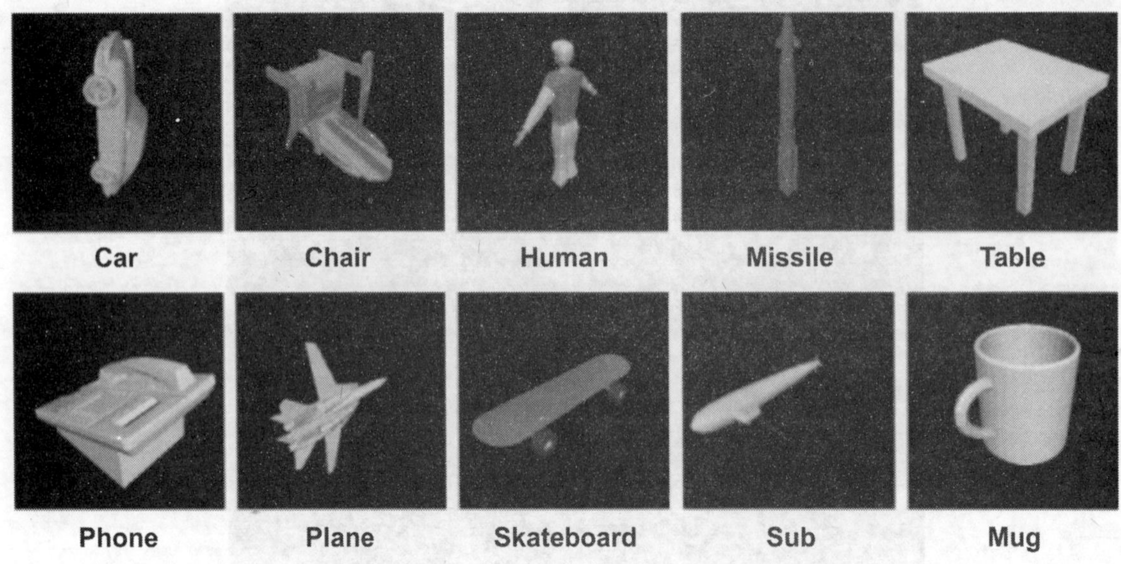

Car Chair Human Missile Table

Phone Plane Skateboard Sub Mug

4.2 2D VERSUS 3D GRAPHICS

2D Graphics	*3D Graphics*
• 2D software uses images called bitmaps that consist of blocks of colour stacked together to make a picture. The limitation is that only one angle can be seen at any given time.	• 3D software uses computer-generated lines, surfaces, or solids to create 3 dimensional models. It is also a more difficult technique to perfect.
• Extraspective: In 2D animation, the extraspective aspect removes you from the scenario and presents the virtual environment as a layered stack of images.	• Introspective: The introspective aspect of 3D animation allows you to change your point of view within a given scenario. This is what gives 3D its "realistic" perspective when viewed in video and computer games.

Summary of Comparison

While 3D animation gives a better image, cost and time constraints make 2D techniques a bit more attractive for most budgets.

Transition: Most viewers appreciate a combination of both 3D and 2D styles in order to maximize the artistic truth and freedom of movement and sensation.

2D and 3D Representation of Objects

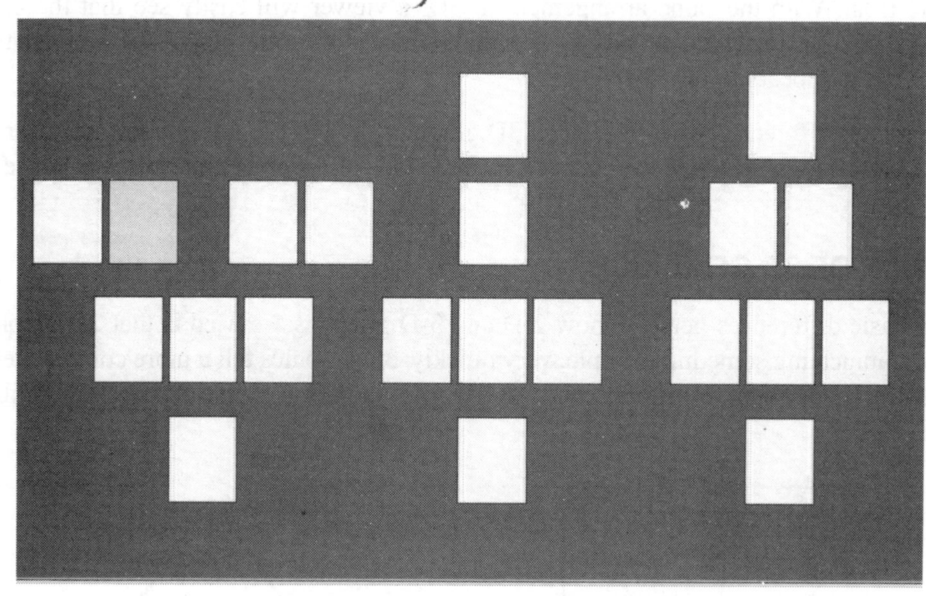

2D Arrangement of Objects (Cards)

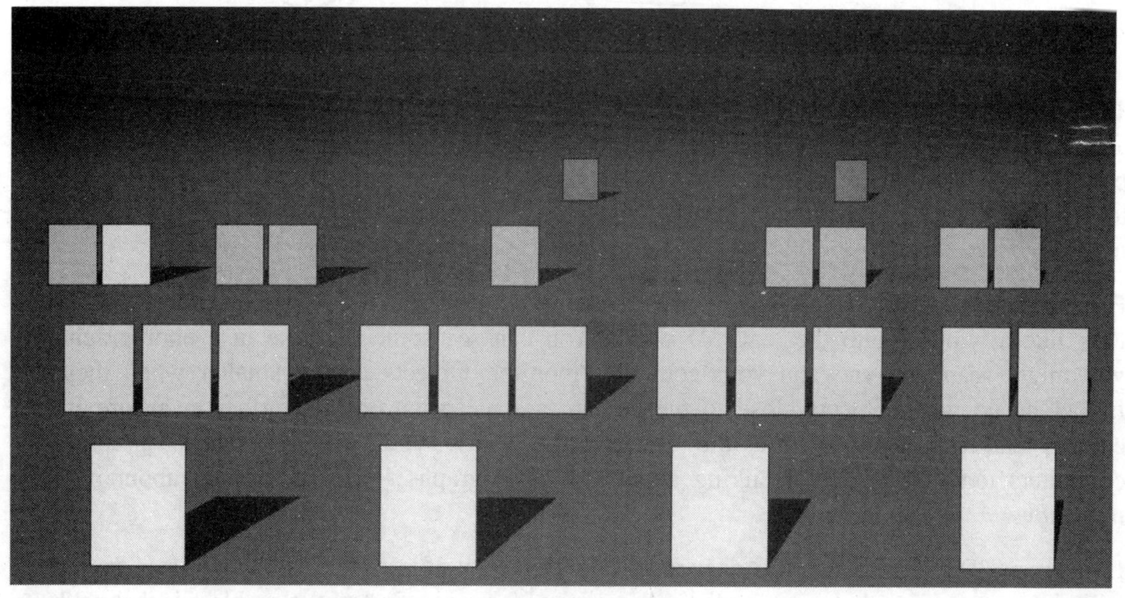

3D Arrangement of Objects (Cards)

This presents an actual view of the sequence & arrangement of cards.

From the above 2D picture, the viewer may not know the image of the cards taken from the surface or from the front. With the same arrangement in 3D, a viewer will easily see that the cards are arranged in row wise sequence as well as that the picture is the front-upper view rather than the surface view as it appears in the 2D picture.

This is the major difference between 2D and 3D graphics. In a 2D representation, the user simply knows the object, but in 3D the viewer gets an accurate idea of the object like size, sequence, depth, etc.

4.3 BASICS OF 3D GRAPHICS

One of the basic differences between how 2-D and 3-D graphics are used is that 2D graphics are good at communicating something simple, very quickly. 3D graphics tell a more complicated story, but have to carry much more information in order to do so. Thus some pictures are deliberately shown in 2-D.

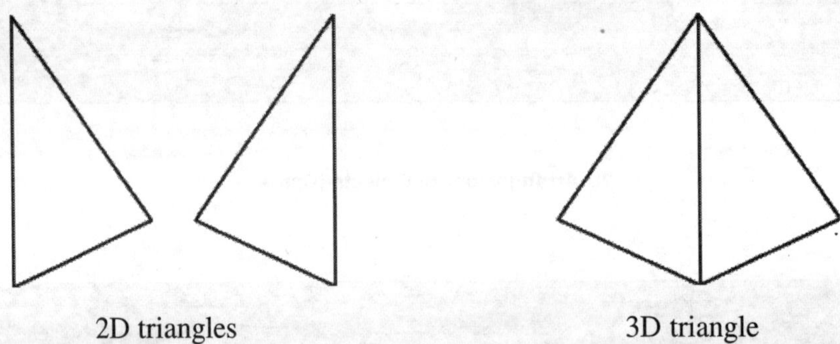

2D triangles 3D triangle

Take a look at the triangles above. Each of the triangles on the left has three lines and three angles - all that is needed to tell the story of a triangle. We see the image on the right as a pyramid - a 3D structure with four triangular sides. Note that it takes five lines and six angles to tell the story of a pyramid - nearly twice the information required to tell the story of a triangle.

For hundreds of years, artists have known some of the tricks that can make a flat, 2D painting look like a window into the real, 3D world. You can see some of these in a photograph that you might scan and view on your computer monitor. Objects appear smaller when they are farther away; when objects close to the camera are in focus, objects farther away are fuzzy; colours tend to be less vibrant as they move farther away. When we talk about 3D graphics on computers today, we are not talking about still photographs – we are talking about *pictures that move*.

If making a 2D picture into a 3D image requires adding a lot of information, then the step from a 3D still picture to images that move realistically requires far more. Part of the problem is that we have grown to expect a high degree of realism in everything we see.

Today, we compare game screens to DVD movies, and want the games to be as smooth and detailed as what we sec in a movie theatre. This poses a challenge for 3D graphics on PCs, Macintoshes, and, increasingly, game consoles like the Dreamcast and the Playstation II.

3D Graphic View (Box)

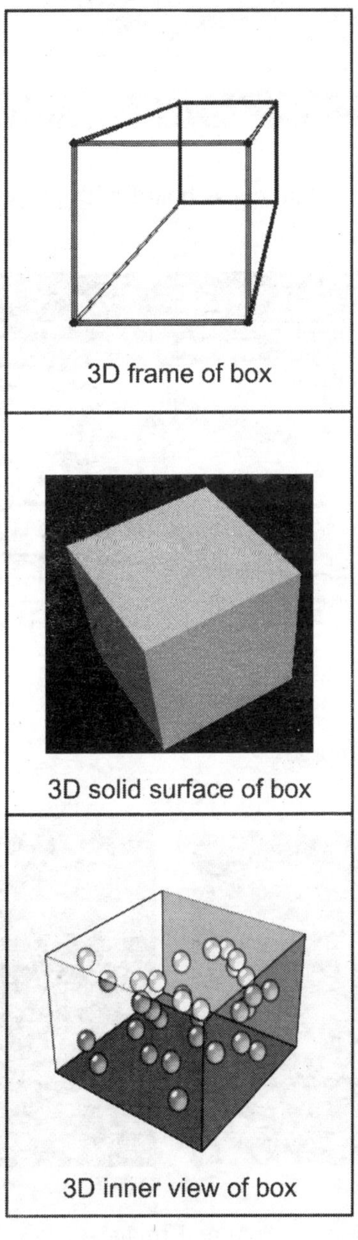

3D frame of box

3D solid surface of box

3D inner view of box

Comparison: Actual View and 3D Graphics

Actual chess board with player

3D chess board

Integrating 3D Graphics with Image

Actual images

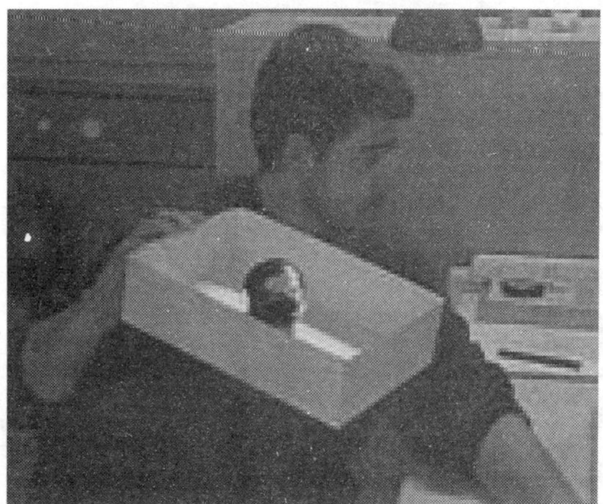

Integrated image (3D ball in box)

4.4 STEPS TO CREATE 3D GRAPHICS

A virtual 3D world is not the same thing as one picture of that world. This is true of our real world also. Take a very small part of the real world - your hand and a desktop under it. Your hand has qualities that determine how it can move and how it can look. The finger joints bend toward the palm, not away from it. If you slap your hand on the desktop, the desktop does not splash – it is always solid and it is always hard. Your hand cannot go through the desktop.

Structure of 3-D Objects

A number of image parts go into making an object seem real. Among the most important of these are shapes, surface textures, lighting, perspective, depth of field and anti-aliasing.

Shapes

When we look out of our windows, we see scenes made up of all sorts of shapes, with straight lines and curves in many sizes and combinations. Similarly, when we look at a 3D graphical image on our computer monitor, we see images made up of a variety of shapes, although most of them are made up of straight lines. We see squares, rectangles, parallelograms, circles and rhomboids, but most of all we see triangles. However, in order to build images that look as though they have the smooth curves often found in nature, some of the shapes must be very small, and a complex image - say, a human body - might require thousands of these shapes to be put together into a structure called a wireframe. At this stage the structure might be recognizable as the symbol of whatever it will eventually picture, but the next major step is important: The wireframe has to be given a surface.

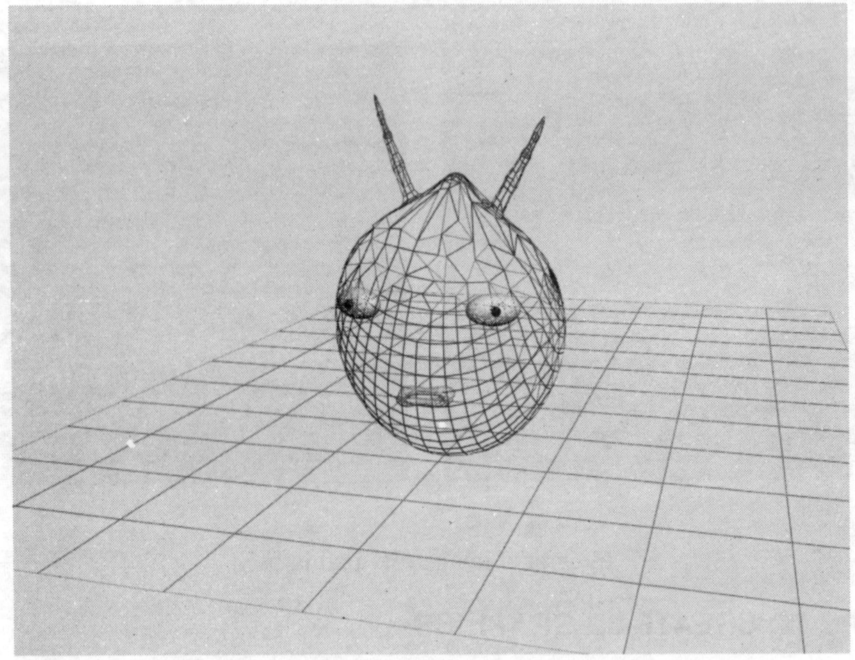

This illustration shows the wireframe of an object made from relatively few polygons

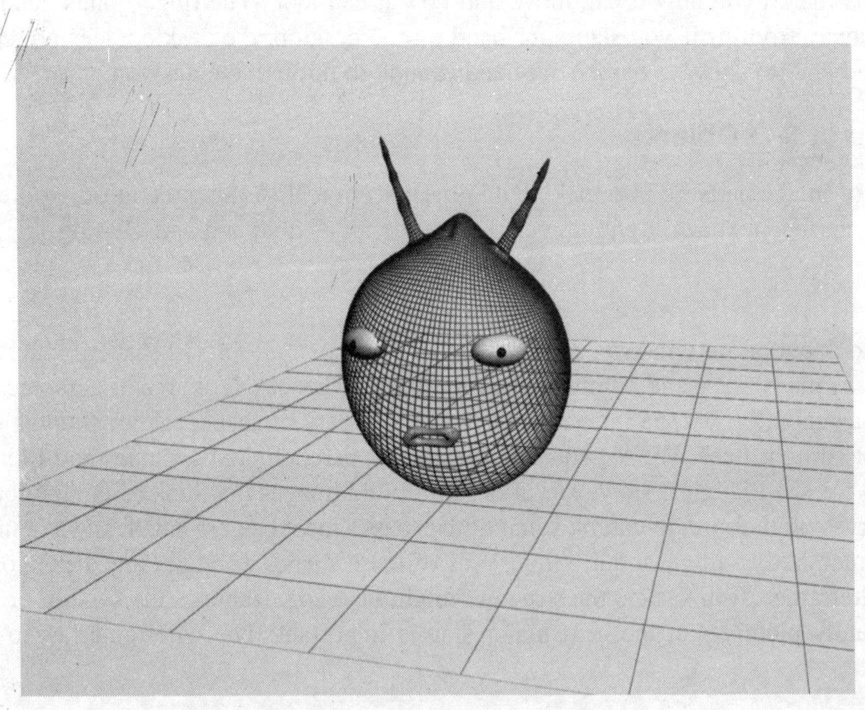

The outline of the wireframe can be made to look more natural and rounded

Surface Textures

When we see a surface in the real world, we can get information about it in two key ways. We can look at it, sometimes from several angles, and we can touch it to see whether it is hard or soft. In a 3D graphic image, however, we can only look at the surface to get all the information possible. All this information comes from three areas:

- **Colour:** What colour is it? Is it the same colour all over?
- **Texture:** Does it appear to be smooth, or does it have lines, bumps, craters or some other irregularity on the surface?
- **Reflectance:** How much light does it reflect? Are reflections of other items in the surface sharp or fuzzy?

One way to make an image look "real" is to have a wide variety of these three features across the different parts of the image. Look around you now: Your computer keyboard has a different colour/texture/reflectance than your desktop, which has a different colour/texture/reflectance than your arm.

For realistic colour, it is important for the computer to be able to choose from millions of different colours for the pixels making up an image. Variety in texture comes both from mathematical models for surfaces ranging from frog skin to Jell-o gelatin to stored "texture maps" that are applied to surfaces.

We also associate qualities that we cannot see - soft, hard, warm, cold - with particular combinations of colour, texture and reflectance. If one of them is wrong, the illusion of reality is shattered.

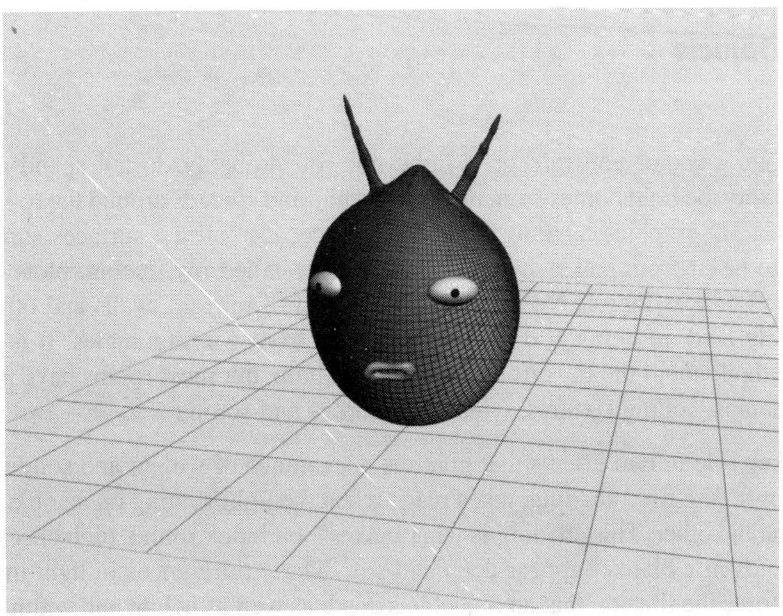

Adding a surface to the wireframe

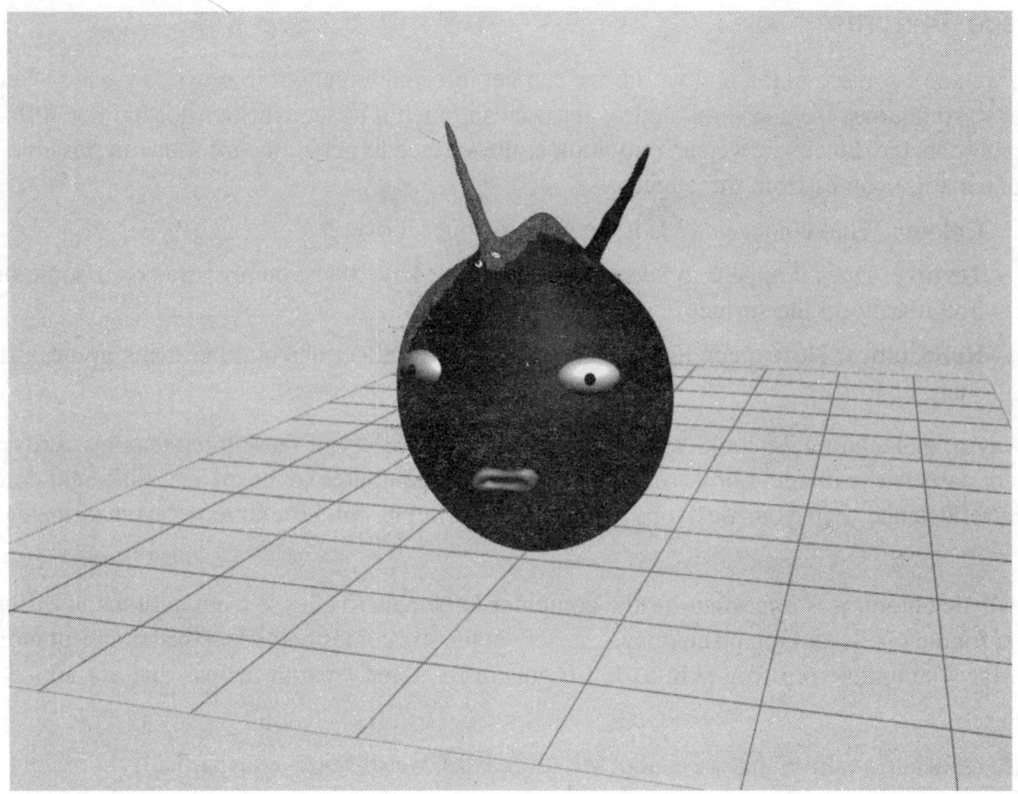

Effects in 3D Objects

Lighting

When you walk into a room, you turn on a light, but you probably do not spend a lot of time thinking about the way the light comes from the bulb or tube and spreads around the room. However, persons involved in 3D graphics have to think about it, because all the surfaces surrounding the wireframes have to be lit from somewhere. One technique, called ray-tracing, plots the path that imaginary light rays take as they leave the bulb, bounce off of mirrors, walls and other reflecting surfaces, and finally land on items at different intensities from varying angles. It is complicated enough when you think about the rays from a single light bulb, but most rooms have multiple light sources - several lamps, ceiling fixtures, windows, candles and so on.

Lighting plays a key role in two effects that give the appearance of weight and solidity to objects: shading and shadows. The first, shading, takes place when the light shining on an object is stronger on one side than on the other. This shading is what makes a ball look round, high cheekbones seem striking and the folds in a blanket appear deep and soft. These differences in light intensity work with shape to reinforce the illusion that an object has depth as well as height and width. The illusion of weight comes from the second effect - shadows.

Lighting in an image not only adds depth to the object through shading, it "anchors" objects to the ground with shadows.

Adding lighting and shadow to an object

Solid bodies cast shadows when a light shines on them. You can see this when you observe the shadow that a sundial or a tree casts onto a sidewalk. And because we are used to seeing real objects and people cast shadows, seeing the shadows in a 3D image reinforces the illusion that we are looking through a window into the real world, rather than at a screen of mathematically generated shapes.

Perspective

Perspective is one of those words that sounds technical but that actually describes a simple effect everyone has seen. If you stand on the side of a long, straight road and look into the distance, it appears as if the two sides of the road come together at a point on the horizon. Also, if trees are growing next to the road, the trees farther away will look smaller than the trees close to you. As a matter of fact, the trees will look as if they are converging to the point formed by the side of the road. When all the objects in a scene appear to eventually converge at a single point in the distance, it is perspective. There are variations, but most 3D graphics use the "single point perspective" just described.

For example, the hands are separate, but most scenes feature some items in front of, and partially blocking the view of, other items. For these scenes the software must not only calculate the relative sizes of the items but must also know which item is in front and how much of the other items it hides. The most common technique for calculating these factors is the Z-Buffer. The Z-buffer gets its name from the common label for the axis, or imaginary line, going from the screen back through the scene to the horizon. (There are two other common axes to consider: the x-axis, which measures the scene from side to side, and the y-axis, which measures the scene from top to bottom.)

The Z-buffer assigns, to each polygon, a number based on how close an object containing the polygon is to the front of the scene. Generally, lower numbers are assigned to items closer to the screen, and higher numbers are assigned to items closer to the horizon. For example, a 16-bit Z-buffer would assign the number -32,768 to an object rendered as close to the screen as possible and 32,767 to an object that is as far away as possible.

In the real world, our eyes cannot see objects behind others, so we do not have a problem of what we should be seeing. But the computer faces this problem constantly and solves it in a straightforward way. As each object is created, its Z-value is compared to that of other objects that occupy the same x- and y-values. The object with the lowest z-value is fully rendered, while objects with higher z-values are not rendered where they intersect. The result ensures that we do not see background items appearing through the middle of characters in the foreground. Since the Z-buffer is employed before objects are fully rendered, pieces of the scene that are hidden behind characters or objects do not have to be rendered at all. This speeds up graphics performance. Next, we look at the depth of field element.

Depth of Field

Another optical effect successfully used to create 3D is depth of field. Using our example of the trees beside the road, another interesting thing happens as that line of trees gets smaller. If you look at the trees close to you, the trees farther away will appear to be out of focus. This is especially true when you are looking at a photograph or movie of the trees. Film directors and computer animators use this depth of field effect for two purposes. The first is to reinforce the illusion of depth in the scene you are watching. It is certainly possible for the computer to make sure that every item in a scene, no matter how near or far it is supposed to be, is perfectly in focus. Since we are used to seeing the depth of field effect, though, having items in focus regardless of distance would seem foreign and would disturb the illusion of looking at a scene in the real world.

The second reason directors use depth of field is to focus your attention to the items or actors they feel are most important. To direct your attention to the heroine of a movie, for example, a director might use a "shallow depth of field," where only the actor is in focus. A scene that is designed to impress you with the grandeur of nature, on the other hand, might use a "deep depth of field" to get as much as possible in focus and so be more noticeable.

View to array of object (Clear view)

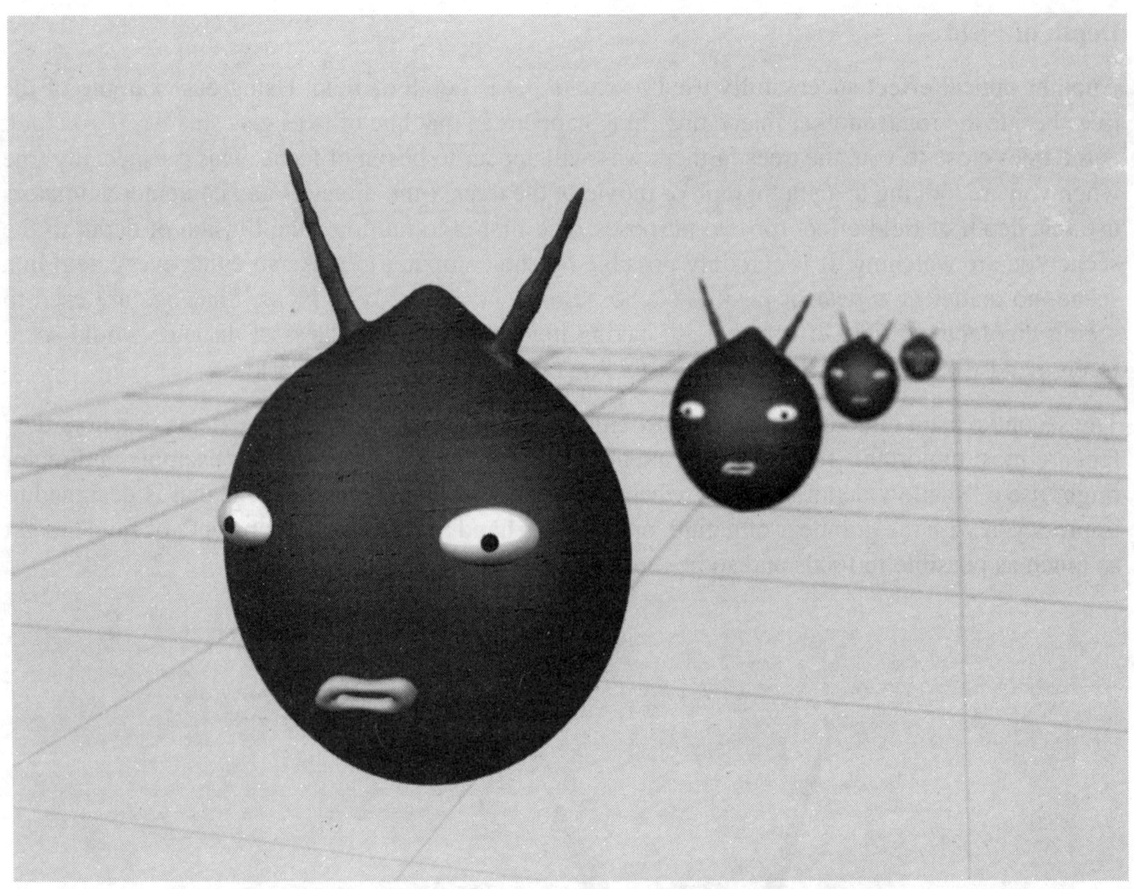

View to array of object (Deem view for distance object)

Anti-aliasing

A technique that also relies on fooling the eye is anti-aliasing. Digital graphics systems are very good at creating lines that go straight up and down the screen, or straight across. But when curves or diagonal lines show up (and they show up pretty often in the real world), the computer might produce lines that resemble stair steps instead of smooth flows. So to fool your eye into seeing a smooth curve or line, the computer can add graduated shades of the colour in the line to the pixels surrounding the line. These "grayed-out" pixels will fool your eye into thinking that the jagged stair steps are gone. This process of adding additional coloured pixels to fool the eye is called anti-aliasing, and it is one of the techniques that separate computer-generated 3D graphics from those generated by hand. Keeping up with the lines as they move through fields of colour, and adding the right amount of "anti-jaggy" colour, is yet another complex task that a computer must handle as it creates 3D animation on your computer monitor.

The jagged "stair steps" that occur when images are painted from pixels in straight lines mark an object as obviously computer-generated.

Drawing gray pixels around the lines of an image - "blurring" the lines - minimizes the stair steps and makes an object appear more realistic.

3D Animation

A 3D graphics object animated in a sequence of effects and in combination with other 3D objects creates 3D animation.

3D animation is the creation of moving pictures in a three-dimensional digital environment. This is done by sequencing consecutive images, or "frames", that simulate motion by each image showing the next in a gradual progression of steps, filmed by a virtual "camera" and then outputting to video by a rendering engine. The eye can be "fooled" into perceiving motion when these consecutive images are shown at a rate of 24 frames per second or faster.

Producing animation by using computer technology, without doubt, is closely related to the computer technology technique and a series of capabilities of this technique. Computers give an opportunity to the animator to use time, technique and creativeness at a higher level and enables high quality products to be produced.

Production Pipeline

In the process of 3D computer animation production, it is necessary to understand some series of steps related to production technique and methods based on both technique and expression style. The information about these steps is as follows.

- Design
- Producing the models (modelling)

- Determining the surface qualities of models
- Scene arrangement
- Transformation
- Rendering the objects
- Assembling and special effects
- Transferring to video, CD, or film.

Animation is used for:

- Education
- Entertainment
- Represent intuition, myths
- Movies
- Simulations
- Demonstrations of product
- Internal architecture of an entity (like home)

4.5 SUMMARY

- 3D computer graphics are graphics that use a three dimensional representation of geometric data.
- A picture having height, width and depth is three-dimensional (or 3D). A picture that has height and width but no depth is two-dimensional (or 2D).
- 3D animation is a process where characters or objects are created as moving images.
- Rather than traditional flat or 2D characters, these 3D animation images give the impression of being able to move around and can be observed from all angles, just as in real life
- Computer graphics generates & displays a 3D object in 2-dimensional space like a computer screen. For this purpose 2-dimensional X-axis and Y-axis graphics properties like position, colour and brightness along with an additional 3-D pixel that adds depth, indicating where the point lies on an imaginary Z-axis, are used.
- When many 3-D pixels are combined, each with its own depth value, the result is a three-dimensional surface, which is called a texture.
- A number of image parts go into making an object seem real. Among the most important of these are shapes, surface textures, lighting, perspective, depth of field and anti-aliasing.

4.6 REVIEW QUESTIONS

1. Develop a procedure, based on a back-face detection technique, for identifying all the visible faces of a convex polyhedron that has different coloured surfaces. Assume that the object is defined in a right-handed viewing system with the xy-plane as the viewing surface.
2. Implement a back-face detection procedure using an orthographic parallel projection to

view visible faces of a convex polyhedron. Assume that all parts of the object are in front of the view plane, and provide a mapping onto a screen viewport for display.

3. Implement a back-face detection procedure using a perspective projection to view the visible faces of a convex polyhedron. Assume that all parts of the object are in front of the view plane, and provide a mapping onto a screen viewprt for display.
4. Write a program to produce an animation of a convex polyhedron. The object is to be rotated incrementally about an axis that passes through the object and is parallel to the view plane. Assume that the object lies completely in front of the view plane. Use an orthographic parallel projection to map the views successively onto the view plane.
5. Implement the depth-buffer method to display the visible surfaces of a given polyhedron. How can the storage requirements for the depth buffer be determined from the definition of the objects to be displayed?
6. Implement the depth-buffer method to display the visible surfaces in a scene containing any number of polyhedrons. Set up efficient methods for storing and processing the various objects in the scene.
7. Implement the A-buffer algorithm to display a scene containing both opaque and transparent surfaces. As an optional feature, your algorithm may be extended to include antialiasing.
8. Develop a program to implement the scan-line algorithm for displaying the visible surfaces of a given polyhedron. Use polygon and edge tables to store the definition exercises of the object, and use coherence techniques to evaluate points along and between scan lines.
9. Write a program to implement the scan-line algorithm for a scene containing several polyhedrons. Use polygon and edge tables to store the definition of the object, and use coherence techniques to evaluate points along and between scan lines.
10. Set up a program to display the visible surfaces of a convex polyhedron using the painter's algorithm. That is, surfaces are to be sorted on depth and painted on the screen from back to front.
11. Write a program that uses the depth-sorting method to display the visible surfaces of any given object with plane faces.
12. Develop a depth-sorting program to display the visible surfaces in a scene containing several polyhedrons.
13. Write a program to display the visible surfaces of a convex polyhedron using the BSP-tree method.
14. Give examples of situations where the two methods discussed for test 3 in the area subdivision algorithm will fail to identify correctly a surrounding surface that obscures all other surfaces.
15. Develop an algorithm that would test a given plane surface against a rectangular area to decide whether it is a surrounding, overlapping, inside, or outside surface.
16. Develop an algorithm for generating a quadtree representation for the visible surfaces of an object by applying the area-subdivision tests to determine the values of the quadtree elements.

17. Set up an algorithm to load a given quadtree representation of an object into a frame buffer for display.
18. Write a program on your system to display an octree representation for an object so that hidden-surfaces are removed.
19. Devise an algorithm for viewing a single sphere using the ray-casting method.
20. Discuss how antialiasing methods can be incorporated into the various hidden-surface elimination algorithms.
21. Write a routine to produce a surface contour plot for a given surface function $f(x, y)$.
22. Develop an algorithm for detecting visible line sections in a scene by comparing each line in the scene to each surface.
23. Discuss how wireframe displays might be generated with the various visible-surface detection methods discussed in this chapter.
24. Set up a procedure for generating a wireframe display of a polyhedron with the hidden edges of the object drawn with dashed lines.

CHAPTER 5

2D & 3D Transformations

5.1 OVERVIEW OF 2D TRANSFORMATION

Transformations are a fundamental part of computer graphics. With the help of geometric transformations we can change the orientation, size and shape of output primitives.

In 3D graphics, we must use 3D transformations. However, 3D transformations can be quite confusing so it helps to first start with 2D transformations.

The basic geometric transformations are:

1. Translation
2. Rotation
3. Scaling

Other transformations are also available such as:

4. Reflection
5. Shear

5.2 REPRESENTATION OF POINTS

A point p in 2 dimensions is represented as a pair of numbers: p = (x, y) where x is the x-coordinate of the point p and y is the y-coordinate of p. 2D objects are often represented as a set of points (vertices), $\{p_1,p_2,...,p_n\}$, and an associated set of edges $\{e_1,e_2,...,e_m\}$. An edge is defined as a pair of points e = $\{p_i,p_j\}$.

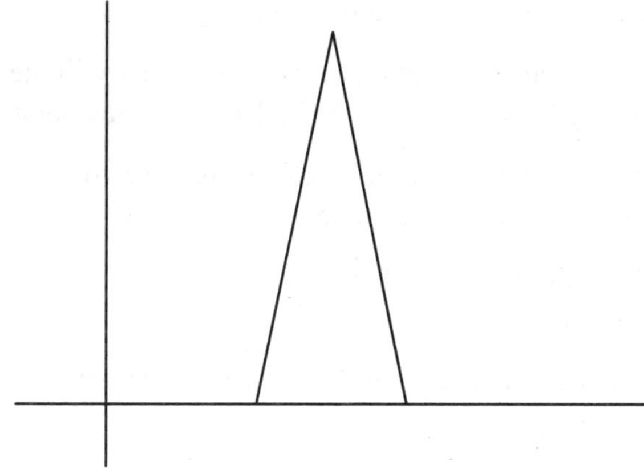

We can also write points in vector/matrix notation as:

$$P = \begin{vmatrix} x \\ y \end{vmatrix}$$

5.3 TRANSLATION

A translation is the process of changing the position of an object along a straight line path from one coordinate location to another.

We can translate a 2D point by adding translation distances, t_x and t_y to the original coordinate position (x, y) to move the point to the new position (x', y').

$$x' = x + t_x$$

$$y' = y + t_y \qquad (5.1)$$

The translation distance pair (t_x, t_y) is called a translation vector or shift vector.

Matrix/Vector Representation of Translations

A translation can also be represented by a pair of numbers, $t = (t_x, t_y)$ where t_x is the change in the x-coordinate and t_y is the change in the y coordinate. To translate the point p by t, we simply add the values to obtain the new (translated) point q = p + t.

$$q = p + t = \begin{vmatrix} x \\ y \end{vmatrix} + \begin{vmatrix} t_x \\ t_y \end{vmatrix}$$

where the value of x is $x + t_x$ and the value of y is $y + t_y$

Translation is a rigid body transformation that moves the object without deformation. It means that every point on the object is translated by the same amount.

For example, assume you are given a point at $(x, y) = (2, 1)$. Where will the point be if you move it 3 units to the right and 1 unit up? Ans: $(x', y') = (5, 2)$. How was this obtained? -

$(x', y') = (x + 3, y + 1)$. That is, to move a point by some amount t_x to the right and t_y up, you must add t_x to the x-coordinate and t_y to the y-coordinate.

What is the required transformation to move the green triangle to the red triangle? Here the green triangle is represented by 3 points.

To identify the triangles paint the first triangle with green colour and the second i.e. below line with red colour.

triangle = {p = (1 0) p = (2 0) p = (1.5, 2)}

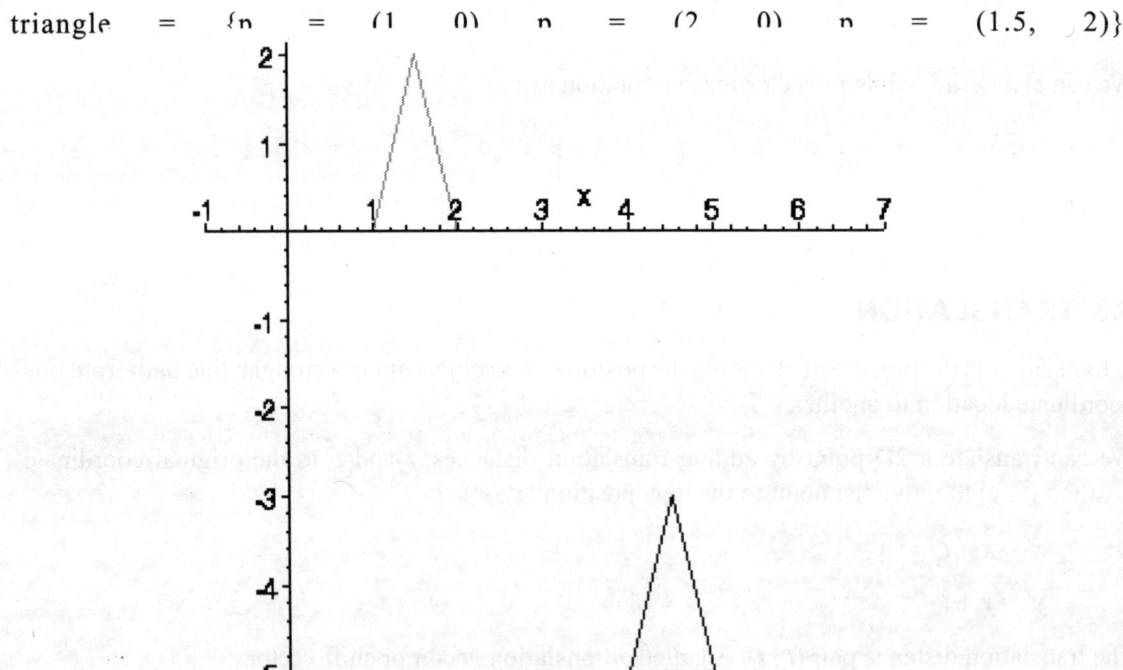

What are the points and edges in the picture of a house shown below? What transformation is required to move this house so that the peak of the roof is at the origin?

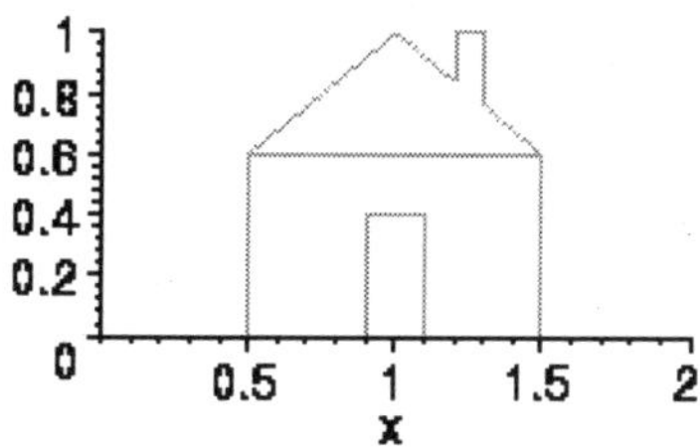

Program

```
/* Program to move the house
________________________________________________
*/
#include<stdio.h>
# include <iostream.h>
# include <conio.h>
# include <graphics.h>
# include <math.h>

char IncFlag;
int PolygonPoints[4][2] =
        {{10,10},{10,100},{100,100},{100,10}};


void PolyLine()
{
        int i;
        cleardevice();

        for (i=0; i<=3; i++)
        {
                line(320+PolygonPoints[i][0],
```

```
                240-PolygonPoints[i][1],
                320+PolygonPoints[(i+1)%4][0],
                240-PolygonPoints[(i+1)%4][1]);
    }
}
void Translate(int tx,int ty)
{
    int i;

    for (i=0; i<50; i++)
    {
        PolygonPoints[i][0] += tx;
        PolygonPoints[i][1] += ty;
    }
}

void main()
{
    int gDriver = DETECT, gMode;
    int i;
    int tx,ty;

    initgraph(&gDriver, &gMode, "C:\\TC\\BGI");

    PolyLine();
    printf("\n Before traslation:");

    getch();
    printf("\n Now, enter both Translation vector :");
    scanf("%d%d",&tx,&ty);

    Translate(tx,ty);
```

```
    PolyLine();
    printf("\n\n\n After traslation :");
    getch();
}
```

5.4 ROTATION

A 2D rotation is applied to an object by reposting it along a circular path in the xy plane either in the clockwise or anti-clockwise direction.

To generate a rotation, we have to specify the rotation angle θ and the position (x_r, y_r) of the rotation point about which the object is to be rotated.

Now consider the rotation of the object about the origin as shown in the figure below.

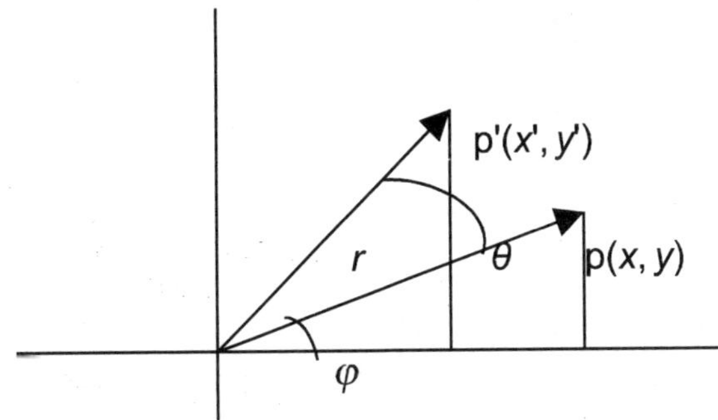

Here r is the constant distance of the point from the origin, the angle φ is the original angular position of the point from the horizontal and θ is the rotation angle.

We can express the transformed coordinates in terms of the angle θ and as:

$$x' = r\cos(\varphi + \theta) = r\cos\varphi - r\sin\varphi$$

$$\boldsymbol{y' = r\sin(\varphi + \theta) = r\cos\varphi + r\sin\varphi} \qquad (5.2)$$

Our original coordinates are:

$$x = r\cos\varphi$$

$$\boldsymbol{y = r\sin\varphi} \qquad (5.3)$$

Substituting Equation (5.2) into Equation (5.1), we obtain the transformation equation for rotating a point at position (x, y) through an angle θ about the origin as:

$$x' = x\cos\theta - y\sin\theta$$

$$\boldsymbol{y' = x\sin\theta + y\cos\theta} \qquad (5.4)$$

Matrix/Vector Representation of Translations

$$q = p + r = \begin{vmatrix} x \\ y \end{vmatrix} * \begin{vmatrix} \cos\theta & -\sin\theta \\ \sin\theta & \cos\theta \end{vmatrix}$$

Below, we see objects that have been rotated by 25 degrees.

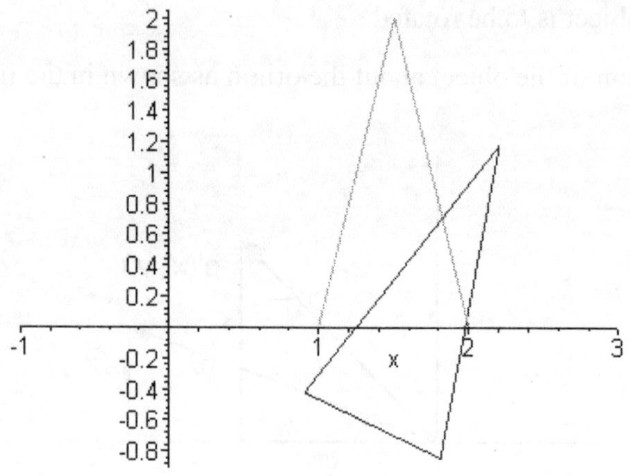

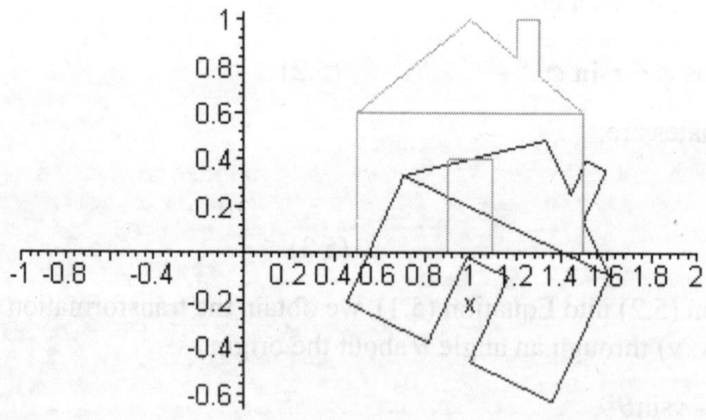

Again, we see that basic rotations are with respect to the origin:

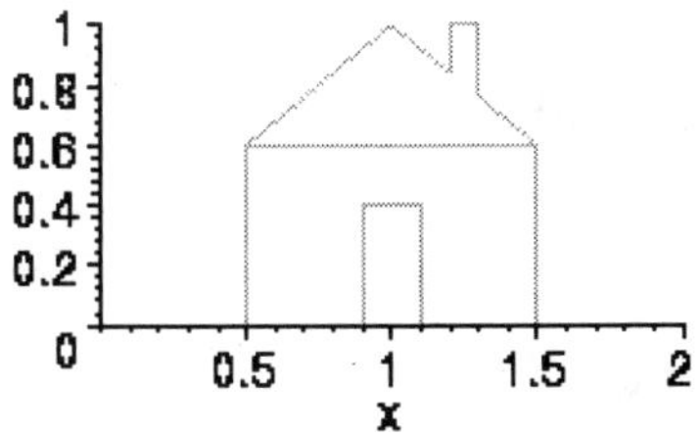

Program

```
/*
Rotate About Origin
*/
# include <iostream.h>
# include <conio.h>
# include <graphics.h>
# include <math.h>
#include<stdio.h>
int PolygonPoints[4][2] =
        {{10,100},{110,100},{110,200},{10,200}};
void PolyLine()
{
        int I;
        cleardevice();

                for (i=0; i<=3; i++)
        {
                line(PolygonPoints[i][0],PolygonPoints[i][1],
                  PolygonPoints[(i+1)%4][0],PolygonPoints[(i+1)%4][1]);
        }
}
void Rotate()
{
```

```
        float Angle;
        int I;
        int Tx,Ty;

        Angle = 30.0*(22.0/7.0)/180.0;
        for (i=0; i<=3; i++)
        {
                Tx = PolygonPoints[i][0];
                Ty = PolygonPoints[i][1];
                PolygonPoints[i][0] = (Tx – 320)*cos(Angle) –
                                        (Ty – 240)*sin(Angle) + 320;
                PolygonPoints[i][1] = (Tx – 320)*sin(Angle) +
                                        (Ty – 240)*cos(Angle) + 240;
        }
}

void main()
{
        int gDriver = DETECT, gMode;
        int iCnt;
        initgraph(&gDriver, &gMode, "C:\\TC\\BGI");
        for (iCnt=0; iCnt<4; iCnt++)
        {
                PolygonPoints[iCnt][0] += 320;
                PolygonPoints[iCnt][1] = 240 – PolygonPoints[iCnt][1];
        }
        PolyLine();
        printf("\n Before Rotation :");
        getch();
        Rotate();
        PolyLine();
        printf("\n After rotation:");
        getch();
}
```

5.5 SCALING

Suppose we want to double the size of a 2D object. First we have to be clear as to what we mean by double? Usually when we talk of scaling it means the same amount of scaling along each dimension. That is, we must specify how much the size should be changed along each dimension.

Thus we can say that scaling is the process of changing the size of the object. This operation can be carried out by multiplying the coordinate values (x, y) of each vertex by the scaling factors S_x and S_y to produce the transformed coordinates (x', y')

$$x' = x.S_x$$

$$y' = y.S_y \qquad (5.5)$$

Below we see a triangle and a house that have been doubled in both width and height. (Note: The area is more than doubled).

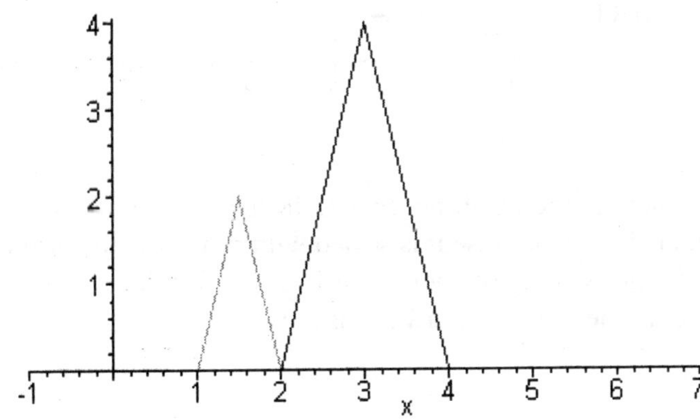

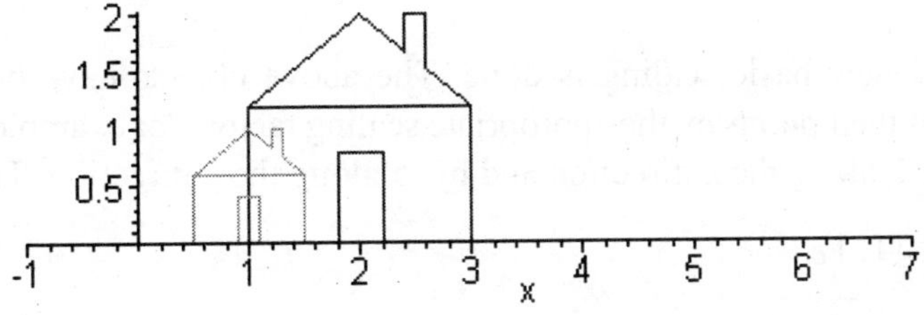

The scaling for the x dimension does not have to be the same as the y dimension. If they are different, then the object is distorted. What is the scaling in each dimension of the pictures below?

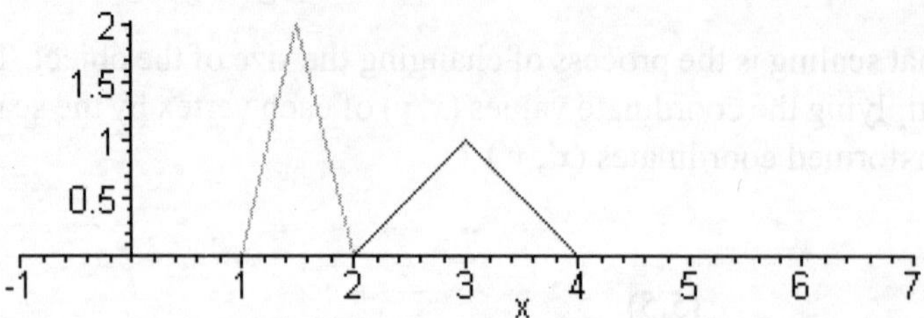

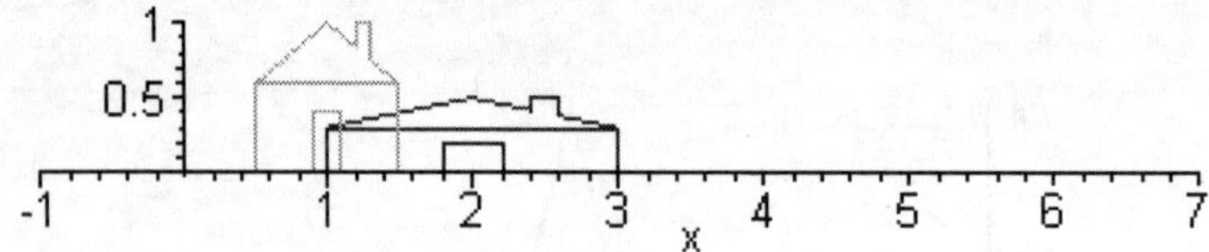

If we double the size, where is the resulting object? In the pictures above, the scaled object is always shifted to the right. This is because it is scaled with respect to the origin. That is, the point at the origin is left fixed. Thus scaling by more than 1 moves the object away from the origin and scaling of less than 1 moves the object toward the origin.

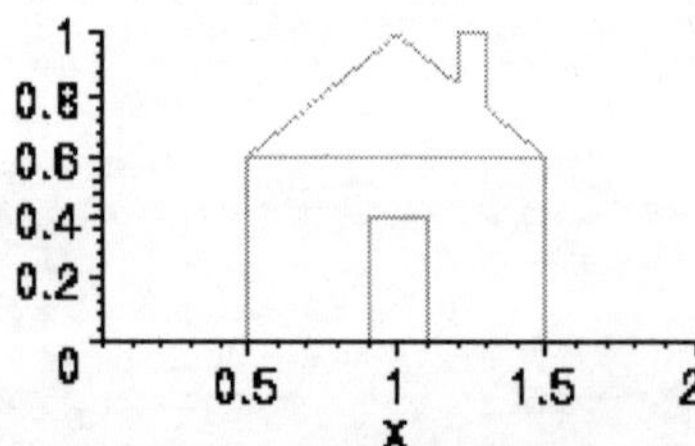

This is because of how basic scaling is done. The above objects have been scaled simply by multiplying each of their points by the appropriate scaling factor. For example, the point p = (1.5, 2) has been scaled by 2 along the x direction and by .5 along the y direction. Thus, the new point is

q = (2*1.5, .5*2) = (1, 1).

Matrix/Vector Representation of Translations

Scaling transformations are represented by matrices. For example, the above scaling of 2 and .5 is represented as a matrix:

$$\text{scale matrix: s} = \begin{bmatrix} sx & 0 \\ 0 & sy \end{bmatrix} = \begin{bmatrix} 2 & 0 \\ 0 & 5 \end{bmatrix}$$

$$\text{new point: q} = \text{s*p} = \begin{bmatrix} sx & 0 \\ 0 & sy \end{bmatrix} \begin{bmatrix} x \\ y \end{bmatrix} = \begin{bmatrix} sx\ x \\ sy\ y \end{bmatrix}$$

Scaling about a Particular Point

Below we show how objects are scaled about their centre point.

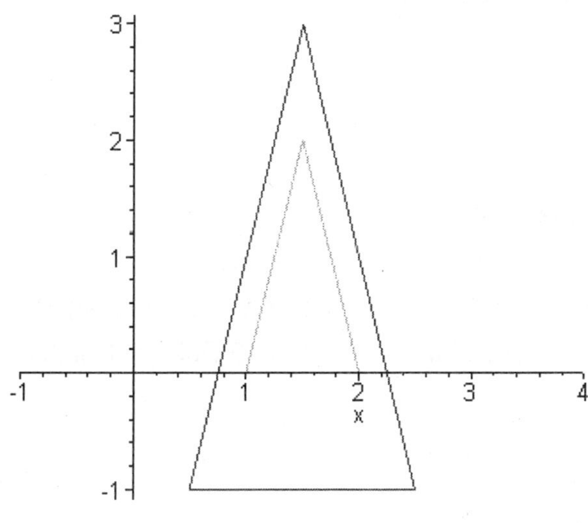

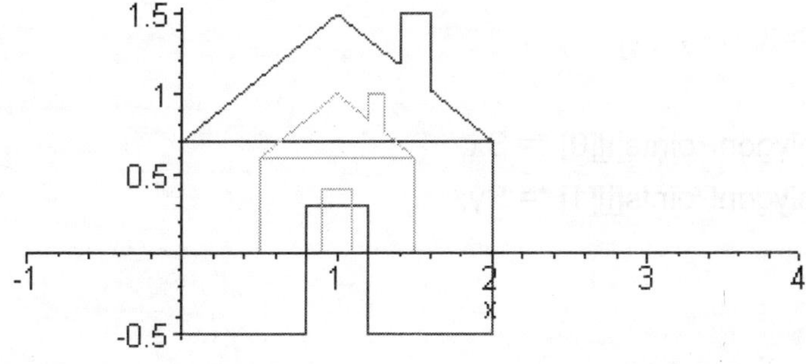

Program

```
/*
Scaling about Origin
*/

# include <iostream.h>
# include <conio.h>
# include <graphics.h>
# include <math.h>
#include<stdio.h>
int PolygonPoints[4][2] =
        {{10,10},{10,100},{100,100},{100,10}};
void PolyLine()
{
        int i;
        cleardevice();
                for (i=0; i<=3; i++)
        {
                line(320+PolygonPoints[i][0],240-PolygonPoints[i][1],
                 320+PolygonPoints[(i+1)%4][0],240-PolygonPoints[(i+1)%4][1]);
        }
}
void Scale(float Sx,float Sy)
{
        int i;

        for (i=0; i<=3; i++)
        {
                PolygonPoints[i][0] *= Sx;
                PolygonPoints[i][1] *= Sy;
        }
}
```

```
void main()
{
        int gDriver = DETECT, gMode;
        float sx,sy;
        initgraph(&gDriver, &gMode, "C:\\TC\\BGI");
        PolyLine();
        printf("\n Before Scaling :");
        printf("\n Now enter both scaling factor:");
        scanf("%f%f",&sx,&sy);
        getch();
        Scale(sx,sy);
        PolyLine();
        printf("\n After scaling:");
        getch();
}
```

5.6 REFLECTION

Reflection is a transformation that produces a mirror image of an object. It is relative to an axis of reflection and is carried out by rotating the object 180° about the reflection axis.

Reflection about the x axis (horizontal axis) can be expressed as:

$$\begin{vmatrix} 1 & 0 & 0 \\ 0 & -1 & 0 \\ 0 & 0 & 1 \end{vmatrix}$$

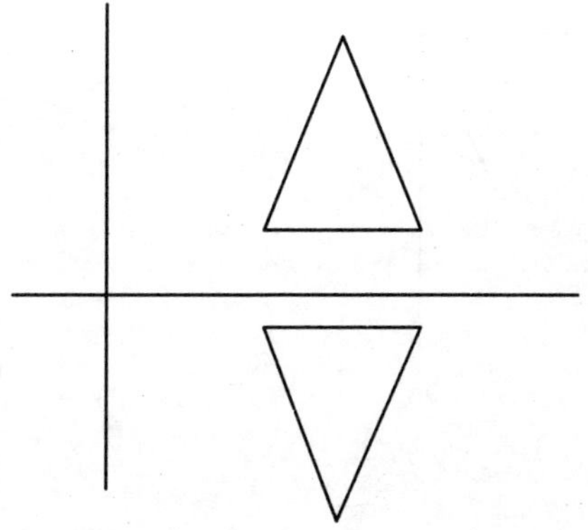

Reflection about the y axis (vertical axis) can be expressed as:

$$\begin{vmatrix} -1 & 0 & 0 \\ 0 & 1 & 0 \\ 0 & 0 & 1 \end{vmatrix}$$

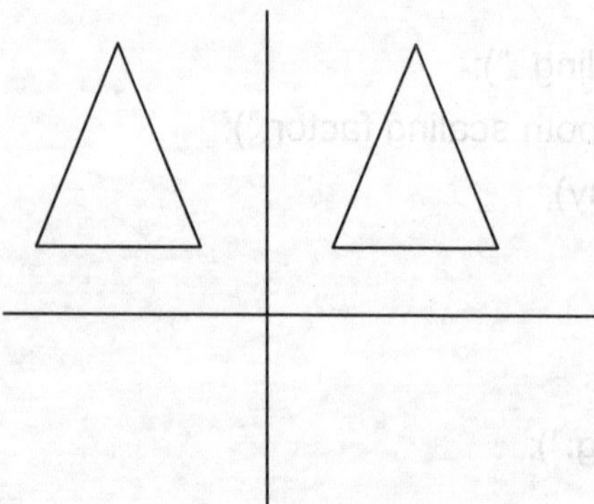

In this way we can also obtain the transformation matrix for reflection image about the vertical axis and horizontal axis as:

$$\begin{vmatrix} -1 & 0 & 0 \\ 0 & 1 & 0 \\ 0 & 0 & 1 \end{vmatrix}$$

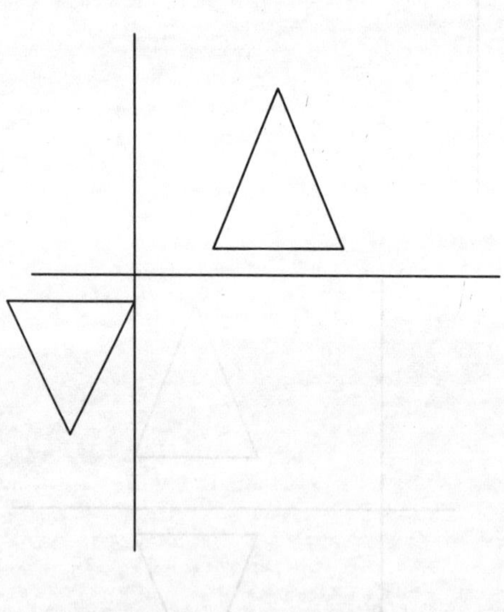

Program

```
/*
______________________________________________________________

Reflection about the x axis
______________________________________________________________

*/

# include <iostream.h>
# include <conio.h>
# include <graphics.h>
# include <math.h>
#include<stdio.h>


int PolygonPoints[3][2] =
        {{10,100},{110,100},{110,200}};

void PolyLine()
{
        int i;
        cleardevice();

        for (i=0; i<3; i++)
        {
                line(PolygonPoints[i][0],PolygonPoints[i][1],
                 PolygonPoints[(i+1)%3][0],PolygonPoints[(i+1)%3][1]);
        }
}
void Reflect()
{

        int i;
```

```
        for (i=0; i<3; i++)
                PolygonPoints[i][1] = (480 - PolygonPoints[i][1]);
}

void main()
{
        int gDriver = DETECT, gMode;
        int i;
        initgraph(&gDriver, &gMode, "C:\\TC\\BGI");
        for (i=0; i<3; i++)
        {
                PolygonPoints[i][0] += 320;
                PolygonPoints[i][1] = 240 - PolygonPoints[i][1];
        }
        PolyLine();
        printf("\n Before Reflection :");
        getch();
        Reflect();
        PolyLine();
        printf("\n After Reflection ");
        getch();
}
```

5.7 SHEAR

Shear is a transformation that distorts the shape of an object. In the distorted image it appears that some layers of the image have been sheared off from the original image. Basically there are two common shearing transformations.

1) x shear: This preserves the y co-ordinates but changes the x values.

We can express x shear as:

$$x' = x + sh_x . y$$

$$y' = y \qquad (5.6)$$

The transformation matrix for x shear is given below.

$$\begin{vmatrix} 1 & sh_x & 0 \\ 0 & 1 & 0 \\ 0 & 0 & 1 \end{vmatrix}$$

2) y shear: This preserves the x co-ordinates but changes the y values.

We can express y shear as:

$$x' = x$$

$$y' = y + sh_y.x \qquad (5.7)$$

The transformation matrix for y shear is given below:

$$\begin{vmatrix} 1 & 0 & 0 \\ sh_y & 1 & 0 \\ 0 & 0 & 1 \end{vmatrix}$$

5.8 USE OF A HOMOGENEOUS CO-ORDINATE SYSTEM

In real life, graphics transformations are required in almost all situations. However, the transformations are not necessarily simply the translation type, rotation type or scaling type. Real life transformations are generally made up of sequential combinations of these three, i.e. a sequential combination of translation and rotation, scaling and translation, scaling, rotation and translation etc. Though these combinations can be represented by the combinations of the corresponding matrix equations, it will definitely be easier if we use a co-ordinate system represented by the general form as:

(x_h, y_h, h)

Where, $x_h = x.\ h \qquad (5.8)$

$y_h = y.\ h \qquad (5.9)$

Where, h = a factor to convert a Cartesian co-ordinate to the homogeneous co-ordinate system, and (x, y) = original co-ordinate of the pixel in Cartesian form.

For all practical purposes of a two dimensional co-ordinate system we will assume the value of $h = 1$. Thus, the homogeneous co-ordinate of the original Cartesian co-ordinate (x, y) will be changed to $(x, y, 1)$.

In case of a three dimensional working system the value of h may be different from 1, but for all practical purposes of a two dimensional working environment, it will be accepted as 1.

The advantage of using a homogeneous co-ordinate system is that it helps us to represent all sorts of geometric transformation very easily. Thus all types of transformations can be represented by using standard 3 x 3 matrices.

For example, at the time of translation we used the matrix equation:

$p' = p.t$ (5.10)

Or,

$$\begin{vmatrix} X' \\ Y' \end{vmatrix} = \begin{vmatrix} X \\ Y \end{vmatrix} \bullet \begin{vmatrix} t_x \\ t_y \end{vmatrix}$$

Converting this equation to its equivalent homogeneous co-ordinate form we can write it as:

$$\begin{vmatrix} X' \\ Y' \\ 1 \end{vmatrix} = \begin{vmatrix} 1 & 0 & t_x \\ 0 & 1 & t_y \\ 0 & 0 & 1 \end{vmatrix} \bullet \begin{vmatrix} X \\ Y \\ 1 \end{vmatrix}$$

This expression can be expressed in a simplified form as:

$p' = t(t_x, t_y)p$

Where the term $t(t_x, t_y)$ is called a Translation matrix of size 3 * 3

5.9 COMPOSITE AND COMBINED TRANSFORMATIONS

As mentioned above a real life problem of transformation does not normally contain only the basic transformations, but consists of sequential transformations of the basics. Thus it will always be better to use the standardized form of the equation for all types of transformations, using the homogeneous form of co-ordinate system.

We will now develop the matrix equations for the sequential combinations of the basic types of transformations. But before that, let us see the methods of composite transformations, i.e. translations with more than one step, e.g. scaling and rotation in sequence.

In this context we introduce a term 'Matrix Concatenation'. This term refers to the product of two transformation matrices, which is often required.

Composite Translation

Suppose the original position of the co-ordinate was $p(x_h, y_h, h)$ in the homogeneous form of representation. Assume a translation of $t(t_{x1}, t_{y1})$ to a position p′. Now assume a further translation $t(t_{x2}, t_{y2})$, which will cause a further shift to the position p″.

Then

$p' = t(t_{x1}, t_{y1}).\ p$

and $p'' = t(t_{x2}, t_{y2}).p'$

By concatenation of these two equations we can write the equation of the final position of the co-ordinate as:

$p'' = t(t_{x2}, t_{y2}).\ \{t(t_{x1}, t_{y1}).p\}$

$\quad = \{t(t_{x2}, t_{y2}).\ \{t(t_{x1}, t_{y1}).p\}$

If we now find the product of these two translation vectors we can write it as:

$$t(t_{x2}, t_{y2}).\ t(t_{x1}, t_{y1}) = \begin{vmatrix} X' \\ Y' \\ \end{vmatrix} = \begin{vmatrix} 1 & 0 & t_{x2} \\ 0 & 1 & t_{y2} \\ 0 & 0 & 1 \end{vmatrix} \bullet \begin{vmatrix} 1 & 0 & t_{x1} \\ 0 & 1 & t_{y1} \\ 0 & 0 & 1 \end{vmatrix}$$

$$\textbf{Or} = \begin{vmatrix} 1 & 0 & t_{x2} + t_{x1} \\ 0 & 1 & t_{y2} + t_{y1} \\ 0 & 0 & 1 \end{vmatrix}$$

$$= t(t_{x1} + t_{x2},\ t_{y1} + t_{y2})$$

Composite Scaling

Using the same principle, we can write the general equation for two successive scaling operations.

Suppose the two successive scaling matrices are:

$S(s_{x1}, s_{y1})$ and $S(s_{x2}, s_{y2})$

After applying these two successive scaling operations to a pixel having a co-ordinate $p(x, y)$, we will obtain:

$p'' = S(s_{x2}, s_{y2}).\{s_{x1}, s_{y1}).p\}$

$= \{S(s_{x2}, s_{y2}). S(s_{x1}, s_{y1}).P\}$ (5.11)

$$\text{Now, } S(s_{x2}, s_{y2}). S(s_{x1}, s_{y1}) = \begin{vmatrix} S_{X2} & 0 & 0 \\ 0 & S_{X2} & 0 \\ 0 & 0 & 1 \end{vmatrix} \bullet \begin{vmatrix} S_{X1} & 0 & 0 \\ 0 & S_{X1} & 0 \\ 0 & 0 & 1 \end{vmatrix}$$

Or more simply we can write:

$S(s_{x2}, s_{y2}). S(s_{x1}, s_{y1}) = S(s_{x1}.s_{x2}, s_{y1}.s_{y2})$ (5.12)

From this expression we can understand that successive scaling operations will produce a multiplicative effect.

Composite Rotation

Using the same principle of operation, we can write the general expression of the transformations if two successive rotations are carried out.

In the case of a rotation through an angle β_1, the original co-ordinate $p(x_h, y_h, 1)$ will be moved to a co-ordinate p', after which it can be expressed as:

$p' = R(\beta_1).p$

After two successive rotations through the angles β_1 and $\beta_{2,}$ the equation can be expressed as:

$p'' = R(\beta_1).p'$

$= R(\beta_2).\{R(\beta_1). p\}$

$= R(\beta_2).\{R(\beta_1).\} p$

$= R(\beta). P$

Where $R(\beta) = R(\beta_1). R(\beta_2)$

$$= \begin{vmatrix} \cos\beta_1 & -\sin\beta_1 & 0 \\ \sin\beta_1 & \cos\beta_1 & 0 \\ 0 & 0 & 1 \end{vmatrix} \bullet \begin{vmatrix} \cos\beta_2 & -\sin\beta_2 & 0 \\ \sin\beta_2 & \cos\beta_2 & 0 \\ 0 & 0 & 1 \end{vmatrix}$$

$$= \begin{vmatrix} \cos\beta_1 . \cos\beta_2 - \sin\beta_1 . \sin\beta_2 + 0 & \cos\beta_1 . \sin\beta_2 - \sin\beta_1 . \cos\beta_2 + 0 & 0 \\ \sin\beta_1 . \cos\beta_2 - \cos\beta_1 . \sin\beta_2 + 0 & \sin\beta_1 . \sin\beta_2 - \cos\beta_1 . \cos\beta_2 + 0 & 0 \\ 0 & 0 & 1 \end{vmatrix}$$

$$R(\beta) = \begin{vmatrix} \cos(\beta_1 + \beta_2) & -\ \sin(\beta_1 + \beta_2) & 0 \\ \sin(\beta_1 + \beta_2) & \cos(\beta_1 + \beta_2) & 0 \\ 0 & 0 & 1 \end{vmatrix}$$

In a more simple form it can be written as:

$R(\beta_1). R(\beta_2) = R(\beta_1 + \beta_2)$

Or, the expression can be written as:

$p'' = R(\beta_1 + \beta_2) .p$

This expression represents two successive rotations, where the effect will be the same as the sum of the angles of the two rotational matrices.

Combination of Transformations

So far we have seen the three basic types of transformations, the use of homogeneous co-ordinates and composite transformations.

We will now study real life transformations of graphics objects, which are normally a combination of these basic transformations. In this case, we would concatenate the respective matrices one after another in order to obtain the required effect.

Combination of Translation and Rotation

Suppose we want to obtain the effect of rotation with respect to a selected co-ordinate (x', y'), which is not the origin. The object which we want to rotate and the respective co-ordinates are given in the figure below.

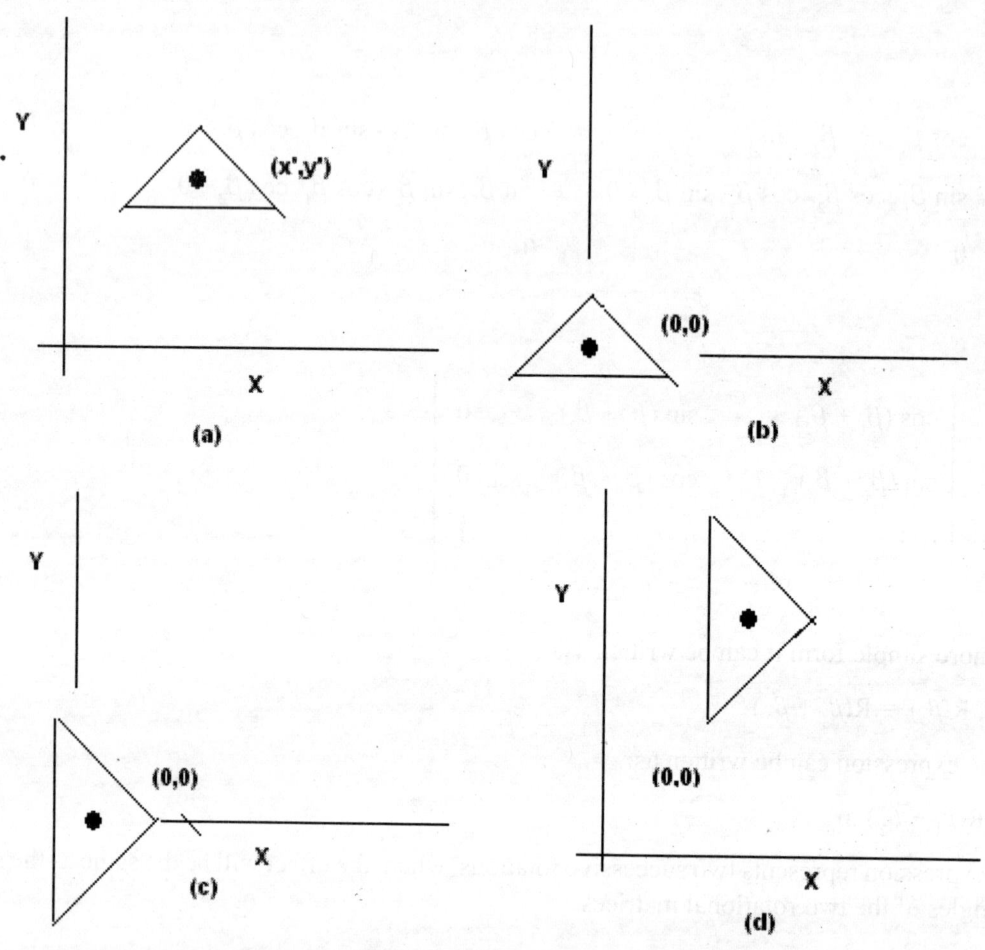

In this case, the steps of the operation will be as follows:

Step-1: Translate the object in a direction and value such that the co-ordinate (x', y') comes to the origin as shown in the figure above.

Step-2: Rotate the object through 90° in the clockwise direction with respect to the origin as shown in Fig. -c

Step-3: After this again allow a translation towards the co-ordinate (x', y') as shown in Fig. – d

Following these three steps successively, we can obtain the effect of rotation of the object with respect to the co-ordinates (x', y'), which are not the origin. To obtain these effects, we have to concatenate their corresponding matrices as shown below:

$$T(x',y') \,.\, R(-\beta) \,.\, T(-x', y') = \begin{vmatrix} 1 & 0 & x' \\ 0 & 0 & y' \\ 0 & 1 & 1 \end{vmatrix} \bullet \begin{vmatrix} \cos\beta & -\sin\beta & 0 \\ \sin\beta & \cos\beta & 0 \\ 0 & 0 & 1 \end{vmatrix} \bullet \begin{vmatrix} 1 & 0 & -x' \\ 0 & 1 & -y' \\ 0 & 0 & 1 \end{vmatrix}$$

$$= \begin{vmatrix} \cos\beta & -\sin\beta & x'(1-\cos\beta) + y'\sin\beta \\ \sin\beta & \cos\beta & y'(1-\cos\beta) - x'\sin\beta \\ 0 & 0 & 1 \end{vmatrix}$$

Or simply, $t(x, y').R(-\beta).t(-x', -y') = R(x', y, \theta)$

Combination of Translation and Scaling

For the combinational effect of translation and scaling we have to follow the steps given below:

Step-1: Translate the object to the origin.

Step-2: Scale it as per requirement.

Step-3: Again translate it to its original position.

The concatenated matrix will be:

$t(x, y) .S(x, y). t(-x, -y) =$

$$\begin{vmatrix} 1 & 0 & X_c \\ 0 & 1 & Y_c \\ 0 & 0 & 1 \end{vmatrix} \bullet \begin{vmatrix} S_x & 0 & 0 \\ 0 & S_y & 0 \\ 0 & 0 & 1 \end{vmatrix} \bullet \begin{vmatrix} 1 & 0 & -X_c \\ 0 & 0 & -Y_c \\ 0 & 0 & 1 \end{vmatrix}$$

$$= \begin{vmatrix} S_x & 0 & X_c(1 - S_x) \\ 0 & S_y & Y_c(1 - S_y) \\ 0 & 0 & 1 \end{vmatrix}$$

5.10 THREE DIMENSIONAL TRANSFORMATION

We have already seen in 2D systems that the transformation area normally includes the three basic operations, (1) translation (2) rotation and (3) scaling. In 3D systems also, these same three basic types of transformations are used, along with other transformations like reflection and shear.

1) Translation

In 2D, we have seen that if a point p having the co-ordinates (x, y) is translated through a distance, the new co-ordinates will be changed to (x', y'). Using a homogeneous co-ordinate system we can represent it as a 3*3 matrix.

In 3D this 3*3 will automatically change to a 4*4 matrix as shown below:

P′ = T * P

$$\begin{vmatrix} x' \\ y' \\ z' \\ 1 \end{vmatrix} = \begin{vmatrix} 1 & 0 & 0 & t_x \\ 0 & 1 & 0 & t_y \\ 0 & 0 & 1 & t_z \\ 0 & 0 & 0 & 1 \end{vmatrix} \bullet \begin{vmatrix} x \\ x \\ z \\ 1 \end{vmatrix}$$

Where the original co-ordinate of the point p is (x, y, z) and the new transformed position p' has the co-ordinates (x', y', z'). The parameters, t_x, t_y, t_z represent the translation distance of the point p in the x, y and z directions respectively.

We can also write:

$x' = x + t_x$

$y' = y + t_y$

$z' = z + t_z$

This situation is shown in the figure below.

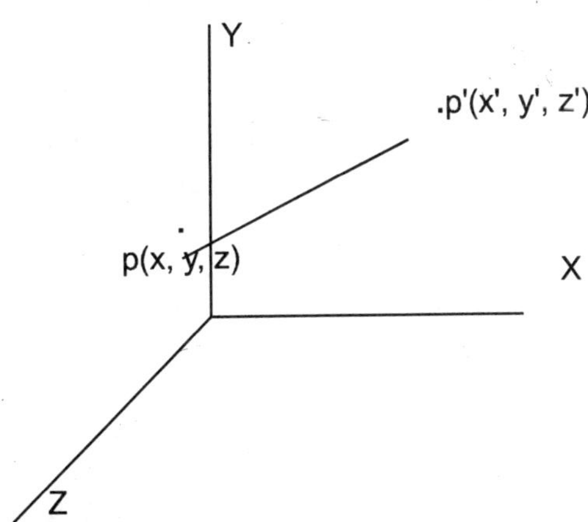

Thus for the translation of a 3D object we have to transform each component of the co-ordinates separately in the proper direction.

1) Rotation

Rotation in 3-D applications is somewhat different than that in 2D applications. In 2D fields, the rotation of the object is always in the xy plane. But in the case of a 3D system rotation may be carried out around any axis of the 3D system. For rotation in a 3D system, we first have to select an axis of rotation and then specify the angle of rotation. In 3D, the axis of rotation may be of 3 types as shown in the figure below.

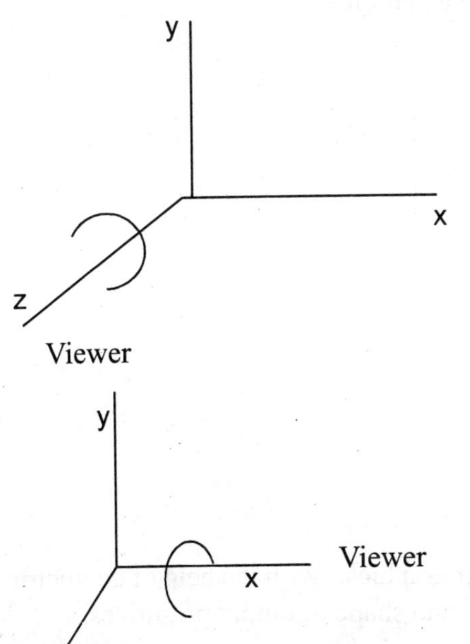

Rotation about the z axis in the anti-clockwise direction

Rotation about the x axis in the anti-clockwise direction

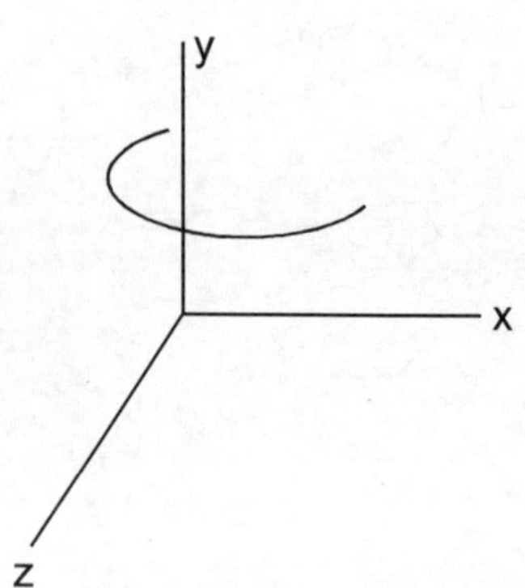

Rotation about the y axis in the anti-clockwise direction

From the first figure we can find the equation of rotation about the z-axis in the anti-clockwise direction as:

$$x' = x\cos\theta - y\sin\theta$$

$$y' = x\sin\theta + y\cos\theta$$

$$z' = z$$

Where (x', y', z') are the new co-ordinates of a point p whose original co-ordinates were (x, y, z) and θ is the angle of rotation about the z axis in the positive direction.

Using the homogeneous co-ordinate form, we can write the equation as:

$$\begin{vmatrix} x' \\ y' \\ z' \\ 1 \end{vmatrix} = \begin{vmatrix} \cos\theta & -\sin\theta & 0 & 0 \\ \sin\theta & \cos\theta & 0 & 0 \\ 0 & 0 & 1 & 0 \\ 0 & 0 & 0 & 1 \end{vmatrix} * \begin{vmatrix} x \\ y \\ z \\ 1 \end{vmatrix}$$

In compact form we can write it as:

$$p' = r_z(\theta) * p$$

5.11 SUMMARY

- Transformations are a fundamental part of computer graphics. With the help of geometric transformations we can change the orientation, size and shape of output primitives.
- Translation is a rigid body transformation that moves the object without deformation. It means that every point on the object is translated by the same amount.

- A 2D rotation is applied to an object by reposting it along a circular path in the xy plane either in the clockwise or in the anti-clockwise direction.
- To generate a rotation, we have to specify the rotation angle è and the position (x_r, y_r) of the rotation point about which the object is to be rotated.
- In real life graphics transformations are required in almost all situations. But these transformations are not necessarily simply of the translation type, rotation type or scaling type.
- Real life transformations are generally made up of sequential combinations of these three, i.e. a sequential combination of translation and rotation, scaling and translation, scaling, rotation and translation etc.
- The advantage of using a homogenous co-ordinate system is that it helps us to represent all sorts of geometric transformation very easily. Thus all types of transformation can be represented by using standard 3 x 3 matrices.

5.12 REVIEW QUESTIONS

1. Write procedures to implement the buildTransformationMatrix and the composeTransformationMatrix functions to produce a composite transformation matrix for any set of input transformation parameters.
2. Write a program that applies any specified sequence of transformations to a displayed object. The program is to be designed so that a user selects the transformation sequence and associated parameters from displayed menus, and the composite transform.
3. Modify the transformation matrix for scaling in an arbitrary direction, to include coordinates for my specified scaling fixed point h, y_o.
4. Prove that the multiplication of transformation matrices (or each point of the following sequence of operations is commutative:
   (a) Two successive rotations.
   (b) Two successive translations.
   (c) Two successive scaling.
5. Prove that a uniform scaling (5, 5) and a rotation form a commutative pair of operations, but that in general, scaling and rotation are not commutative operations.
6. Multiply the individual scaling, rotation and translation matrices to verify the elements in the composite transformation matrix.
7. Determine the form of the transformation matrix for a reflection about an arbitrary line with the equation $y = m + b.1$. Show that two successive reflections about any line passing through the coordinate origin is equivalent to a single rotation about the origin.
8. Determine a sequence of basic transformations that are equivalent to the x-direction shearing matrix.
9. Determine a sequence of basic transformations that are equivalent to the y direction shearing matrix.

10. Show that the transformation matrix for a reflection about the line $y = x$, is equivalent to a reflection relative to the x axis followed by a counter clockwise rotation of 90°.
11. Show that transformation matrix for a reflection about the line $y = -x$, is equivalent to a reflection relative to the y axis followed by a counter clockwise rotation of 90°.
12. Show that the two successive reflections about either of the coordinate axes is equivalent to a single rotation about the coordinate origin.
13. Determine the form of transformation matrix for a reflection about an arbitrary line with equation $y = m.x + b$.
14. Show that the two successive reflections about any line passing through the coordinate origin is equivalent to a single rotation about the origin.
15. Prove that 2D rotation and scaling commute if $s_x = s_y$ or if $\theta = n\pi$ for integral n, but otherwise do not.
16. Use the midpoint method to derive decision parameters for generating a point along a straight line path with the slope in the range $0 < m < 1$. Show that the midpoint decision parameters are the same as those in the Bresenham line algorithm.
17. Using the midpoint method, and taking symmetry into account, develop an efficient algorithm for scan conversion of the following curve over the interval $-10 \leq x \geq 10$:

$$y = 1/12x^3$$

18. Using the midpoint method and symmetry considerations to scan convert the parabola

$$y = 100 - x^2$$

over the interval $-10 \leq x \geq 10$.

19. Using the midpoint method and symmetry considerations to scan convert the parabola

$$x = y^2$$

over the interval $-10 \leq x \geq 10$.

20. Given a unit cube with one corner at (0, 0, 0) and the opposite corner at (1, 1, 1), derive the transformations necessary to rotate the cube by θ degrees about the main diagonal (from (0, 0, 0) to (1, 1, 1)) in the counter clockwise direction when looking along the diagonal toward the origin.

CHAPTER 6

Curves

6.1 INTRODUCTION

The real world is not made up of stick figures. Many of the objects that we might like to model and display involve curves. Display of curved lines and surfaces can be generated from an input set of mathematical functions defining objects or from a set of user specified data points. When functions are specified, a package can project the defining equations for a curve to be displayed in a plane and plot pixel positions along the path of the projected function.

When a set of discrete coordinate points is used to specify the shape of an object, a functional description is obtained that best fits the designed points according to the constraints of the application. Spline representations are examples of this class of curves and surfaces. These methods are commonly used to design new object shapes and to digitize drawings to describe animation path. We shall develop spline interpolation algorithms for drawing curved lines and fractal curve generators for rough, natural looking objects.

6.2 CURVE GENERATION

There are two approaches which can be taken to draw curved lines. One approach is to develop a curve generation algorithm such as DDA and with this approach, a true curve is created. The second method is to approximate a curve by a number of small straight-line segments.

Suppose we want to draw a curve, such as the arc of a circle. If we know the differential equation for this curve, we can write a digital differential analyzer algorithm, which will calculate the coordinates of points on the curve. We can then change the intensity values of the pixels which contain these points and an image of the curve will appear on the screen.

The differential equations of simple curves such as circles and ellipses are fairly easy to solve, and algorithms for their generation can be implemented in hardware. A display device may be capable of drawing arcs as well as line segments.

Let us go through the development of a DDA algorithm for generating circular arcs. The equations for the arc coordinates can be written in terms of an angle parameter A as follows:

$$x = r\cos A + x_0$$

$$y = r\sin A + y_0 \qquad (6.1)$$

Where (x_0, y_0) is the centre of curvature and r is the arc radius.

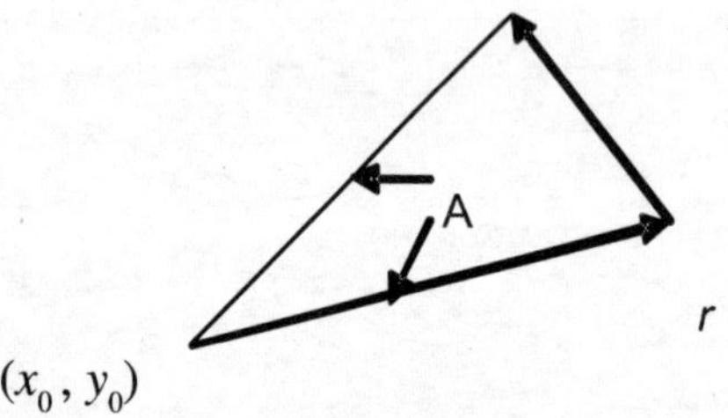

Differentiating equation (6.1) gives:

$$dx = -r\sin A\, dA$$

$$dy = r\cos A\, dA \qquad (6.2)$$

Equation 1 gives

$$r\cos A = x - x_0$$

$$r\sin A = y - y_0 \qquad (6.3)$$

So that,

$$dx = -(y - y_0)dA$$

$$dy = (x - x_0)dA \qquad (6.4)$$

Now the changes dx and dy tell us the amount to add to the original point on the arc to get the new point. Thus the coordinates of the new point are:

$$x_2 = x_1 + dx = x_1 - (y_1 - y_0)dA$$

$$y_2 = y_1 + dy = y_1 + (x_2 - x_0)dA \qquad (6.5)$$

This equation forms the basis for an arc generation algorithm. In this algorithm, we can start with the centre of curvature (x_0, y_0), the total angle of the arc to be drawn A, a point at which the arc drawing should begin (x, y), and the intensity at which to set the pixels. The step size of the parameter dA should be small enough not to leave gaps in the arc and to give a good approximation of a circle.

The arc-generating algorithm is as follows:

Algorithm ARCDDA (x_0, y_0, A, x, y, INTENSITY) counter clockwise circular arc generation.

Arguments: (x_0, y_0) the centre of curvature.

(A) the arc angle.

(x, y) the starting point for drawing the arc

Global FRAME the frame buffer array

Local XARC, YARC the next point to draw A-DRAWN the part of the angle currently covered

dA the angle increment

Constant ROUNDOFF some small number greater than any round off error

```
Begin
        IF|x- x0| + |y – y0|< ROUNDOFF THEN RETURN;
A-      DRAWN ← 0;
Find a suitable angle increment
dA ← MIN (0.01, 1/(3.2*(|x - x0| + |y -y0|)));
set the first point of the arc
XARC ← X;
YARC ← Y;
generate the arc until desired angle is covered
WHILE A-DRAWN < A DO
BEGIN
            Find new point
XARC ← XARC + (Y0 - YARC) *DA;
YARC ← YARC + (XARC – X0)*DA;
A-  DRAWN ← A-DRAWN + DA;
see the corresponding pixel
FRAME [INT(XARC), INT(YARC)] ← INTENSITY;
END;
RETURN;
END;
```

There are some problems which arise when curves are generated at this level. To specify a curve, we need more information than just its end points. This may mean that a different display file structure should be used. Another problem can arise from transformations. A line segment when scaled is still a line segment, but other curves may behave differently, for example a circle when scaled in only one direction becomes an ellipse. Another problem is that our clipping algorithm would have to be developed.

6.3 INTERPOLATION

We can express a curve, which has no simple mathematical definition. We can draw an approximation to a curve if we have an array of sample points. We can then guess what the curve should look like between the sample points. If the curve is smooth and our samples are close enough together, we can make a fairly good guess as to what the missing portions should look like.

Our guess will probably not be exactly right, but it will be close enough for all appearances. We fill in portions of the unknown curve with pieces of known curves which pass through the nearby sample points. Since the known and unknown curves share these sample points in a local region, we assume that in this region, the two curves look pretty much alike. We fit a portion of the unknown curve with a curve that we know. Now we can fill in a gap between the sample points by finding the coordinates of points along the known approximating curve and connecting these points with line segments.

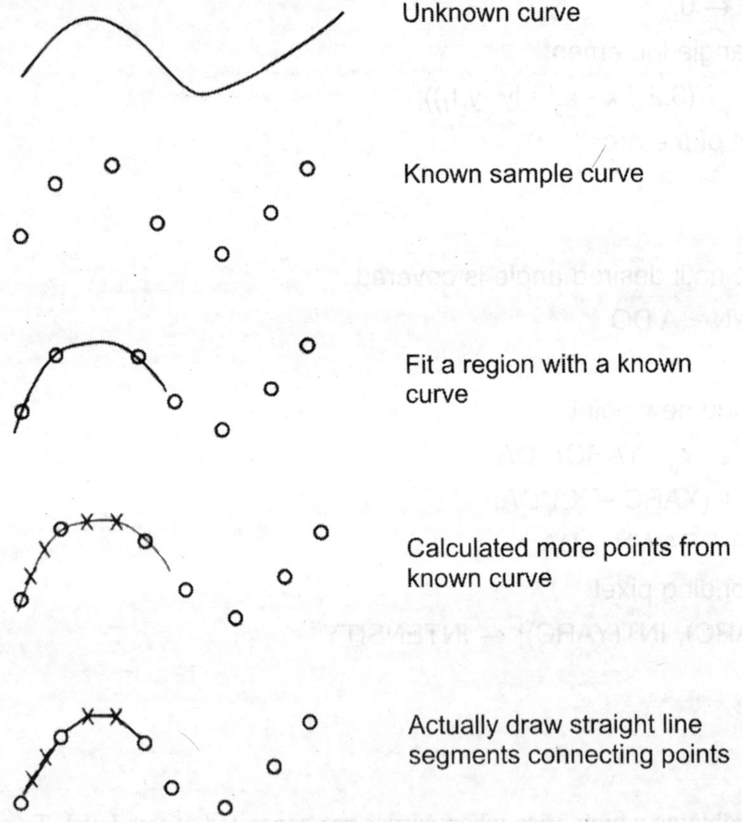

Fig. 6.1: The interpolation process

Functions are often expressed in the form $y = f(x_0)$, but we prefer a parametric form:

$x = f_x(u)$

$Y = f_y(u)$

$z = f_z(u)$ (6.6)

There are two reasons why the parametric form is preferable, (i) the difference between two and three dimensions is just the addition of a third equation for z and (ii) the parametric form treats all three directions equally and it allows multiple values (several y or z values for a given x) so that curves can double back or even cross themselves as shown in the figure below.

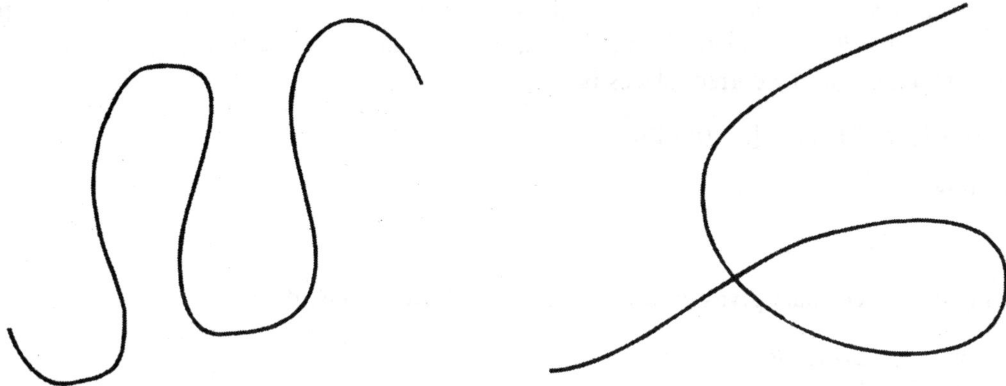

Now let us write a function that can be used for interpolation. There will be a number of things wrong with this first attempt, but it will nevertheless serve to illustrate the approach.

Suppose we want a polynomial curve that will pass through sample points.

$(x_{1,} y_{1,} z_1), (x_{2,} y_2, z_2) \ldots\ldots\ldots\ldots (x_n, y_n, z_n)$ (6.7)

We shall construct the function as the sum of terms, one term for each sample point. The parametric form allows representation of curves which double back or cross themselves.

$$FX(u) = \sum_{i=1}^{n} XiBi(u)$$

$$FY(u) = \sum_{i=1}^{n} XiBi(u)$$

(6.8)

$$FZ(u) = \sum_{i=1}^{n} XiBi(u)$$

The functions $B_i(u)$ are called blending functions. For each value of u, they determine how much the ith sample points affect the position of the curve. We can think of each sample point as trying to pull the curve in its direction. The $B_i(u)$ function tells us now hard the ith sample point is pulling. If for some value of u, $B_i(u) = 1$ and for each $j \neq i$, $B_j(u) = 0$, then the ith sample has complete control of the curve. The curve will pass through the ith sample point. If at a different value of u, one of the other sample points has complete control, then the curve will pass through the ith sample point. If at a different value of u, one of the other sample points has complete control, then the curve will pass through this point as well. What we want then are blending functions which for curve passes through each of the sample points are not very important just so long as the sample points get control of the curve in proper order. We shall create blending functions for which the first sample point (x_1, y_1, z_1) has complete control when $u = -1$, the second when $u = 0$, the third when $u = 1$, and so on. The reason, for this selection of u values is to make the actual implementation a bit simpler for this choice, we need for $B_1(u)$ a function which is 1 at $u = -1$, and 0 for u = 0, 1, 2, 3. . . . n - 2. An expression which is 0 at the correct places is

$$u(u - 1)(u - 2) \ldots\ldots [u - (n - 2)]$$

At $u = -1$ it is

$$(-1)(-2)(-3) \ldots\ldots (1 - n)$$

So dividing by this constant gives us 1 at $u = -1$, and behaves in just the way we want.

$$B_1(u) = \frac{u(u - 1)(u - 2) \ldots [u - (u - 2)]}{(-1)(-2)(-3) \ldots\ldots (1 - n)}$$

The ith blending function can be constructed in the same way to be 1 at $u = i - 2$, and 0 and at the other integral values.

$$B_1(u) = \frac{u(u + 1)(u)(u - 1) \ldots [u - (i - 3)[u - (i - 1)] \ldots [u - (i - 2)]}{(i - 1)(i - 2)(i - 3) \ldots\ldots (1)(-1) \ldots (i - n)}$$

Using these expressions to approximate the curve is called Lagrange interpolation.

Let us consider the case where there are four sample points. Then we will need four blending functions. Using these functions and four sample points, we can construct a curve which passes through the four sample points.

$$x = x_1B_1(u) + x_2B_2(u) + x_3B_3(u) + x_4B_4(u)$$

$$Y = y_1B_1(u) + y_2B_2(u) + y_3B_3(u) + y_4B_4(u)$$

$$z = z_1B_1(u) + z_2B_2(u) + z_3B_3(u) + z_4B_4(u) \qquad (6.9)$$

This curve lies fairly close to the actual curve in the region of these four points, particularly in the middle, between the second and third sample points. This is the position of the curve followed as u varies between 0 and 1.

For example, suppose that we wish to approximate the curve between the second and the third sample points by three straight line segments. We have as sample points the values at $u = 0$ and $u = 1$. If we use our equation to calculate points at $u = 1/3$ and $u = 2/3$, we will have four points which will serve as the end points of the three approximating segments. The entire curve can be approximated by repeating this process. We take four consecutive sample points (1, 2, 3, 4) and approximate the curve between the middle two (2, 3). Then we step up one sample point, picking up a new sample point at one end and discarding a point at the other end, to obtain (2, 3, 4, 5).

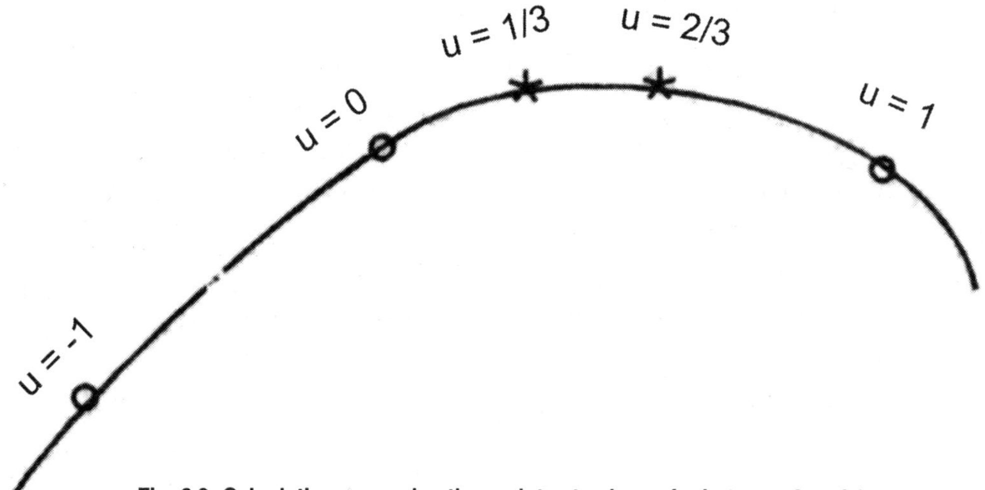

Fig. 6.2: Calculating approximation points at values of *u* between 0 and 1.

We can then approximate the next portion of the curve (3, 4) and continue moving through the sample points until the curve is drawn. The initial and the final portions of the curve will require special handling, for the first four points (1, 2, 3, 4) we need to draw the region between points 1 and 2 with u values between -1 and 0. Likewise the blending functions for the very last step of curve should be evaluated with u values between 1 and 2. There is nothing particularly difficult about these special cases; they must just be handled separately.

Interpolating Algorithm

Before discussing the shortcomings of these blending functions and presenting an improved set, let us see how this curve-drawing program might be implemented. The first thing which we notice is that the same blending function values are needed for each section of the curve that is drawn. If each section is approximated by three straight-line segments, then each section will require the blending function values for u at 0, 1/3, 2/3 and 1.

These values can be calculated once and saved in an array for use in drawing each curve section. The first algorithm which we shall present allows the user to specify how many straight line segments should be used to complete a section of the curve. This number (NUMBER-OF-LINES) will tell us the u values at which to calculate and save the blending function values. The value of $B_i(u)$ is stored in the BLEND array at BLEND[I,U]. The blending function values needed for the first and last sections of the curve are also calculated and stored in arrays FIRST-BLEND and LAST-BLEND.

Algorithm: SET-SMOOTH (NUMBER–OF-LINES) user routine to set the number of line segments per curve section.

Argument: NUMBER-OF-LINES the number of line segments per curve section.

Global: LINES-PER-SECTION storage for the NUMBER-OF-LINES specification BLEND, FIRST BLEND, LAST BLEND, LAST BLEND array size 4 by MAX-NUMBER-OF-LINES for blending function values.

Local: U.V.W parameters for blending function evaluation I a variable for stepping through need curve points.

Constant: MAX–NUMBER-OF-LINES the maximum allowed number of line segments per curve section.

```
BEGIN
            If NUMBER-OF-LINES <1
            OR NUMBER-OF-LINES>MAX-NUMBER-OF-LINES THEN
            OF LINE SEGMENTS':
FOR         I=1 to NUMBER-OF-LINES DO
BEGIN
            blending function values for the middle section
            U ← I / NUMBER-OF-LINES;
            BLEND[1,I] ← U*(U-1)*(U-2)/(-6);
            BLEND [2,1] ← (U+1) *(U-1)*/ (U-2) /2;
            BLEND [3,1] ← (U+1) *U*(U-2) / (U-2) ;
            BLEND [4,1] ← (U+1) *U* (U-1) /6;
            V ← U-1 ;
            blending function values for the first section of curve
            FIRST – BLEND [1,I] ← V*(V-1)*(V-2)/ (-6);
            FIRST – BLEND [2,I] ← (V+1)*V*(V-1)*(V-2)/2;
            FIRST – BLEND [3,I] ← (V+1)*V*(V-2) /(-2);
            FIRST – BLEND[4,I] ← (V+1)*V*(V-1) /6;
            blending function values for the last section of the curve
            LAST – BLEND [1,I] ← W*(W-1)*(W-2) /(-6);
            LAST – BLEND [2,I] ← (W+1)*(W-1)*(W-2)/2;
            LAST – BLEND [3-I] ← (W+1)*W*(W-2)/(-2);
            LAST – BLEND [4,I] ← (W+1) *W*(W-1)/6;
```

```
END:
RETURN;
END;
```

The next routine we write multiplies the sample points and blending functions to give points on the approximation curve. These points are then connected by line segments. The sample points are assumed to be in the global arrays x_{sm}, y_{sm} and z_{sm} while the array of blending function values is passed as an argument.

Algorithm MAKE-CURVE(B) A routine to fill in a section of the curve

Argument B a 4 by LINES-PER-SECTION array of blending function values.

Global LINES-PER-SECTION the number of line segments per curve section Xsm, Ysm,Zsm four elements arrays containing the sample points.

Local I for stepping through the four sample points I for stepping through the lines segments of the curve section X, Y, Z the coordinates of a point on the approximation curve

```
BEGIN
        FOR J=1 TO LINES-PER-SECTION DO
BEGIN
        X ← 0;
        Y ← 0;
        Z ← 0;
        sum the contribution from each sample point.
        For I = 1 TO 4 DO
BEGIN
        X ← X + XSM [I] *B [I,J];
        Y ← Y YSM [I] *B[I,J];
        Z ← Z + ZSM [I]*B[I,J];
END;
        draw the approximation line segment
        LINE – ABS-3 (X,Y,Z);
END;
RETURN;
END;
```

After a section of the curve has been drawn, we will shift the sample points so that our blending function can be applied to the next section. This is accomplished by the following routine.

Algorithm NEXT-SECTION Routine to shift the sample points to get ready for next curve section

Global XSM,YSM,ZSM, the four elements sample points arrays

Local I a variable for stepping through the sample points

```
BEGIN
    FOR I = 1 TO 3 DO
BEGIN
    XSM [I] ← XSM[I+1];
    YSM [I] ← YSM[I+1];
    ZSM [I] ← ZSM [I+1];
END;
RETURN;
END;
```

To start drawing the curve, we require the first four sample points. With the values of these points, we can use the FIRST-BLEND and BLEND arrays to draw the first two curve sections. The START-CURVE algorithm does this. As arguments it expects arrays containing the first four sample points. It loads these points into the XSM, YSM and ZSM arrays. The pen is positioned at the first sample point, and the MAKE-CURVE routine is used to draw the first two sections of the curve. The sample points are then shifted to prepare to draw the next curve section.

Algorithm START-CURVE(XA,YA,ZA) User routine to start drawing a curve

Arguments XA,YA,ZA four elements arrays containing the first four sample points

Global XSM, YSM, ZSM four elements arrays for holding the sample points FIRST – BLEND, BLEND 4 by LINES-PER-SECTION arrays containing blending function values.

Local I for stepping through the sample points

```
BEGIN
    load the sample points
    for I = 1 to 4 DO
BEGIN
    XSM [I] ← XA [I];
    YSM [I] ← YA [I];
    ZSM [I] ← ZA [I];
END;
    move to the start of the curve
```

```
MOVE – ABS – 3(XA [I]; YA[I];ZA[I]);
draw the first two sections
MAKE –CURVE (FIRST-BLEND);
MAKE –CURVE (BLEND);
prepare for the next section
NEXT-SECTION;
RETURN;
END;
```

Once the curve has been started, new sections can be added one at a time as shown in the figure below.

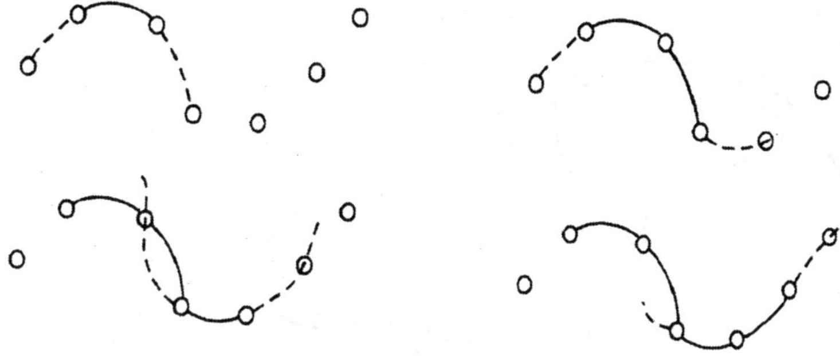

For each new sample point, a new section of the curve can be drawn; but since we are adding the fourth sample point while interpolating between the second and third sample points, the section of the curve being drawn always lags one sample point behind the points entered. The following is a routine (utility) to place a new sample point in the XSM, YSM, ZSM arrays.

Algorithm PUT-IN-SM (X,Y,Z) Routine to place a new sample point in the XSM, YSM, ZSM ARRAYS

Arguments X,Y,Z the new sample point

Global XSM, YSM, ZSM four element arrays for saving sample points

```
BEGIN
        XSM [4] ← X;
        YSM [4] ← Y;
        ZSM [4] ← Z;
        RETURN;
END;
```

The routine to extend the curve takes a new sample point as its argument and stores it in the XSM, YSM, ZSM arrays. It then uses the MAKE-CURVE routine to draw the next curve section. Finally, it shifts the sample points to make ready for the next curve section. The algorithm which does this is called CURVE-ABS-3.

Algorithm CURVE-ABS-3(X,Y,Z) user routine to extend the curve

Argument X,Y,Z the new sample point for the curve

Global BLEND 4 by LINES-PER-SECTION array of blending function valuation

```
BEGIN
    PUT-IN-SM (X,Y,Z);
    MAKE-CURVE (BLEND);
    RETURN;
END;
```

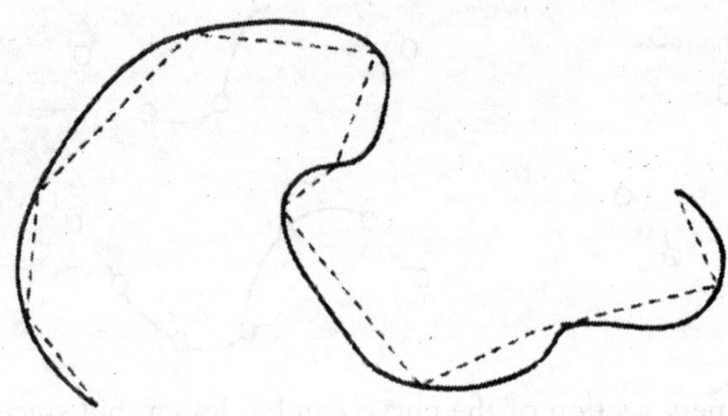

Fig. 6.3: Interpolation smoothing

Interpolating Polygons

The sides of a polygon can also be rounded by means of our blending functions. In fact, a polygon is conceptually easier to deal with, since no special initial or final sections occur. We just step around the polygon, smoothing out each side by replacing it with several small line segments. We start out with a polygon that has only a few sides and end up with a polygon which has many more sides and appears smoother. (See the figure below).

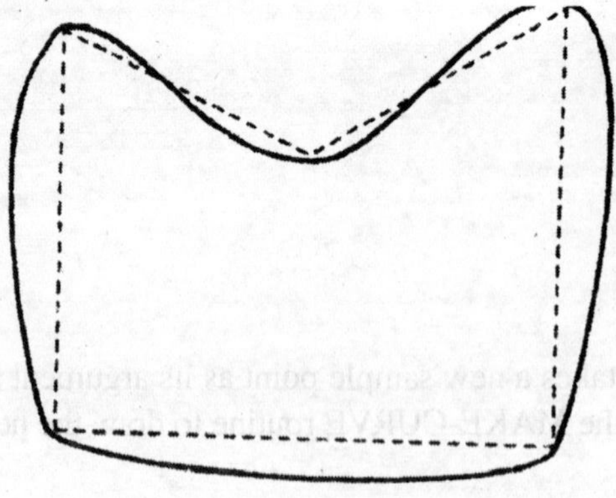

The system will have some limit to the total number of sides a polygon can have. The algorithm SMOOTH-POLY-ABS-3 given below smoothens a polygon. It assumes that a call has been made to the SET-SMOOTH routine to set up the proper blend array values and that the system is capable of handling the resulting polygons. The size of the resulting polygon will be the number of sides in the original polygon times the LINES-PER-SECTION factors. The algorithm steps through the sides of the original polygon and builds the new smoother polygon, which is drawn.

Algorithm	SMOOTH-POLY-ABS-3(AX,AY,AZ,M) User routine to draw a smoothed polygon.
Argument	AX,AY,AZ arrays containing vertices of original polygon. M the original number of polygon sides.
Global	BLEND the array of blending function values LINES-PER-SECTION the number of line segments per original polygon side.
Local	BX,BY,BZ arrays to hold smoothed polygon vertices NSIDES number of sides for the smoothed polygon J index variable for saving the smoothed polygon sides K to step through the small segments for each polygon side I, II variables for stepping through the four blending functions.

```
BEGIN
        IF M<3THEN RETURN ERROR 'POLYGON SIZE ERROR';
        NSIDES ← LINES-PER-SECTION*M;
        IF LINES_PER_SECTION=1THEN POLYGON-ABS-3
        (AX,AY,AZ,M)
        ELSE
        BEGIN
        J ← 1;
        FOR II = 1 to M Do
        smooth all sides
        FOR K = 1 to LINES-PER-SECTION DO
        Smooth a side of the original polygon
BEGIN
        BX [J] ← 0;
        BY [J] ← 0;
        BZ [J] ← 0;
        FOR L=1to 4 DO
        One side of the smooth polygon
BEGIN
        BX [J] ← BX [J] + AX [I] *BLEND [L,K];
```

```
BY [J] ← BY [J] + AY [I] *BLEND [L,K];
BZ [J] ← BZ [J] + AZ [I] *BLEND [L,K];
IF I=M THENI ← 1 ELSE I ← I+1;
END;
draw the result
POLYGON-ABS-3(BX,BY,BZ,NSIDES);
END;
RETURN;
END;
```

6.4 B-SPLINES

We have implemented a larger interpolation program using our home-made blending functions. Now we examine some of its inadequacies. One thing to notice is that the sum of the blending function is not 1 at every value of *u*. The blending functions were designed to sum to 1 at integer values of *u*, but not at fractional values. What does this mean? Suppose that all points had the same *x* value, $x = x_0$.

We would then want the approximating curve to also have constant values for *x* at the points in between sample points but the approximating curve is,

$$X = \sum_{i=1}^{n} XiBi(u) \tag{6.10}$$

Which for $x_i = x_0$ gives

$$X = X_0 \sum_{i=1}^{n} B_i(u) \tag{6.11}$$

We will get the flat behaviour we want only if the sum of the blending functions is 1 for all values of *u*. This shortcoming also means that curves which should lie in a plane may in fact move in and out of the plane. This particular problem might be dealt with by dividing the blending function values calculated in SET-SMOOTH by their sum for each value of u, thereby normalizing the functions. However this is not the only problem. Each section of the curve is connected to the next section at a sample point, but the slopes of the two sections need not match at this point. This means that there can be corners at the sample points and that we may not have a completely smooth curve. Finally, in pulling the curve all the way over to pass through one of the sample points, we had to reduce the effect of all other points to zero; but as we leave the vicinity, the sample points in the region have control over the curve. Thus, we saw that the curve was controlled by the sample point pulsating in and out as we move along in *u*.

A more natural behaviour might be to have the sample points' control vary smoothly from zero far away from the point to a maximum near the point. We can do this if we do not try to force the curve through the sample point, but rather gently pull it into the neighbourhood of the sample point. The result will be a curve which follows the general contours indicated by the sample points but may not actually pass through the points themselves. A set of blending functions which take this approach and also always sum to 1 are called B splines. They generate curve sections which have continuous slopes so that they fit together smoothly. (See the figure below).

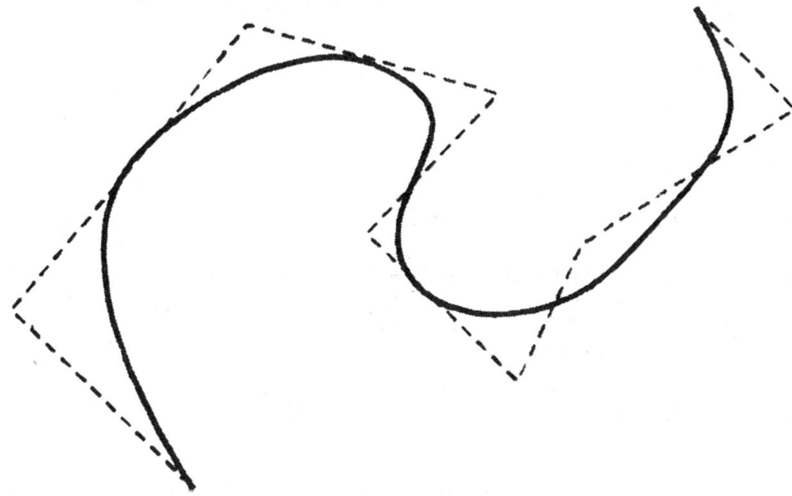

The derivation of the B-spline functions is beyond the scope of this book, but we shall present and implement the cubic B-spline functions, which are adequate for most applications. The cubic B-spline blending functions interpolate over four sample points and are cubic polynomials in u, just as our home-made blending functions. The cubic B-spline functions for the middle of the curve are as follows:

$B_1(u) = (1 - u)^3/6$

$B_2(u) = (u)u^3/2 - u^2 + 2/3$

$B_3(u) = -u^3/2 + u^2/2 + u/2+1/6$ (6.12)

$B_4(u) = u^3/6$

Starting or stopping the cubic B-spline blending functions require two special curve sections. The following functions should be used for the very first section of the curve.

$\beta'_1(u) = (1 - u)^3$

$\beta'_2(u) = 21u^3/12 - 9u^2/2+3u$

$\beta'_3(u) = -11u^3/12 + 3u^2/2$ (6.13)

$\beta'_4(u) = u^3/6$

The last section of the curve would reverse these functions,

$B_1' R(u) = B_4' (1 - u)$

$B_2' R(u) = B_3' (1 - u)$

$B_3' R(u) = B_2' (1 - u)$

$B_4' R(u) = B_1' (1 - u)$ (6.14)

The second section of the curve also has special blending functions,

$B_1' R(u) = (1 - u)^3/4$

$B_2' R(u) = 7u^3/12 - 5u^2/4 + u/4 + 7/12$

$B_3' R(u) = u^3/2 + u^2/2 + u/2 + 1/6$

$B_4' R(u) = u^3/6$ (6.15)

The next-to–last section of the curve uses the reverse of these functions

$B''_{1R}(u) = B_4''(1- u)$

$B''_{2R}(u) = B_3''(1- u)$

$B''_{3R}(u) = B_2''(1- u)$

$B''_{4R}(u) = B_1''(1- u)$ (6.16)

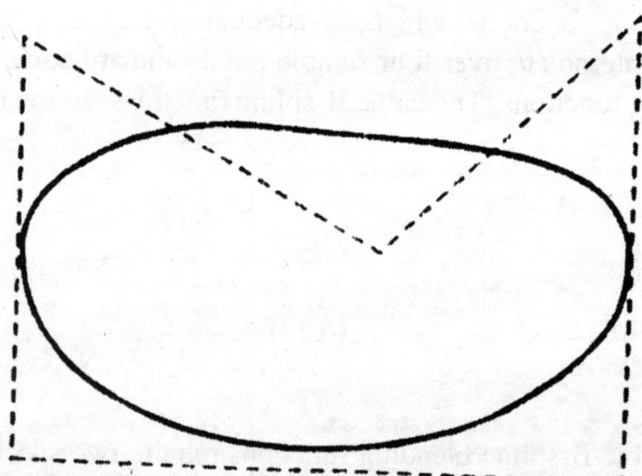

B-Splines and Corners

The B-splines bending functions were designed to eliminate sharp corners in the curve, and the curve does not usually pass through sample points. However, a sharp corner and passage through a sample point can be produced in a B-spline curve, if desired. This is done by using several identical sample points.

CURVE-ABS-3 (X0,Y0,Z0)

Produces one sample point at (X0, Y0, Z0) pulling the curve in that direction. (See the figure below).

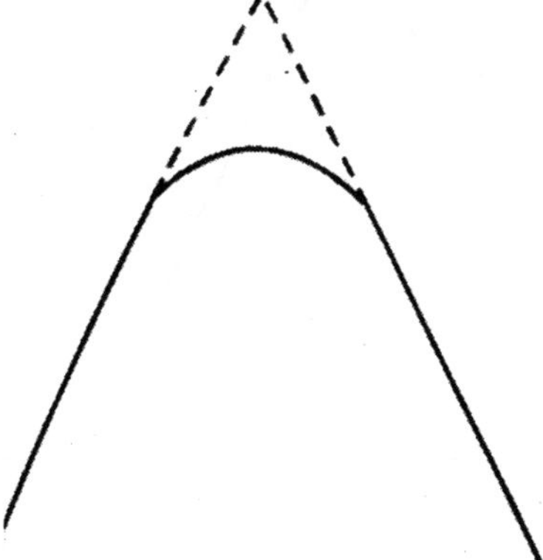

The two calls

CURVE-ABS-3(X0,Y0,Z0)

CURVE-ABS-3 (X0,Y0,Z0)

produce two sample points, both pulling the curve to the same place. The curve will be pulled closer to this point, and the corner will be little sharper. (See the figure below).

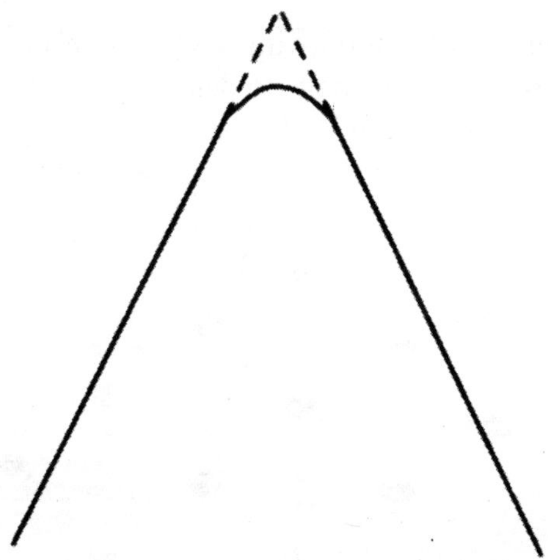

If three identical sample points are used

CURVE-ABS-3 (X0,Y0,Z0)

CURVE-ABS-3 (X0,Y0,Z0)

CURVE-ABS-3 (X0,Y0,Z0)

the curve will be forced through this point. (See the figure below).

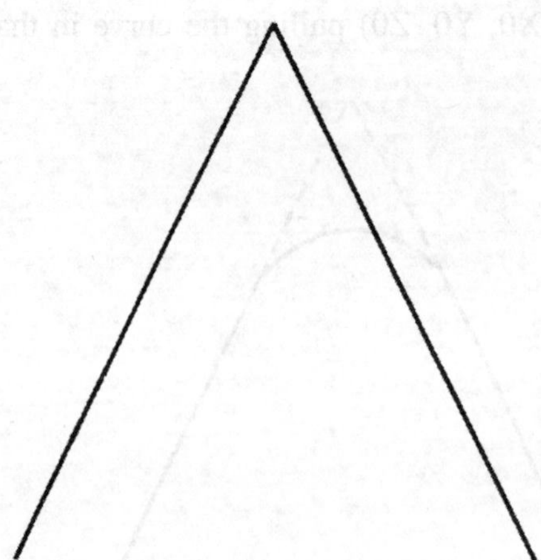

Blending-function interpolation and approximation by small straight-line segments allow us to draw curves which may not have simple mathematical forms. The technique also allows us to use the simple straight line transformation and clipping methods which we have developed. The major drawback of this technique is the amount of display-file storage required. For each sample point, 5 or 10 small line segments may be produced, so care must be taken to assure sufficient display-file storage when curves are drawn.

6.5 CURVED SURFACE PATCHES

We have seen a way of specifying curved lines with B splines. We use a set of sample points or control points and the B-spline blending functions to determine points on the curve. This method can be generalized to describe curved surfaces such as aeroplane wings or car fenders. To describe a surface we shall need a grid of control points $((x_{ij}, y_{ij}, z_{ij}))$, as shown in the figure below.

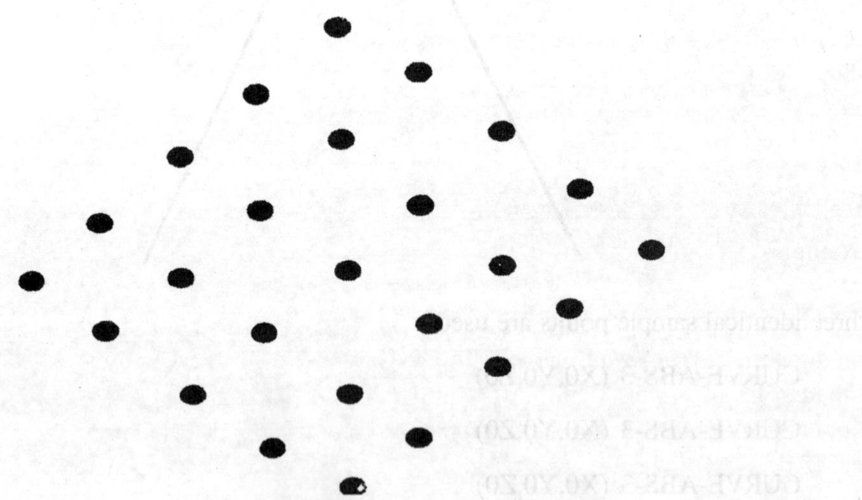

Stepping through i moves along one direction on the gird, while changing j moves in the other direction. Such a grid can be used to define patches which will fit together to form a smooth surface, just as we previously defined curve sections which fit together to make the curve.

The coordinate values for points on the surface of a patch are given by:

$$X = FX(u,v) = \sum_{i=1}^{n} \sum_{j=1}^{m} XijBi(u)Bj(v)$$

$$Y = FY(u,v) = \sum_{i=1}^{n} \sum_{j=1}^{m} YijBi(u)Bj(v) \qquad (6.17)$$

$$Z = FZ(u,v) = \sum_{i=1}^{n} \sum_{j=1}^{m} ZijBi(u)Bj(v)$$

There are two parameters which specify the position on the surface patch, u and v. Just as for curves, each varies from 0 to 1. Changing u will cause movement along the patch in the same direction as changing i on the grid of control points. Changing v causes movement in the same direction as changing j.

$$X = \sum_{i=1}^{n} \sum_{j=1}^{m} XijBi(u)Bj(v)$$

$$X = \sum_{i=1}^{n} \sum_{j=1}^{m} XijBi(u)Bj(v) \qquad (6.18)$$

As with curves, we can move from one patch to the next by simply re-labelling the control points. For bicubic surface patches (cubic splines in both directions) the B functions are those presented in Equations 6.14 through the special functions 6.15 through 6.18 are used at the boundary of the overall surface. They should be used for B_i when the patch is first or second (last or next-to-last) in the i direction on the grid, and similarly for B_j in the j direction.

To present a curved surface on a display, we must either rely on shading techniques or show the curves which result from lines drawn on the surface.

For example, for a given patch

X=FX (U,V), Y=FY(U,V) Z=FZ(U,V)

we can draw the curves resulting from fixing v at a constant and letting u vary from 0 to 1. We could draw the curves for several values of v and similarly, we could draw curves for fixed values of u, letting v change from 0 to 1. Notice that for this kind of display, our B-spline curve drawing algorithms suffice. If x for the surface is given as:

$$X = \sum_{i=1}^{n} \sum_{j=1}^{m} XijBi(u)Bj(v)$$

and v is held constant at vc, then $B_j(vc)$ is a constant, so we can write

$$X = \sum_{i=1}^{n} \left[\sum_{j=1}^{m} XijBi(v) \right] Bi(u)$$

$$= \sum_{i=1}^{n} \widehat{X}iBi(u)$$

where

$$\widehat{X}i = \sum_{j=1}^{m} XijBj(vc)$$

This is just the expression used for the B-spline curve, provided the control point at each i is replaced by the weighted sum over j of the grid points with index i. Thus for a fixed vc, we can find the values of $B_j(vc)$ and perform the weighted sum of grid points in the j direction to determine the values of x_i, and use these as the control points in our curve drawing routines. The same thing can be done for the y and z coordinates.

If we want to employ shading to display the curved surface, one approach is to approximate the surface by a number of flat polygons. Each polygon can have a slightly different direction and shade. We have already developed the machinery for shading flat polygons, so the only thing new is the automatic decomposition of the curved surface into a patch work of flat surfaces. This is analogous to approximating a curved path by a series of straight line segments. One way would be to find the rectangular polygons formed by lines of constant u and v, but there is no guarantee that four corner points of a small rectangular patch will all lie in the same plane. This may not be a problem if the patch is small, as the point may be nearly planar and the shading software may not require planar points. An alternative is to decompose the surface into triangular pieces. Triangles are necessarily planar. One method for converting to triangles is as follows. We have a unit square in the uv parameter space which generates the surface patch. We first imagine the diagonal (0, 0) to (1, 1) on this unit square. (See the figure below).

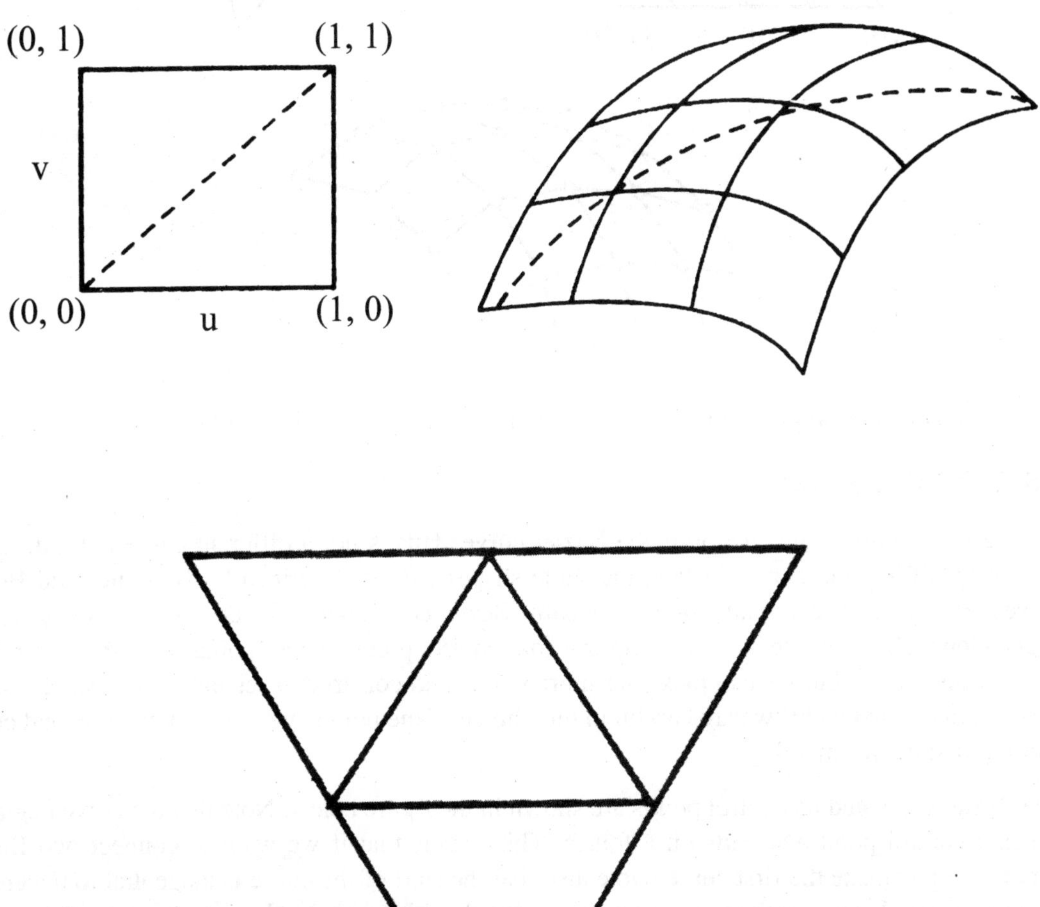

This divides the square into two triangles. The second step is to find a rule which divides a triangle into smaller triangles. The rule is to find the midpoints of each of the three sides of the triangles and to connect them.

This divides the triangle into four smaller triangles (as shown in the above figure). We can recursively apply this rule to break up the area uv into a mesh of small triangles. Finally we can use the vertices of the uv triangles in our B-spline surface equation to find the corresponding x, y, z points.

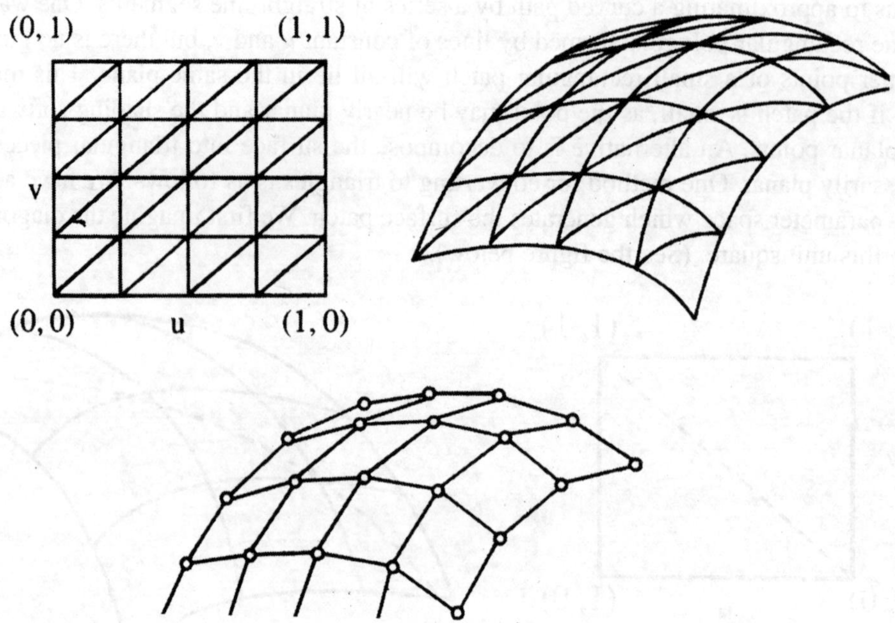

These points form triangles which can be shaded and entered into the display file.

6.6 BEZIER CURVES

An alternative curve construction is the Bezier curve. This is not a different curve but a different way of specifying the curve. In fact, the same shapes can be described by B-splines and Bezier curves. We shall restrict our attention to the cubic Bezier curve, which is adequate for most graphics applications. The cubic Bezier curve requires four control points. These points smoothly extend the cubic Bezier curve, but we can pick four more points and construct a second curve, which can be attached to the first and if we are careful in our choice of the points, we can make the second curve join the first curve smoothly.

The Bezier curve and its control points are shown in the figure below. Note that the curve begins at the first control point and ends on a fourth. This means that if we want to connect two Bezier curves, we just make the first curve. Note also that the start of the curve is tangential to the end of the curve; it is also tangential to the line connecting the third and fourth control points. This means that if we want to join two Bezier curves smoothly, we must arrange for the third and fourth control points of the first curve to be on the same line as the first and second points of the second curve.

Equations describing the Bezier curve are as follows

$x = x4u^3 + 3x3u^2(1 - u) + 3x_2u(1 - u^2) + x_1(1 - u)^3$

$y = y4u^3 + 3y3u^2(1 - u) + 3y_2u(1 - u^2) + y_1(1 - u)^3$

$z = z4u^3 + 3z3u^2(1 - u) + 3z_2u(1 - u^2) + z_1(1 - u)^3$

In these expressions, as *u* goes from 0 to 1, the curve goes from the first to the fourth control. (This is slightly different from our previous curves, where we only covered the region between two control points when the parameter changed from 0 to 1). From the expression, we could extract the blending functions for the Bezier curve and proceed as we did above. However, one of the most amazing things about Bezier curves is that they can be constructed without reference to the above defining equations.

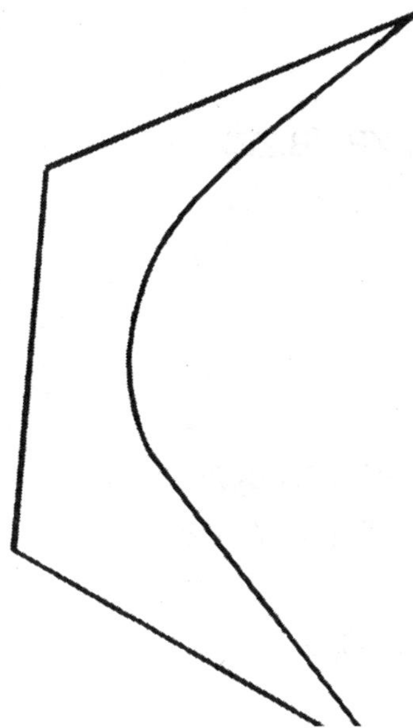

In fact, a Bezier curve can be constructed simply by taking midpoints. Consider the above figure, where we have drawn the lines connecting the four control points A, B, C, and D. We have determined the midpoints of these segments AB, BC, and CD. We connect these mid points with line segments and find their midpoints, ABC and BCD. Finally we connect these two points and find the midpoint ABCD. Now the point ABCD is on the Bezier curve. It divides the curve into two sections. Further more, the points A, AB, ABC and ABCD are the control points for the first section and the points ABCD, BCD, CD, and D are the control points for the second section. Thus by taking midpoints we can find a point on the curve and also split the curve into smaller sections so short that they can be replaced by straight lines, or even by individual pixels.

Algorithms for adding Bezier curves to our system are given below. They assume that the first control point is at the current pen position, so only three additional points must be specified. They use the recursive subdivision approach.

Algorithm BEZIER – ABS – (XB, YB, ZB, XC, YC, ZC, XD, YD, ZD, N).

Adds a Bezier curve to the display file.

Arguments XB, YB, XC, YC, ZC, XD, YD, ZD control points N the desired degree of subdivision.

Global DF – PEN-X, OF-PEN-Y, DF-PEN-Z the current pen position.

```
Local         XAB, YAB, ZAB, XBC, YBC, ZBC, XCD,YCD,ZCD first level
              midpoints.
              XABC, YABC, ZABC, XBCD, second-level midpoints XABCD,
              YABCD third-level midpoints
BEGIN
              IF N=0 THEN
              BEGIN
                      LINE-ABC-3(XB,YB,ZB)
                      LINE-ABC-3(XC,YC,ZC)
                      LINE –ABS-3 (XD, YD,ZD)
              END
              ELSE
                      BEGIN
                      XAB ← (DF-PEN-X+B)/2;
                      YAB ← (DF-PEN-Y+YB)/2;
                      ZAB ← (DF-PEN-Z+ZB)/2;
                      XBC ← (XB+XC)/2;
                      YBC ← (YB+YC)/2;
                      ZBC ← (ZB+ZC)/2;
                      XCD ← (XC+XD)/2;
                      YCD ← (YC+YD)/2;
                      ZCD ← (ZC+ZD)/2;
                      XABC ← (XAB+XBC)/2;
                      YABC ← (YAB+YBC)/2;
                      ZABC ← (ZAB+ZBC)/2;
                      XBCD ← (XBC + XCD)/2;
                      YBCD ← (YABC + YBCD)/2;
                      ZABCD ← (ZABC + ZBCD)/2;
BEZIER-ABS-3          (XAB, YAB, ZAB, XABC, YABC, ZABC,XABCD, YABCD,
                      ZABCD, N-1);
BEZIER-ABS-3          (XBCD,YBCD, ZBCD, XCD, YCD, ZCD, XD, YD, ZD, N-1);

END;
RETURN;
END;
```

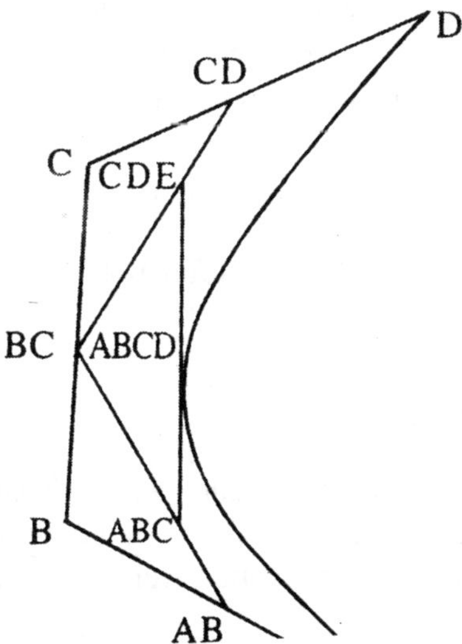

Bezier curves satisfy the convex hull property. This means that the curve lies within the boundary formed by an elastic band stretched over all four of the control points. This property is useful in clipping tests. Like B-splines, the Bezier curves can be extended to surfaces. We can construct a bicubic Bezier surface from a 4 x 4 grid of control points. Recursive subdivision can be used to draw such patches by repeatedly quartering them until they may be replaced by polygons or pixels.

Nonparametric and Parametric Representations

Nonparametric representations

When we write object descriptions directly in terms of the coordinates of the reference frame in use, the representation is called non-parametric. For example, we can represent a surface with either of the following Cartesian functions.

$f(x, y, z) = 0$, or $z = f(x, y)$

The first form of the above equation gives an implicit expression for the surface, and the second form gives an explicit representation, with x and y as the independent variables and z as the dependent variable.

Similarly, we can represent a three dimensional curved line in non-parametric form as the intersection of two surface functions, or we could represent the curve with the pair of functions.

$y = f(x), \quad z = g(x)$

where the coordinate x is selected as the independent variable. Values for the dependent variables y and x are then determined from the equation above as we step through values for x from one line end point to the other end point.

Non parametric representations are useful in describing objects within a given reference frame, but they have some disadvantages when used in graphics algorithms. If we want a smooth plot, we must change the independent variable whenever the first derivative (slope) of either $f(x)$ or $g(x)$ becomes greater than 1. This means that we must continually check values of the derivatives, which may represent multiple valued functions. For instance, the implicit equation of a circle centred on the origin in the xy plane is

$$x^2 + y^2 = r^2$$

And the explicit expression for y is the multivalued function

$$y = \pm \sqrt{r^2 - x^2}$$

In general, a more convenient representation for object and positions along the path of a three dimensional curve can be described with a single parameter u. That is, we can express each of the three Cartesian coordinates in terms of the parameter u, and any point on the curve can then be represented with the following vector point function (relative to a particular Cartesian reference frame):

$$p(u) = (x(u), y(u), z(u))$$

Often the coordinate equations can be set up so that the parameter u is defined over the unit internal from 0 to 1. For example, a circle in the xy plane with its centre at the coordinate origin could be defined in parametric form as:

$x(u) = r\cos(2\pi u)$, $y(u) = r\sin(2\pi u)$, $z(u) = 0$, $0 \le u \le 1$

Other parametric forms are also possible for describing circles and circular arcs.

Curved (or plane) Euclidean surfaces are two-dimensional objects, and positions on a surface can be described with two parameters u and v. A coordinate position on the surface is then represented with the parametric vector function.

$p(u,v) = (x(u,v), y(u,v), z(u,v))$

Where the Cartesian coordinate values for x, y and z are expressed as functions of the parameters u and v.

As with curves, it is often possible to arrange parametric descriptions so that the parameters u and v are defined over the range from 0 to 1. A spherical surface with its centre at the coordinate origin, for example can be described by the equations.

$x(u,v) = r\sin(\pi u)\cos(2\pi u)$

$y(u,v) = r\sin(\pi u)\sin(2\pi u)$

$z(u,v) = r\cos(\pi u)$

Where r is the radius of the sphere. The parameter u describes lines of constant latitude over the surface, and the parameter v describes lines of constant latitude. By keeping one of these parameters fixed while varying the other over a subinterval of the range from 0 to 1, we could plot latitude lines for any spherical section.

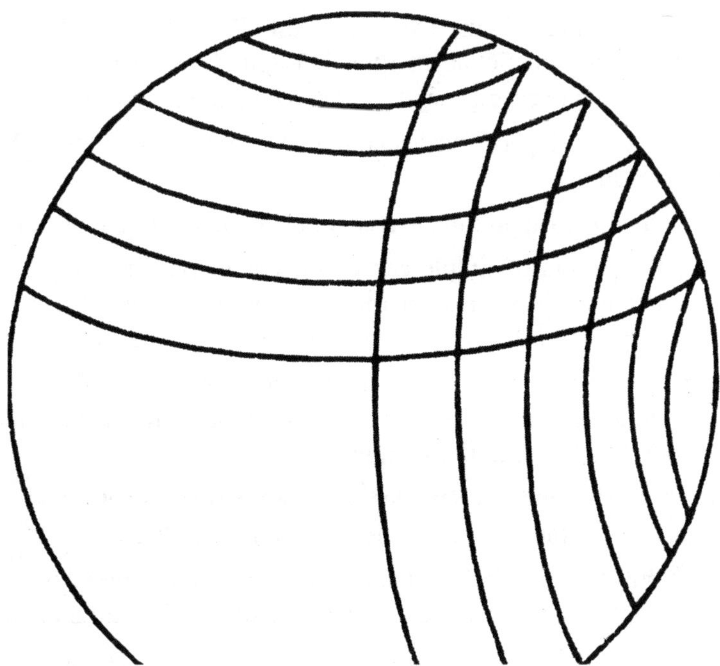

6.7 CUBIC SPLINE

Generation of smooth curves is necessary in many applications. Certain parts of the curve may be modified without affecting other parts of the curve. For example it may be necessary to join the points obtained by digitizing a map by a smooth curve passing through all thc points and also to edit the points occasionally and modify the resulting curve. If we fit only one curve to a set of points, a change in the location of even one point will necessitate the recompilation of the complete curve.

One solution to avoid this problem is as follows. We divide the number of points in a set into subsets and fit a polynomial to the points in each subset. This method is similar to the French curve or spline technique used by draftsmen for joining a set of data points. A mathematical cubic spline is a piecewise polynomial function defined by the following general expression

y_1 = COI + C1IX1 + C2I

6.8 SUMMARY

- A display of curved lines and surfaces can be generated from an input set of mathematical functions defining objects or from a set of user specified data points. When functions are specified a package can project the defining equations for a curve to display the plane and plot pixel positions along the path of the projected function.
- When a set of discrete coordinate points is used to specify the shape of an object, a functional description is obtained that best fits the designed points according to the constraints of the application. Spline representations are examples of this class of curves and surfaces.

- These methods are commonly used to design new object shapes and to digitize drawings to describe the animation path. Spline interpolation algorithms have been developed for drawing curved lines and fractal curve generators for rough, natural looking objects.
- One approach is to develop a curve generation algorithm such as DDA. With this approach, a true curve is created.
- The second method is to approximate a curve by a number of small straight-line segments.
- The differential equation of simple curves such as circles and ellipses are fairly easy to solve, and generation algorithms for them can be implemented in hardware. A display device may be capable of drawing arcs as well as line segments.
- We can express a curve, which has no simple mathematical definition. We can draw an approximation to a curve if we have an array of sample point. We can then guess what the cure should look like between the sample points.
- If the curve is smooth and our samples are close enough together, we can make a fairly good guess as to what the missing portions should look like.
- The sides of a polygon can also be rounded by means of our blending functions. In fact, a polygon is conceptually easier to deal with, since no special initial or final sections occur.
- More natural behaviour might be to have control over the sample points vary smoothly from zero far away from the point to a maximum near the point.
- The derivation of the B-splines functions is beyond the scope of this book, but the cubic B-spline functions have been presented and implemented, which are adequate for most applications.
- The cubic B-spline blending functions interpolate over four sample points and are cubic polynomials in u, just as our homemade blending functions.
- When we write object descriptions directly in terms of the coordinates of the reference frame in use, the representation is called non-parametric.
- Generation of smooth curves is necessary in many applications. Certain parts of the curve may be modified without affecting other parts of the curve. For example it may be necessary to join the points obtained by digitizing a map by a smooth curve passing through all the points and also to edit the points occasionally and modify the resulting curve. If we fit only one curve to a set of points, a change in the location of even one point will necessitate the recompilation of the complete curve.
- One solution to avoid this problem is as follows. We divide the number of points in a set into subsets and fit a polynomial to the points in each subset. This method is similar to the French curve or spline technique used by draftsmen for joining a set of data points.

6.9 REVIEW QUESTIONS

1. Set up an algorithm to converting any specified sphere, ellipsoid, or cylinder to a polygon-mesh representation.
2. Set up an algorithm to convert a specified super ellipsoid to a polygon-mesh representation.

3. Set up an algorithm to convert a meatball representation to a polygon-mesh representation.
4. Write a routine to display a two-dimensional, cardinal-spline curve, given an input set of control points in the xy plane.
5. Write a routine to display a two-dimensional, Koch curve, given an input set of control points in the xy plane.
6. Determine the quadratic Bezier blending functions for three control points. Plot each function and label the maximum and minimum values.
7. Determine the Bezier blending functions for five control points. Plot each function and label the maximum and minimum values.
8. Write an efficient routine to display two-dimensional, cubic Bezier curves, given a set of four control points in the xy plane.
9. Write a routine to design two-dimensional, cubic Bezier curves that have first order piecewise continuity. Use an interactive technique for selecting control-point positions in the xy plane for each section of the curve.
10. Write a routine to design two-dimensional, cubic Bezier curves that have second-order piecewise continuity. Use an interactive technique for selecting control point positions in the xy plane for each section of the curve.
11. Write a routine to display a cubic Bezier curve using a subdivision method.
12. Determine the blending functions for uniform, periodic B-spline curves for $d = 5$.
13. Determine the blending functions for uniform, periodic B-spline curves for $d = 6$.
14. Write a program using forward differences to calculate points along a two-dimensional, uniform, periodic, cubic B-spline curve, given an input set of control points.
15. Write a routine to display any specified conic in the xy plane using a rational Bezier spline representation.
16. Write a routine to display any specified conic in the xy plane using a rational B-spline representation.
17. Develop an algorithm to calculate the normal vector to a Bezier surface at the point p(u, v).
18. Write a program to display any specified quadratic curve using forward differences to calculate points along the curve's path.
19. Write a program to display any specified cubic curve using forward differences to calculate points along the curve's path.
20. Derive expressions to calculate the forward differences for any specified quadratic curve.

CHAPTER 7

Fractals

7.1 INTRODUCTION

Fractals have arisen as an important question twice before the invention of computers. The first time was when British map makers discovered the problem with measuring the length of Britain's coast. As the maps becamc more detailed the coastline appeared to grow longer and at a certain point the length was over double the original. The reason for this is the coastline of Britain on a world map does not have all the bays and harbours. A detailed map of only Britain has more of these, but does not show all the little coves and sounds. The closer they looked, the more detailed and longer the coastline got. At that time they did not realise that this is a property of fractals. (A finite area, in this case Britain, bounded by an infinite line).

The second instance of pre-computer fractals was noted by the French mathematician Gaston Julia. He wondered what a complex polynomial function would look like, such as the ones named after him (in the form of $z^2 + c$, where c is a complex constant with real and imaginary numbers). The idea behind the formula is that you take the x and y coordinates of a point, and substitute them into z in the form of $x + y*i$, where i is the square root of negative one. This number is then squared and a constant 'c' is added. The resulting pair of real and imaginary numbers is then re-substituted into z, and the equation run again. The process is repeated until the result is greater than a particular number. The number of times you have to run the equations to get out of its "orbit" can be assigned a colour and the pixel (x, y) is turned that colour, unless the coordinates cannot get out of their orbit, in which case they remain black.

Later, Benoit Mandelbrot, an employee of IBM, thought about writing a program with a formula such as, $z(n)^2 + c$, and then running it on one of IBM's many computers. Eventually they obtained some good pictures. Mandelbrot was the first person to program computers to do the many repetitive calculations to make a fractal look good.

The basic concept of fractals is that they contain a large degree of self similarity. This means that they usually contain little copies of themselves buried deep within the original, and they also have infinite detail. Like the costal problem, the more you zoom in on a fractal, the more detail (coastline) you get, and this can go on forever.

7.2 USES OF FRACTALS

What good are mathematical pictures that are not even whole dimensions? Well, for one thing they are pretty. As mentioned before, nature is full of fractal-like objects. Twigs on trees look like the branches which they grow on, which look like the tree itself. It is the same thing with fern leaves, and so many other living things. Self-similarity is part of this world, so fractals can make good copies of it. Artists have created very realistic looking landscapes composed of just a few fractal equations.

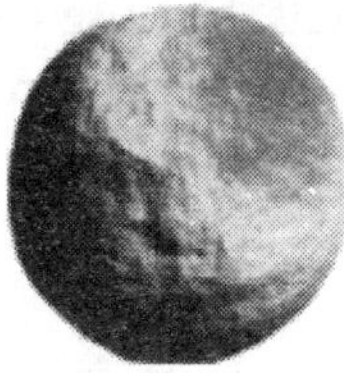

Fractals also have technological applications. Antennae have always been a tricky subject. Many antenna engineers have been reduced to using trial and error methods because of the complex nature of electromagnetism. The usual long, thin wire is not the best antenna. Antenna arrays, another approach, consist of thousands of small antennae, which are either placed randomly or regularly spaced. Fractals provide the perfect mix between randomness and order, and with fewer components. The parts of the fractal provide the disorder, while the fractal as a whole provides the order. By bending wires into the shape of Koch's curve, more wire can be fit into less space, and the jagged shape also generates electrical capacitance and inductance. This eliminates the need for external components to tune the antenna or to broaden its range of frequencies. Motorola has started using fractal antennas in many of its cellular phones, and reports that they are 25% more efficient than the traditional piece of wire. They are also cheaper to manufacture, can operate on multiple bands, and can be put into the body of the phone. The journal *Fractals* showed why fractals work so well as antenna. For an antenna to work equally well at all frequencies, it must be symmetrical around a point and it must be self-similar, both of which fractals can provide.

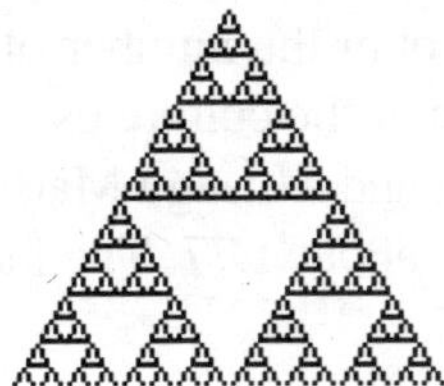

Sierpinski's Triangle

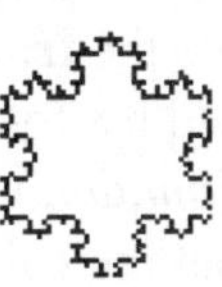

Koch's Curve

Sierpinski's Carpet

Fig. 7.1 : Good Fractal Antennae

7.3 APPLICATION OF FRACTALS

By using fractals it is possible to represent many real-world objects that do not correspond to simple geometric shapes like clouds, mountains, coastlines, roots, branches of trees, turbulence, blood vessels, etc. With the introduction of fractals, many natural phenomena could be expressed analytically having a fractal basis.

Bacteria Cultures

Some of the most amazing applications of fractals can be found in the area of bacteria cultures. A bacteria culture is bacteria that originated from a single ancestor and are living in the same place. When a culture is growing, it spreads outwards in different directions from the place where the original organism was placed. Just like plants, the spreading bacteria can branch and form patterns, which turn out to be fractal. The spreading of bacteria can be modelled by fractals such as the diffusion fractals, because bacteria spread in a manner similar to nonliving materials. Fig. 7.2 is a computer simulation of a growing culture.

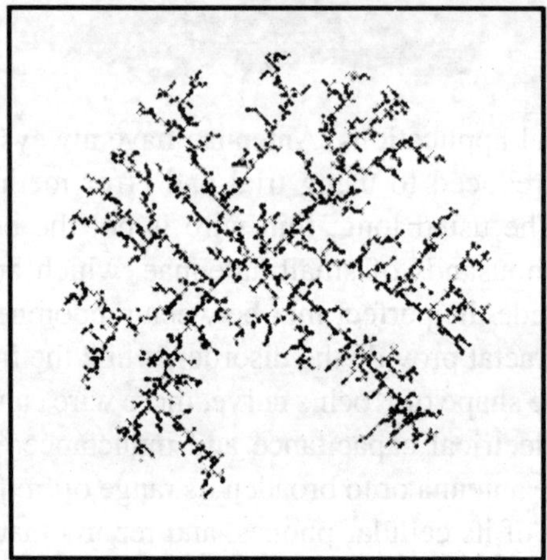

Fig 7.2 : Computer simulation of a growing culture

If you are familiar with fractals, you will probably guess that the above picture is a fractal. You would be right, but we still need a real mathematical proof to be sure of that. The way to do it is quite simple – just place the culture on a piece of graph paper and count the number of occupied squares. This kind of data will let you calculate the **fractal dimension** of the culture using the **box-counting method**. In an experiment performed by Tohey Matsuyama and Mitsugu Matsushita, the fractal dimension of a culture of *Salmonella anatum* was found to be about 1.77. The fact that the dimension is a fraction is enough to prove that the culture is a fractal.

Chemical Reactions

If you know some chemistry, you are probably familiar with the concept of forward and backward reactions. Most reactions are accompanied by a backward reaction, in which the products turn back into the reactants. At equilibrium, the rates of these reactions become equal and the overall composition of the system does not change. However, the fact that is usually missed here is that in talking about the rates of reactions we are talking about *average* rates, since the rates depend on the movement of particles, which involves a lot of chance. Sometimes, however, the rates become different for a short interval of time and the composition of the system changes. As you might guess, these changes would be very chaotic. If we view every three consecutive concentrations of a substance as coordinates of a point in space, we can obtain something that is fractal in shape! Such a fractal is called a **strange attractor** because this type of fractal is based on changing numbers.

Indeed, fractal shapes were found after graphing many different systems, even such common ones as hydrogen and oxygen reacting to form water. One of the scientists who tried to study this mathematically was Otto Rossler. He came up with three formulae that could model chemical reactions. When these three formulae are used to create a **strange attractor**, they create the famous 3-dimensional **Rossler Attractor**.

The Human Body

If you are still not convinced that fractals, being a mathematical topic, are very important in real life, your opinion might change after finding out that you yourself are made of fractals!

The lungs

The pulmonary system, which you use to breathe, is composed of tubes, through which the air passes into microscopic sacks called alveoli. The main tube of the system is the trachea, which splits into two smaller tubes that lead to different lungs, called the bronchi. The bronchi are in turn split into smaller tubes, which are split even further. This splitting continues further and further to the smallest tubes, called the bronchioles which lead into the alveoli. This description is similar to that of a typical fractal, especially a **fractal canopy**, which is formed by splitting lines.

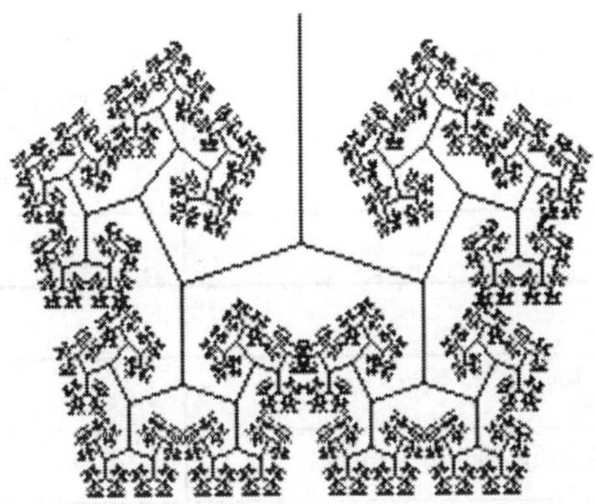

The endpoints of the pulmonary tubes, the alveoli, are extremely close to each other. The property of endpoints being interconnected is another property of **fractal canopies**.

The alveoli

Other supporting evidence that your lungs are fractal comes from measurements of the alveolar area, which was found to be 80 m^2 with light microscopy and 140 m^2 at higher magnification with electron microscopy. From the **geometric method** we know that an increase in size with magnification is one of the properties of fractals!

The blood vessels

Similar to bronchial tubes, splitting can also be found in blood vessels. Arteries, for example start with the aorta, which splits into smaller blood vessels. The smaller ones split as well, and the splitting continues until the capillaries, which, just like alveoli, are extremely close to each other. Because of this, blood vessels can also be described by **fractal canopies**.

The brain

The surface of the brain, where the highest level of thinking takes place, contains a large number of folds. A human, who is the most intellectually advanced animal, has the most folded surface of the brain as well. Geometrically, the increase in folding means an increase in intelligence. Instead of 2, which is the dimension of a smooth surface, the surface of the brain has a dimension greater than 2. In humans, it is obviously the highest, being as large as 2.73 to 2.79.

Membranes

Surface folding similar to that in the brain is found in many other surfaces, such as the ones inside the cell on mitochondria, which is used for obtaining energy and the endoplasmic reticulum, which is used for transporting materials. The same kind of folding was found in the nasal membrane, which allows better sensing of smells by increasing the sensing surface. However, in humans this membrane is less fractal than in other animals, which makes them less sensitive to smells.

The **fractal dimensions** of some anatomical structures are given below. Note that all dimensions are greater than you would expect them to be, and most are fractions, which automatically implies that the structures are fractal.

Anatomical structure	**Fractal dimension**
Bronchial tubes	Very close to 3
Arteries	2.7
Brain	2.73 – 2.79
Alveolar membrane	2.17
Mitochondrial membrane (outer)	2.09
Mitochondrial membrane (inner)	2.53
Endoplasmic reticulum	1.72

Molecules

Fractals can be found in the body on a smaller scale in various **molecules,** in addition to the anatomical structures above.

DNA

DNA is a long sequence of nucleotides that code all the genetic information about us. The nucleotides are adenine, guanine, cytosine, or thymine (abbreviated as A, G, C, and T). One of the fractal patterns that was studied was in the sequence of nucleotides in what is called the DNA walk. The DNA walk is a graphical representation of the DNA sequence in which you move up if you hit C or T and down if you hit A or G. For example, for the sequence CATG you will obtain the following picture:

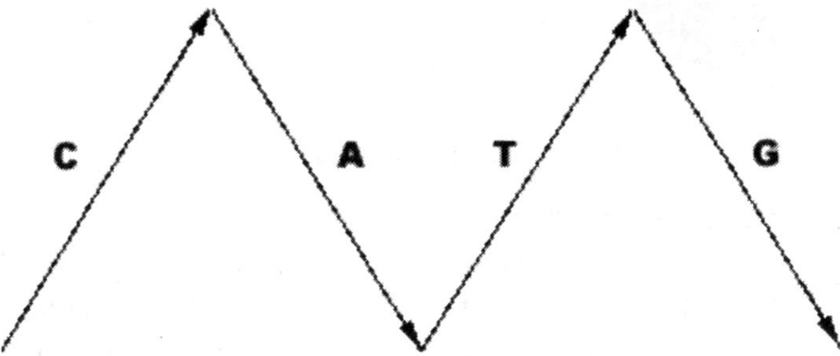

Fractal patterns were found in many DNA walks. These patterns are remarkably similar to **Brownian motion**. The fractal below is a model of a fractal DNA walk:

Chromatin

Chromatin is a fibrous material inside a cell's nucleus that contains the genetic material. As you can see below, chromatin tends to cluster:

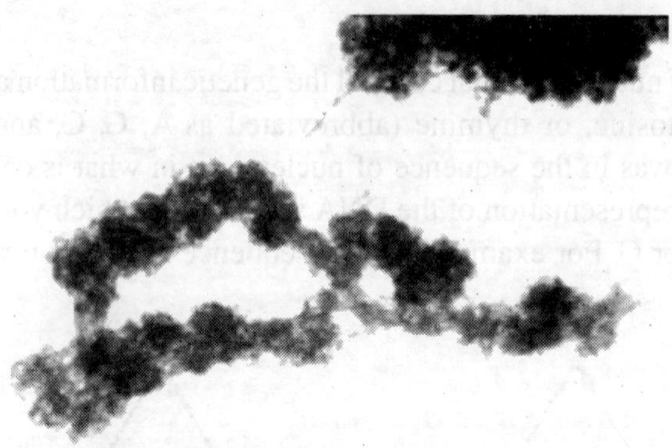

Fig. 7.3 : Chromatin Cluster

We have seen in the example on **galaxies** that **clusters** are fractal in shape. Recently, scientists have found ways to measure the **fractal dimension** of chromatin. Interestingly, experiments performed a few years ago at the Mount Sinai research centre in New York showed that the fractal dimension of chromatin might somehow be connected with cancer. Current experiments are attempting to detect breast cancer by measuring the fractal dimension.

Proteins and polymers

A polymer is a molecule that is composed of a series of "building blocks" (called monomers) connected to one another in a chain. However, you will find that these monomers are not connected in a straight line. Instead, the angles between the monomers can be different and the entire molecule can twist into complicated shapes. The same is true for proteins, which are formed by amino acids bonding together in a chain. Twisting, as well as folding and breaking often implies by itself that the shape is fractal. Proteins and many other polymers are, indeed, fractal and various methods exist for finding their **fractal dimension**. For some interesting proteins the results are shown below. Note that the dimensions are much higher than 1, which you would expect from a linear chain. This is another proof that proteins are fractal.

Table 7.1 : Fractal dimension of Proteins

Protein	Fractal dimension
Lysozyme (egg-white)	1.614
Hemoglobin (oxygen carrier in the blood)	1.583
Myoglobin (muscle protein)	1.728

Spectrum

If you hold any of the above substances in a flame, the flame will turn a colour that is characteristic of that substance. If you then allow the light from that flame pass through a spectroscope, the light will break up into several colours of the rainbow. Shortly after the discovery of fractals, Harter found spectra of some molecules that remarkably resembled the **Cantor Set**. The picture below is a simulation of a spectrum that is perfectly fractal.

Plants

Most plants show some form of branching. This happens when the main stem (of the trunk) splits into a number of branches. Each of these branches splits into smaller branches, and this kind of splitting continues until the smallest branches. You have probably noticed that a tree branch looks similar to the entire tree and a fern leaf looks almost identical to the entire fern. This property, called **self-similarity** is one of the most important properties of fractals. Because of numerous ways branching can be achieved geometrically, there are several ways of creating models of plants as well.

One classic way of creating fractal plants is by means of **l-systems**. Lindenmayer, who is the founder of l-systems, introduced them in a book called *The Algorithmic Beauty of Plants*, where he first used them to create models of plants. Some of the fractal plants he created became classic examples. An example is shown below.

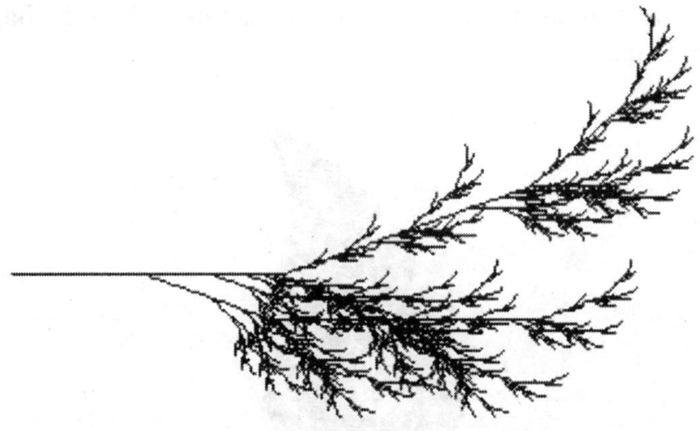

Another way of creating fractal plants is by using **fractal canopies** or **Pythagoras trees**. Fractal canopies are formed by splitting lines, which is very similar to branching. Pythagoras trees, such as the one below do the same more realistically by using squares and triangles instead of lines.

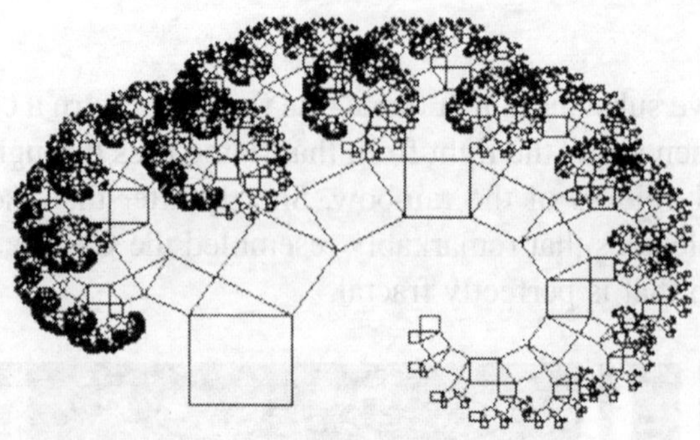

Fig. 7.4 : Fractal canopies or Pythagoras trees

One of the properties of fractal canopies is that the endpoints are interconnected. This is especially interesting in its similarity to broccoli, where the branches' endpoints form an interconnected surface.

The final way of creating plant models is by using **IFS fractals** such as the **Barnsley Fern** below, which resemble plant shapes.

Fig. 7.5 : IFS fractals - the Barnsley Fern

Population Growth

We hear about the rapid growth of population in developing countries all the time. With the problems that it is constantly causing, it is rather obvious how important it is to analyze the population growth. In the last century, Thomas Malthus put forward a theory which stated that with every generation, the population increases a certain amount of times depending on the growth rate. Mathematically, if r is the percent growth rate, and P the population, our formula will become

$$\text{New } P = (1 + r)P$$

For example, if $r = 1/2$ the population will increase by 50%, or become 1.5 times larger. However, according to this theory, the population will increase infinitely, but in fact the population is limited by natural resources, such as space and food. Suppose the maximum possible population the environment can hold is 1, so that P is a number from 0 to 1. As the population gets closer to 1, the growth rate is going to decrease and get close to 0. We can achieve this by multiplying the growth rate by $(1 - P)$. This way, as P gets closer to 1, the growth rate will be multiplied by a number that is getting close to 0. We now determine that the growth rate should really be $r(1 - P)$. Using it in the above formula, we obtain:

$$\begin{aligned}\text{New } P &= [1 + r(1 - P)] \\ &= [1 + r - rP]P \\ &= P + rP - rP^2 \\ &= (1 + r)P - rP^2\end{aligned}$$

Knowing this formula, it is easy to determine what the population will become after a long period of time. For example, when r is between 0 and 2, the population becomes 1 and remains so, no matter what it was at the beginning. When it is 2.25, it will always end up jumping between 1.17 and 0.72. When r is 2.5, it ends up jumping between 1.22, 0.54, 1.16 and 0.70. When it is 2.5, it ends up jumping between 8 values, and when r gets higher, it jumps between 16 values. As we increase r, the number of these values doubles. We call this *bifurcation*. We plot a graph of the population for all values of r from 1.9 to 3.

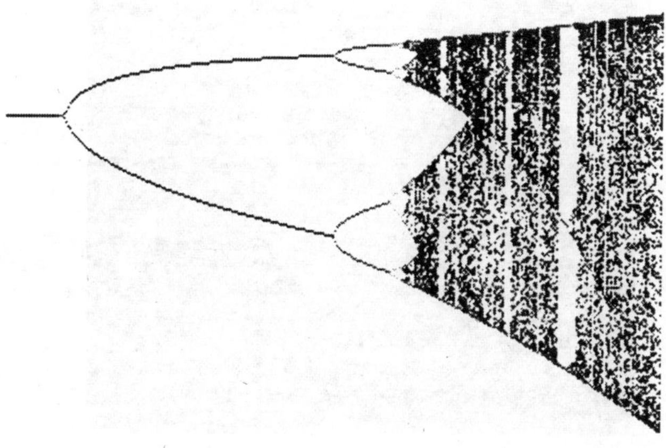

This is identical to the **Feigenbaum Fractal**! Indeed, you can unexpectedly find fractals even in the growth of population.

Note: A *Feigenbaum fractal* is any bifurcation fractal produced by a period-doubling cascade. The 'canonical' Feigenbaum fractal is produced by the logistic map, e.g., a simple population model.

Fig. 7.6 : The Cantor Square

Cluster fractals are formed by repeatedly cutting out pieces of a polygon. The fractal above is obviously not a good model, but making it more random helps a lot. The **fractal dimension** of such fractals can be found very easily using the **similarity method**. In the **Cantor Square**, for example there are 4 smaller squares, the sides of each of which are 1/3rd of the entire picture. The fractal dimension will thus be log 4/log 3 = 1.26. This is remarkably close to the fractal dimension of the universe according to one of the experiments, where it was found to be about 1.23. The fact that this is a fraction is yet another proof of the universe's fractal geometry.

Another way the universe can be modelled is by using **IFS fractals** that resemble the galaxies, such as the one below:

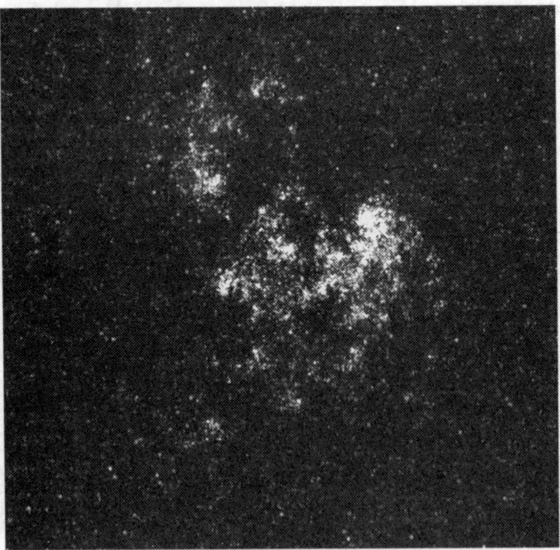

Rings of Saturn

Saturn is perhaps most famous for its rings. Originally, it was believed that there was a single ring. After some time, a break was observed in the middle, and scientists thought that the planet had two rings. However, when Voyager I approached Saturn, it discovered that the two rings were also broken in the middle, and the four smaller rings were broken as well. Eventually, it identified a very large number of breaks, which continuously broke even small rings into smaller pieces. The overall structure is amazingly similar to a **Cantor Set**, which is formed by continuously cutting out the middle of segments.

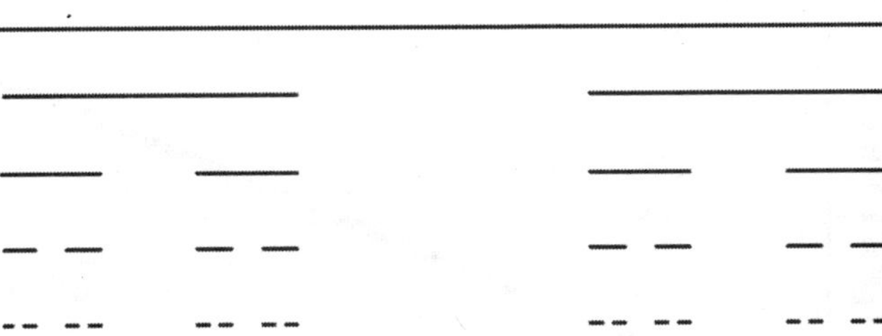

If you put circles through the points in the picture above, you will get a simple model of the rings of Saturn:

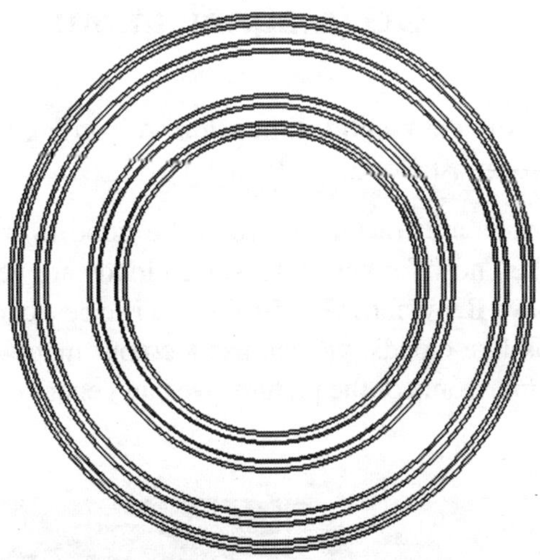

Fig. 7.7 : Model of Rings of Saturn

Clouds

Clouds appear very irregular in shape, you must have often looked at them and noticed how they seemed to resemble many common objects, animals, and people. Clouds, like most other objects in nature, are fractal in shape. Let us first look at experimental evidence that can prove this.

Usually, to prove that something is a fractal it is enough to find its **fractal dimension**. For something like a cloud it is the best to do it using the **geometric method**. Obviously, it cannot be done by measuring the actual cloud, but by measuring its 2D projection, which is the shade. We can make several measurements of the cloud's perimeter using different magnifications. This is achieved by using different sized "yardsticks." If, our yardstick is 1 kilometre long, the magnification is higher and measurement would be more exact than one where the yardstick is 10 kilometres long. We also know that in fractals, more detail adds additional irregularities, which adds to the measurement. If we plot a graph of log(magnification) against log(perimeter) we should get a line with a positive slope since the perimeter of fractals increases with magnification. When we plot such a graph for clouds, we get the figure shown below.

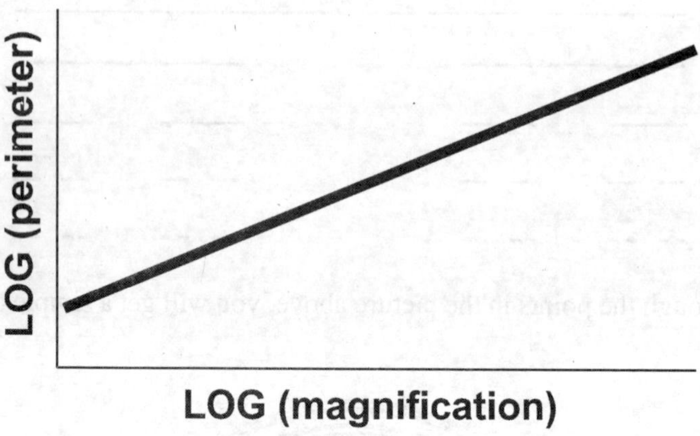

By adding 1 to the slope we find the **fractal dimension**. According to the findings of Lovejoy in 1981, the fractal dimension for most clouds is about 1.164.

Now, having proved that clouds are fractals, it would be good to try using fractals to generate computer models of them. We know for sure that, since clouds are very irregular, we have to use fractals that are random and have **Brownian self-similarity**. The best ones to use are **plasma fractals**. To make plasma fractals look like clouds, we can use a colour map which uses colours similar to ones on a real cloud photograph. Some of the pictures we can generate using this method are shown below.

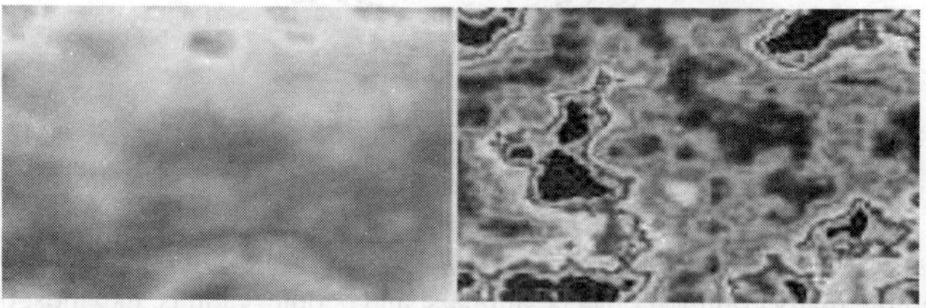

We can control how fragmented the clouds are by changing a parameter in **plasma fractals** called *roughness*.

Coastlines and Borders

Benoit Mandelbrot, the founder of fractals first noticed their properties on the coast of Britain. He realized that no matter how small a piece of the coastline is, it will still have its own bays, harbours, and capes. Basing his work on Richardson's data, he was able to prove that many coasts as well as borderlines are fractal.

Richardson searched many encyclopaedias to find data about the lengths of certain borders. He found enormous differences in data from different countries. For example, Portugal claimed its border with Spain to be 1214 km, while Spain claimed it to be 987 km. Portugal, as a smaller country would definitely measure its border more accurately. Thus, the increased accuracy increased the measurement, which is one of the properties of fractals! This happens because fractals are figures with an infinite amount of detail, and measuring more accurately adds more of these details, which adds to the overall size. Mandelbrot claimed that the difference in the two measurements was due to the fact that Spain used a "yardstick" that was bigger than Portugal's. If, for example, Spain measured the border with a 2 kilometre yardstick, its measurement would be less exact than that of Portugal, which used a 1 kilometre yardstick. If we plot a graph of log(total length) against log(length of yardstick), we get a line with a negative slope, as shown below, since the total length decreases with the increase of the size of the yardstick.

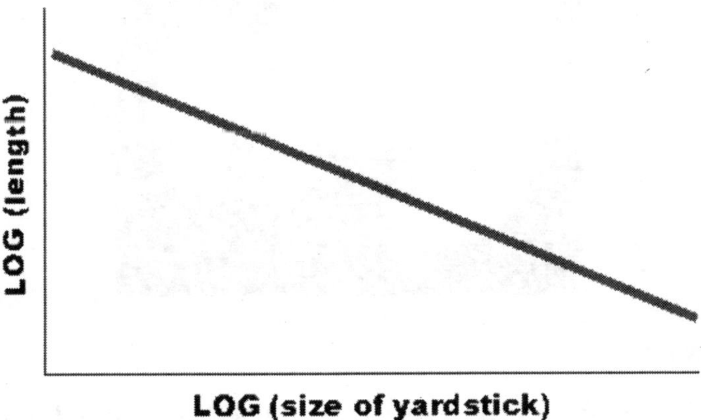

Using this graph, we can find **fractal dimensions** of coasts and borders by using a modified version of the **geometric method**. Since the magnification, used in the geometric method is equal to 1/size of yardstick, the identity log (1/x) = – log (x) will tell you that the slopes of lines, such as the one above, are the negative slopes of the lines in geometric method. A little bit of algebra will tell you that in order to get the fractal dimension, you need to subtract the slope from 1. Note that in the above diagram, the lines of more irregular lines, such as the coast of Britain are steeper than the lines of smoother lines, such as the coast of South Africa. This is due to the fact that the more irregular a curve is, the higher its fractal dimension.

Simple models of coasts can be made with **base-motif** fractals that use polygons for the bases. Such fractals are also called **Koch Islands**. Below are three examples of the **Koch Snowflake**, which uses a triangle, a **Quadric Koch Island** which uses a square, and the **Gosper Island** which uses a hexagon:

These pictures, obviously, are not much use in modelling real-life coasts since they are too perfectly symmetrical and **self-similar**. The solution to this problem is to use fractals with **Brownian self-similarity**, such as the **plasma fractals**. This gives the coasts randomness, which makes them more realistic. Below is an example of a coastline made using a plasma fractal.

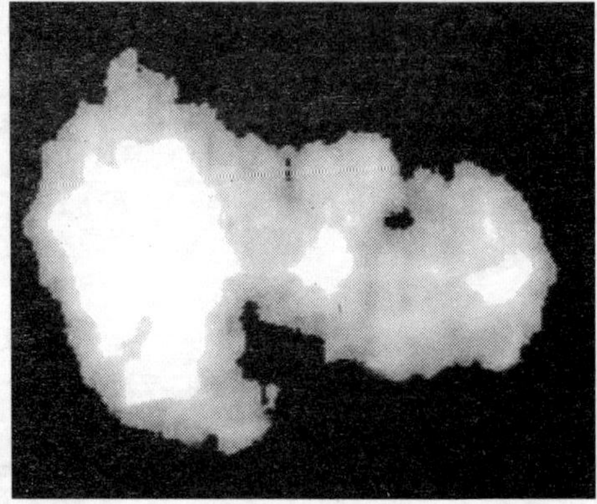

Data Compression

In December 1992, Microsoft released a compact disk entitled the *Encarta Encyclopaedia*. It contains thousands of articles, 7000 photographs, 100 animations, and 800 colour maps. All of this is contained in less than 600 megabytes of data. How was it possible? The answer lies in the mathematics of fractal data compression.

Consider the **Mandelbrot Set**. A full-screen, colour GIF image of it occupies about 35 kilobytes. However, all you need to store it is the formula $z = z^2 + c$, which takes no more than 7 bytes. This is a 99.98% compression! Since it works for the Mandelbrot Set, it could work for a flower diagram, a map of Africa, or a photograph as well. The goal is to find functions, each of which produces some part of the image. For a complex image that is not a fractal, you might need hundreds of such functions. Yet, it would still take up less space than hundreds of thousands of coloured pixels. **IFS** are the functions usually used for compressing data. The mathematical foundation of image compression was established by Michael Barnsley, who is the founder of IFS fractals as well.

Diffusion

Fractals can be used to describe the spreading of substances, such as diffusing gases or oil spills in water. One of the ways this can be modelled is by using **diffusion fractals**. In order to make a diffusion fractal, you need to start from the centre and spread the points outwards. The way this is done is by randomly moving points around the screen, similar to **Brownian motion** of molecules. When a point hits the centre point, it is made to stay there permanently. When some other point hits either the centre point, or the new point, it is also made to stay there.

Diffusion fractals can also be used to model not only diffusion, but the spilling of oil in water as well. Benoit Mandelbrot also found a similarity between the spilling of water and the formation of a **Quadric Koch Island.**

Economy

In economy, perhaps the most important thing is to be able to predict more or less accurately what will happen to the market after some time. Until very recently, the dominant theory that was used for this was the Portfolio Theory. According to this theory, the probability of various changes of the market can be shown using the standard bell curve, given below.

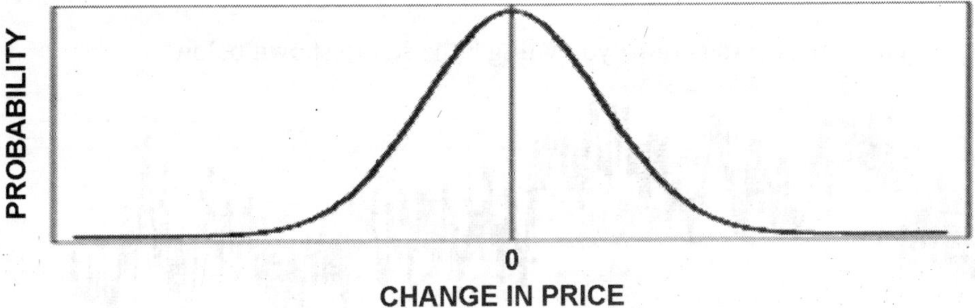

Fig. 7.8 : Standard Bell Curve

Assuming this theory is accurate, we can conclude that very small changes happen most often, while very big changes happen extremely rarely. However, this is not true in practice. While on the bell curve, the probability of rapid changes appears to approach zero, it happens regularly on the market. Recently, about 20 years after discovering fractals, Benoit Mandelbrot introduced a new fractal theory that can be used much more efficiently than the Portfolio Theory to analyze the market. Consider a year of market activity and plotting a graph of the price every month. You will get a broken line with some ups and downs. If you select any one month and plot a more detailed graph showing the variation in price every week, you will get a very similar line, with smaller ups and downs. If you continue in this way to plot more and more detailed graphs showing the variation every day, hour and even every minute or second, you will still get the same line, only with smaller ups and downs. This is **Brownian self-similarity**! Mandelbrot came up with a method of creating fractals that fit the above description. He based it on simple **generator iteration** and created **base-motif fractals** that could model the market. In the February 1999 issue of *Scientific American*, he published some of his fractal "forgeries" next to real market lines, showing how remarkably similar they were. In his method, you start with a shape, called the *generator*. The generator must be composed of three line segments, in order to contain both a rise and a fall in price:

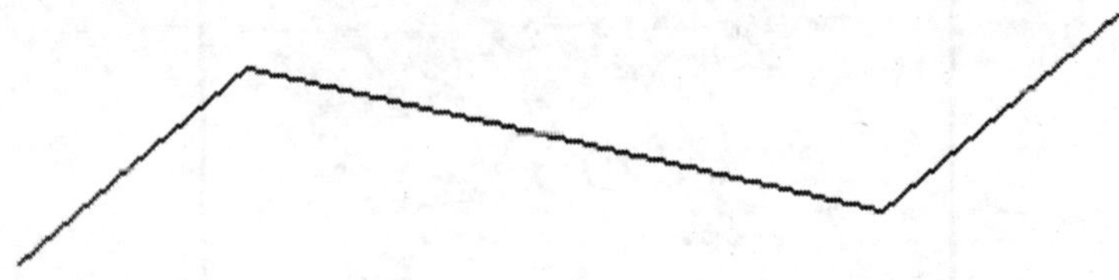

You then take this exact picture and substitute every line segment with it:

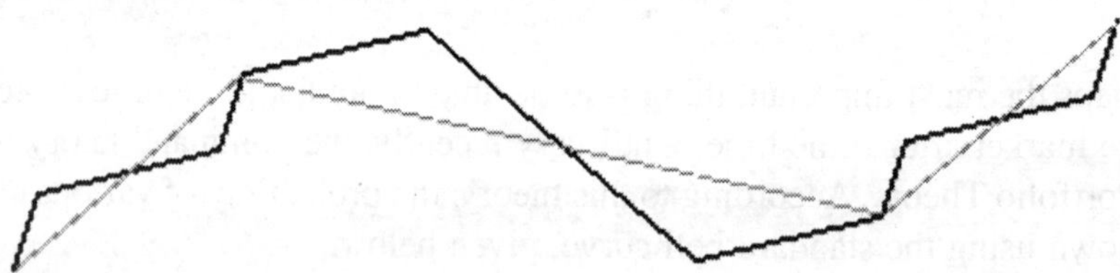

Continuing to substitute (see **iteration**) you will get the figure shown below.

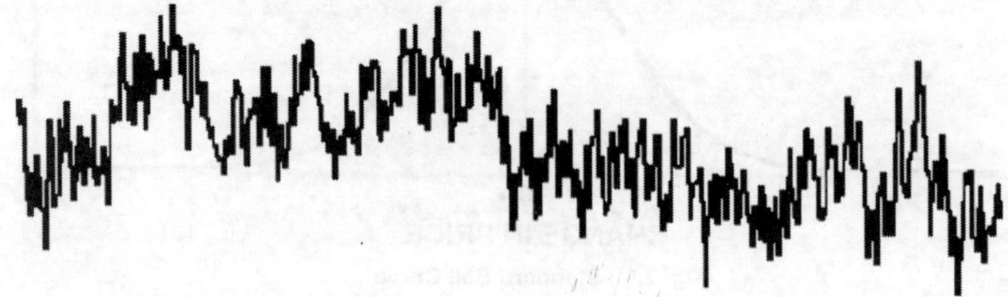

Comparing it to the Portfolio Theory model shown below, the former seems more realistic.

Fractal Art

If you have ever been introduced to fractals, the first things you probably saw were beautiful images as shown below.

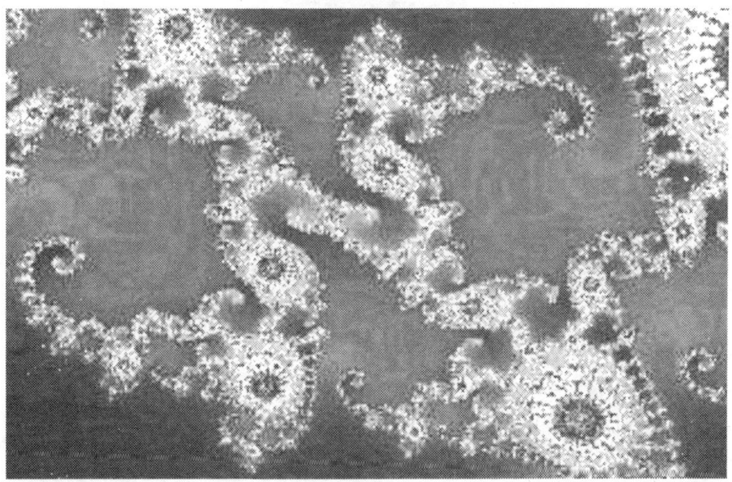

Pictures like the one above are one of the applications of fractals. It is an example of abstract art, which can be used for various decorative purposes when the colours are chosen appropriately. The natural intricate designs of fractals free the artist from worrying about shapes, allowing him to take care of other things such as colours, shading, and 3D effects. A simple 2-dimensional **strange attractor**, for example, can be turned into something very different as shown below.

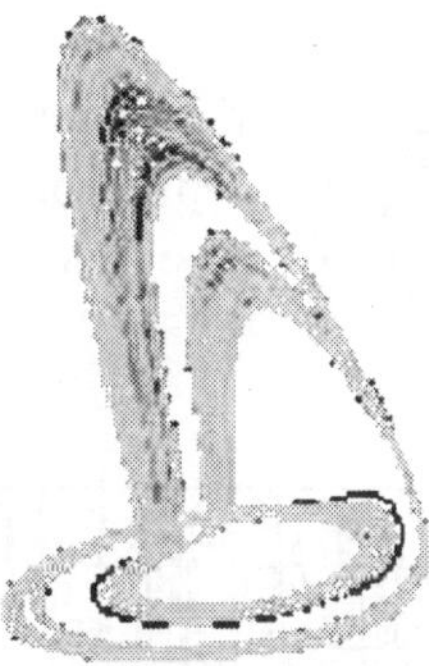

Recently, fractal art has grown in popularity and it has been used to create fractals resembling objects or even to express emotions.

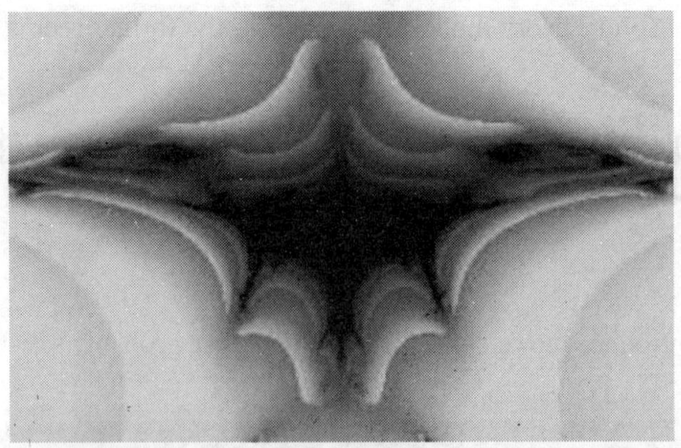

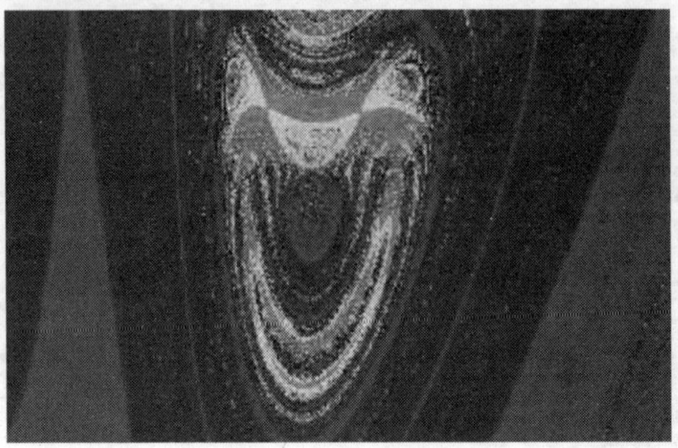

Fractal Music

One of the unusual applications of fractals is turning geometric patterns into sound patterns. We know that the simple formula

$$\text{New } x = bx(1 - x)$$

is capable of creating a fractal. For different values of b, we can see that the value of x changes in different ways. For some values, it remains at a fixed point, while for others it jumps between several values, and for still others it jumps around chaotically. If you plot a graph of the value of x, you obtain a pattern as shown below.

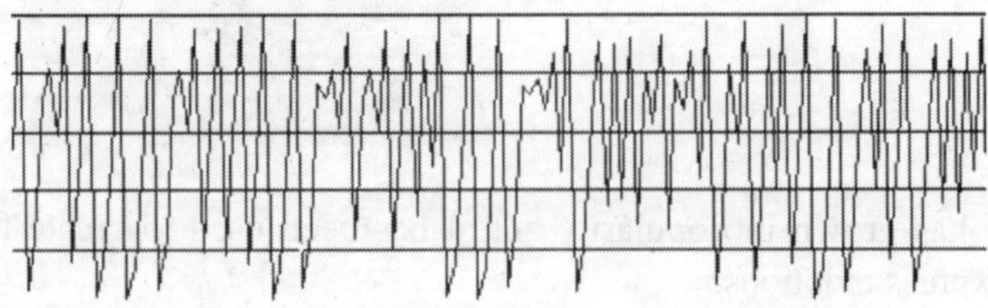

If you now draw five lines through this graph and place a note for every value of x at that point, you will be able to play it as music. Choosing the right value for b, you can make music with a great variety of patterns. Today, there is a lot of fractal music software that allows you to play several patterns at the same time and choose different instruments. You can, for example, make some instruments play a non-repeating pattern and other ones repeat a series of repeating notes. It may not be Beethoven, but it can still compete with many ultra-contemporary composers!

Landscapes

Fractal landscapes are a classic application of fractals. If you look at a mountain, you will not find a complicated shape with smaller hills and valleys. Looking at every hill, you will find it to be composed of even smaller hills and valleys. Even if you pick up a small rock from the mountain, you will find it to be similar to the entire mountain — a property of fractals which we defined as **self-similarity**. To form a 3D landscape out of a fractal, all you have to do is assign a height to every point depending on the colour and draw a picture with those heights. Usually **plasma fractals** are used for landscapes because they give the most realistic pictures. The steps are as follows.

Step 1: Draw a fractal that you will use for the landscape.

Step 2: Change the colours to make it look realistic.

Step 3: Either assign a height to every colour and draw the picture;

Or wrap the picture around a sphere to make a fractal planet.

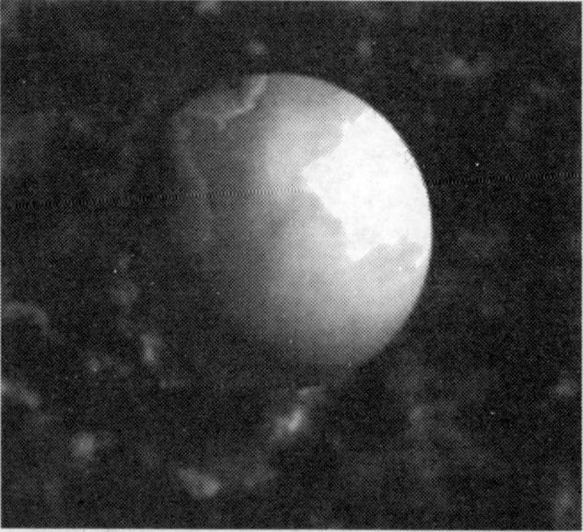

The 3D landscapes that you see are made using Bryce 3D. It allowed us to create light effects and put in appropriate background sky and ocean. However, you can still write programs to create 3D landscapes.

Fractals other than **plasma fractals** are not used very often because they are unable to produce realistic landscapes. However, fractals such as **Julia sets** can still be used to create good non-realistic landscapes for science fiction movies.

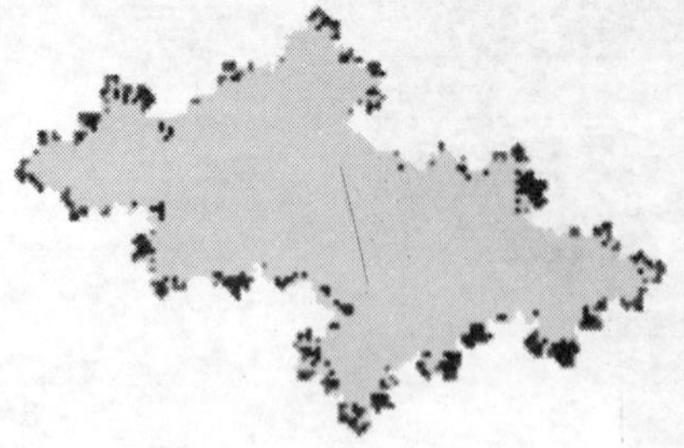

Fractal landscapes and planets were indeed used for **special effects** in many movies, including Star Trek.

Newton's Method

Besides exotic applications in nature, fractals have important mathematical applications as well. One of them is in the analysis of Newton's method, which is used for approximating the roots of an equation. For example, it can be used to solve the equation $x^n = 1$, where n is some positive integer. One of the roots of this equation is always 1, and if *n* is even -1 is also one of the roots. The rest of the roots are complex numbers. If you plot a graph of these numbers on a complex plane, you will see that they are equally spaced on the unit circle. Newton's method is based on making a guess of the root and then **iterating** a certain formula to change that number (it is the method used by computers). The number you end up with is the root that is the closest to the guess, unless you have initially picked a number that is equidistant from two different roots. In such a case the number will jump around chaotically — and create fractal shapes if you plot a graph of them. The fractal will have a different number of "chaos lines" depending on the number of roots (the value of n determines the number of roots). For $n = 3$, for example, the fractal formed is shown below.

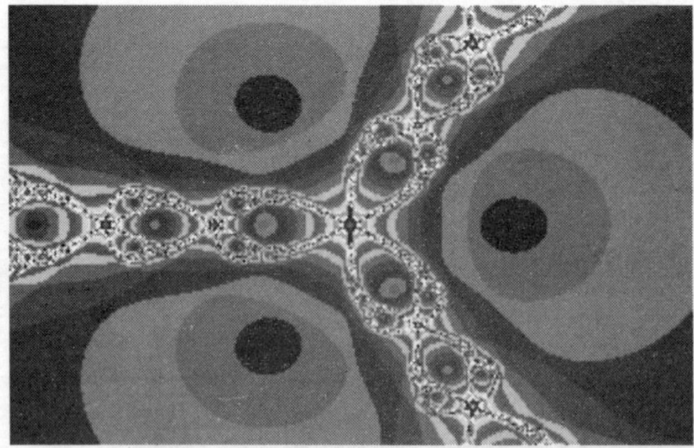

Notice the circles between every chaos line, these are the approximate locations of the roots. This figure is indeed fractal, since magnifying it will give us clearly **self-similar** shapes.

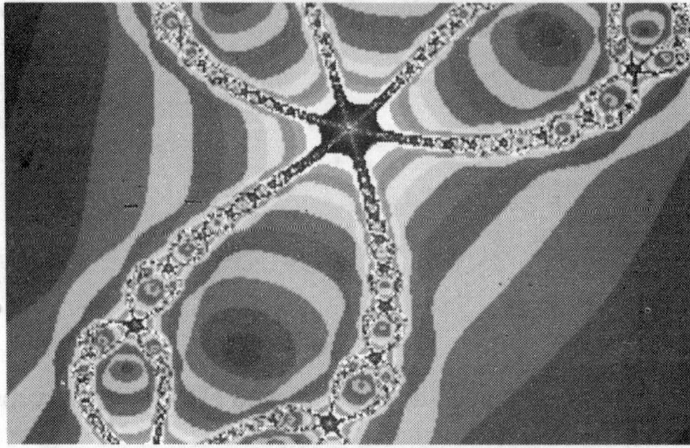

As a different example, consider the fractal for $n = 10$, as shown below.

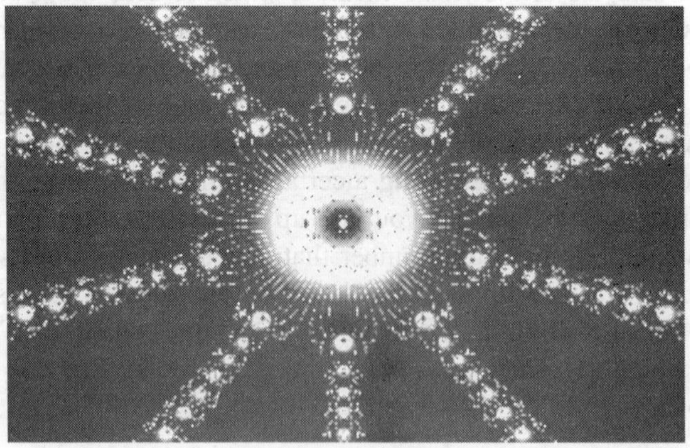

Special Effects

Computer graphics was one of the earliest applications of fractals. Indeed, fractals can achieve realism, beauty, and require very small storage space because of easy **compression**. Very beautiful **fractal landscapes** were published as far back as in Mandelbrot's *Fractal Geometry of Nature*. Although the first algorithms and ideas are owed to the discoverer of fractals, the artistic field of using fractals was started by Richard Voss, who generated the landscapes for Mandelbrot's book. This sparked the imagination of many artists and producers of science fiction movies. A little later, Loren Carpenter generated a computer movie of a flight over a fractal landscape. He was immediately hired by Pixar, the computer graphics division of Lucasfilms. Fractals were used in the movie *Star Trek II: The Wrath of Khan*, to generate the landscape of the Genesis planet and also in *Return of the Jedi* to create the geography of the moons of Endor and the Death Star outline. The success of fractal special effects in these movies lead to making fractals very popular. Today, numerous types of **software** allow anyone who has a basic knowledge of computer graphics and fractals to create such art, an example of which is shown below.

Weather

Weather behaves very unpredictably. Sometimes, it changes very smoothly from day to day, whereas at other times it changes very rapidly. Although weather forecasts are often accurate, they are not one hundred percent accurate, or in other words the weather behaves very chaotically. Weather can create fractal patterns. This was discovered by Edward Lorenz, who was mathematically studying the weather patterns. Lorenz came up with three formulae that could model the changes of the weather. When these formulae are used to create a 3D **strange attractor**, they form the famous **Lorenz Attractor**.

7.4 CLASSIFICATION OF FRACTALS

Fractals can be broadly classified into the following categories:

- Self-Similar Fractals
  - Approximate Self-Similar Fractals
  - Statistically Self-Similar Fractals
- Self-Affine Fractals
- Invariant Fractal Sets
  - Self Squaring Fractals – Mendalbort Set
  - Self Inverse Fractals

Self-Similar Fractals

Self-similar fractals have parts that are scaled down versions of the entire object. Starting with an initial shape, we construct the object subparts by applying a scaling parameter *s* to the overall shape. We can use the same scaling factor *s* for all sub parts, or we can use different scaling factors for different scaled down parts of the object. If we also apply random variations to the scaled down subparts, the fractal is said to be *statistically self similar.* The parts then have the same statistical properties. Statistically self-similar fractals are commonly used to model trees, shrubs and other plants.

Self-Affine Fractals

These have parts that are formed with different scaling parameters, *sx, sx, sz,* in different coordinate directions. We can also include random variations to obtain *self-affine* fractals. Terrain, water and clouds are typically modelled with the statistically self affine fractal construction method.

Invariant Fractal Sets

These are formed with non linear transformations. This class of fractals includes, *self squaring* fractals such as the Mendalbort Set, which are formed with squaring functions in complex space and *self inverse* fractals formed with inverse procedures.

Self-Similarity

Cats, canaries or kangaroos are *similar* if they are alike in some way. In geometry though, similar means something very specific. Geometric figures are ***similar*** if they have the same shape, for example:

The two squares are ***similar.***

The two rectangles are ***not similar.***

But the two rectangles above ***are similar.***

Look carefully at the last black rectangle and you will see that it is twice as wide as the grey rectangle and twice as long. We say that the sides are in proportion and the ratio is 2:1. Since the corresponding sides are in proportion (and the corresponding angles are also of equal measure), the figures are the same shape and are ***similar***.

Consider similarity in another way. In order for one figure to be similar to another, you must be able to zoom in on one of the figures, and it will look exactly like the other one. In some cases you might have to rotate it or turn it over.

How are figures ***self-similar?***

Many figures that are not fractals are self-similar. In the figure below, notice that the outline of the figure is a trapezoid. Now look inside at all the trapezoids that make up the larger trapezoid. This is an example of ***self similarity.***

You can also think of self-similarity as copies. Each of the small trapezoids is a copy of the larger one. Below are five other examples of self-similarity.

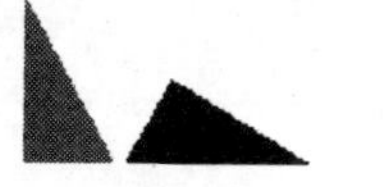

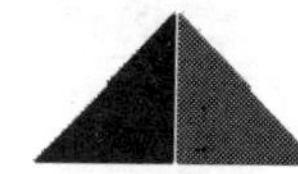

Self-Similarity of Fractals

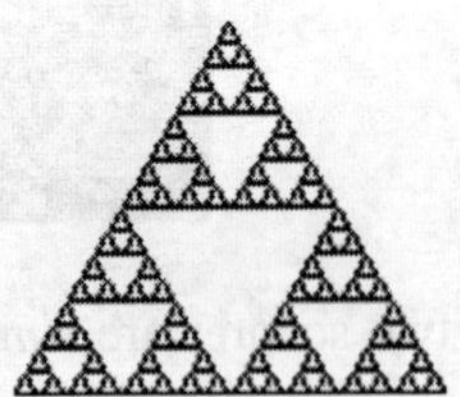

Fig. 7.9 : Sierpinski Triangle

The figure above is known as the Sierpinski Triangle. Notice that the outline of the figure is an equilateral triangle. Now look inside at all the equilateral triangles. Remember that there are infinitely many smaller and smaller triangles inside. How many different sized triangles can you find? All of these are similar to each other and to the original triangle – this is ***self similarity***.

Fractals usually possess what is called self similarity across scales. That is, as one zooms in or out the geometry/image has a similar (sometimes exact) appearance. The following illustrates various types of self similarity as well as present some real world examples.

Exact Self Similarity

The self similarity may be exact, this normally only occurs in mathematically defined fractals where the realities/constraints on structures imposed by the physical world do not apply. The following example is the well known Koch snowflake curve created by starting with a single line segment and on each iteration replacing each line segment by four others shaped as follows:
As one successively zooms in the resulting shape is exactly the same no matter how far in the zoom is applied.

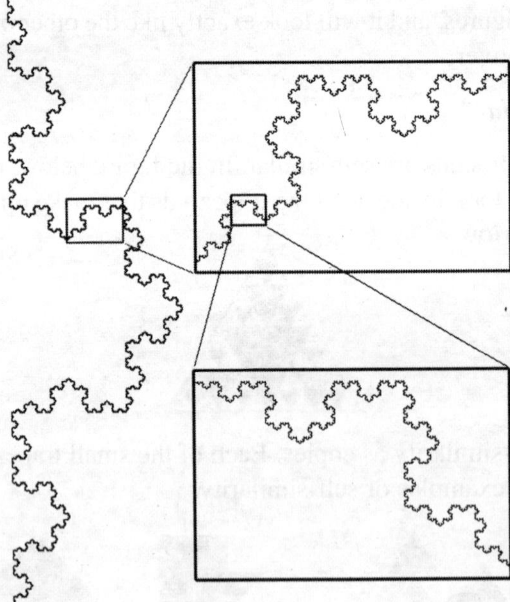

Approximate Self similarity

A far more common type of self similarity is an approximate one, that is, as one looks at the object at different scales one sees structures that are recognisably similar but not exactly so. An example of this in a mathematically defined system can be readily demonstrated by almost all the patterns seen in the **Mandelbrot set**. The following figure shows three successive zooms, and at each level a structure similar but not exactly the same as the whole Mandelbrot set can be found.

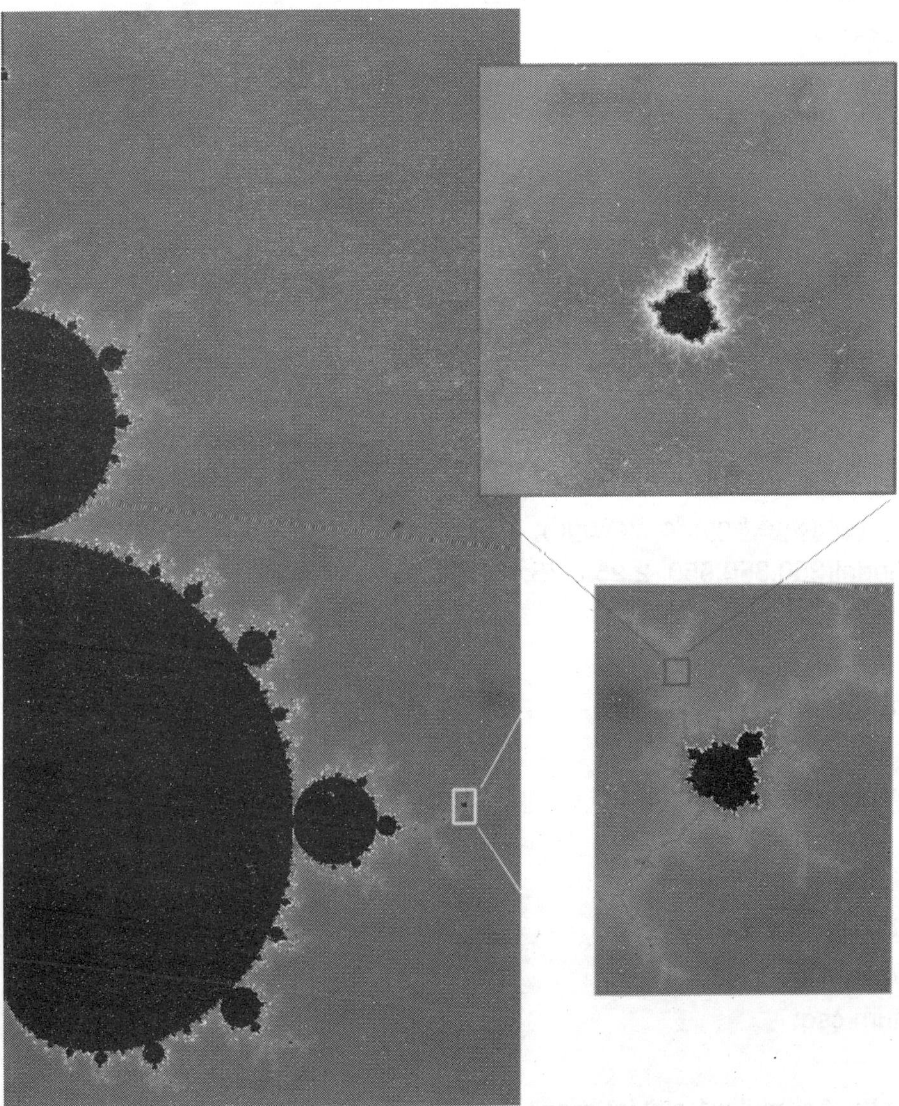

Note that in the above example the self similar structure occurs at discrete levels of scale while other systems like the Koch curve the self similarity occurs at all scales.

Program

```
// Program for Mandelbrot set
#include<stdio.h>
#include<conio.h>
#include<math.h>
#include<graphics.h>
#include<dos.h>

struct complex1
{
        float x;
        float y;
};
void mandel(int nx,int ny,int maxiter,float realmin,float realmax,float imin,float imax);
void main()
{
        int gd=DETECT,gm;
        initgraph(&gd,&gm,"c:\\tc\\bgi");
        mandel(350,350,550,-2.25,0.75,-1.25,1.25);

getch();
        closegraph();
}
struct complex1 complexsqr(struct complex1 c)
{
        struct complex1 csq;
        csq.x= (c.x*c.x)-(c.y*c.y);
        csq.y= 2*c.x*c.y;
        return csq;
}
int iterate(struct complex1 zint,int maxiter)
{
        struct complex1 z;
```

```
        int count=0;
        z=zint;
        while(((z.x*z.x)+(z.y*z.y)<=4.0) && (count< maxiter))
        {
          z = complexsqr(z);
          z.x += zint.x;
          z.y += zint.y;
          count++;
        }
        return count;
}

void mandel(int nx,int ny,int maxiter,float realmin,float realmax,float imin,float imax)
{
        float rinc = (realmax-realmin)/nx;
        float iinc = (imax-imin)/ny;
        struct complex1 z;
        int x1,y1,count;
        for(x1=0,z.x=realmin;x1<nx;x1++,z.x+=rinc)
        {
        for(y1=0,z.y=imin;y1<ny;y1++,z.y+=iinc)
        {
                count= iterate(z,maxiter);
                if(count == maxiter)
                setcolour(0);
                else
             // setcolour(count);
                putpixel(x1,y1,count);
         }
         delay(100);
         }
}
```

Statistical Self Similarity

Sometimes the self similarity is not visually obvious but there may be numerical or statistical measures that are preserved across scales. One obvious measure might be the fractal dimension, in the example below of $1/f$ noise. The fractal dimension is constant as one zooms in.

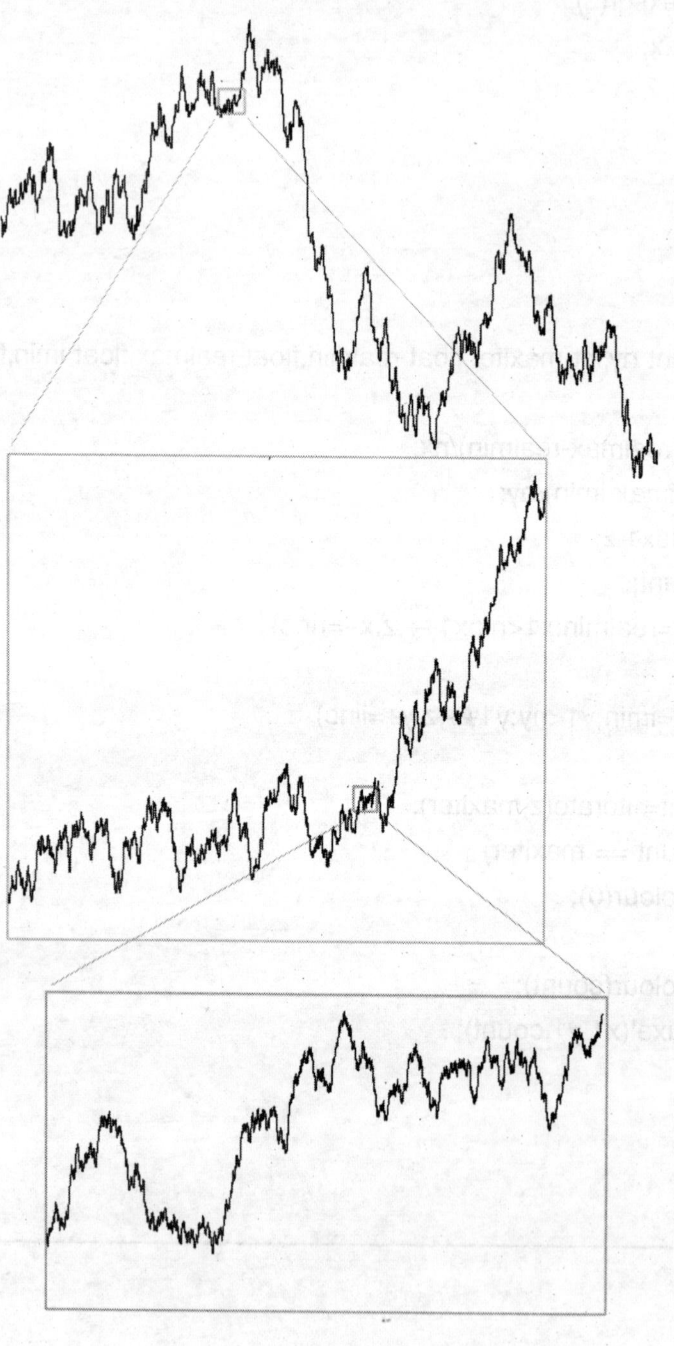

Example 1 - Terrain

Consider the following image, it could bc a large piece of rugged terrain photographed from an aeroplane, or the side of a mountain, or a patch of dirt on a scale of a few meters, or a magnification of the surface of a rough rock. Whichever it is, it could also easily be imagined to be any one of the others. One could start at the large scale view from the air and apply successive zooms down to a microscopic scale and the surface maintains self similarity across those scales.

As with most fractal structures found in nature, the self similarity only occurs over a range of scales. In the above example, there is no self similarity as we zoom out to see the whole planet, or zoom in to microscopic scales.

Example 2 - Fern leaf

In the case of the self similarity found in the fern, not only is there a limit to the range of scales at which the self similarity occurs but it also occurs at only a few discrete scales.

7.5 FRACTAL DIMENSIONS

The detailed variation in a fractal object can be described with a number *D,* called the fractal dimension, which is a measure of the roughness, or fragmentation of the object. More jagged looking objects have larger fractal dimensions. We can set up some iterative procedures to generate fractal objects using a given value for the fractal dimension *D.* With other procedures, we may be able to determine the fractal dimension from the properties of the constructed object, although in general the fractal dimension is difficult to calculate.

There are many methods to determine the fractal dimension. A few of them are listed below:

- Fractal Dimension of Self Similar Fractals obtained with subdivision of Euclidean object.
- Topological Covering object method that approximate object subparts.
- Box – Covering methods

Fractal Dimension of Self Similar Fractals Obtained With Subdivision of Euclidean Object

The following figure shows the relationships between the scaling factor s and the number of subparts n for subdivision of a unit straight-line segment, a square and a cube.

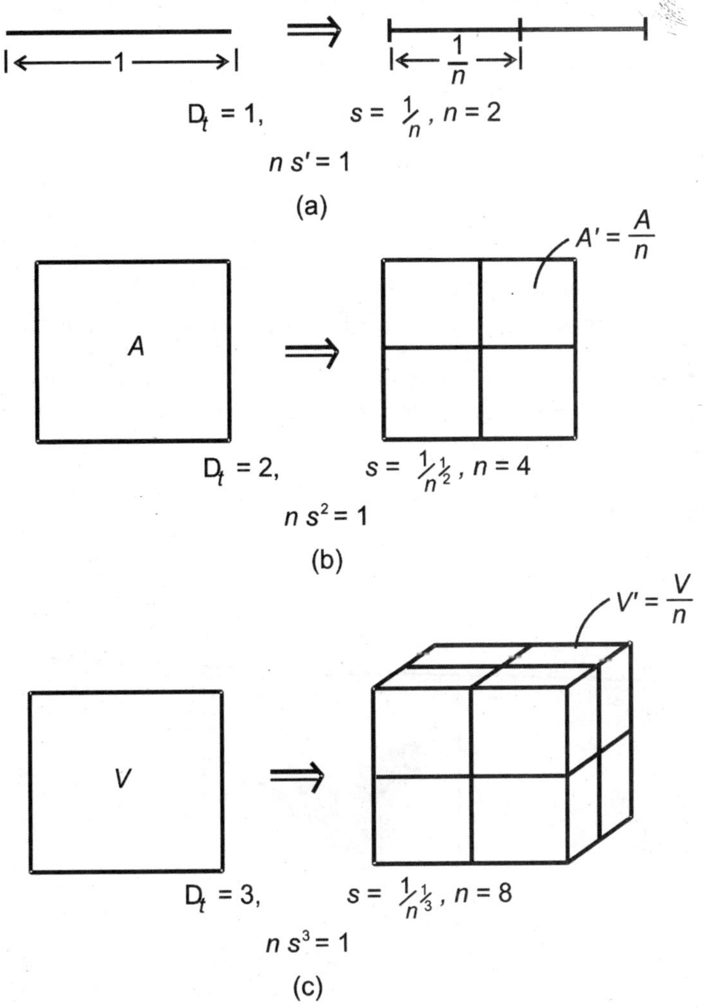

With $s = 1/2$, the unit line segment is divided into two subparts of equal length. Similarly the square is divided into four subparts of equal area and the cube is divided into eight subparts of equal volume.

For each of these objects, the relationship between the number of subparts and scaling factor is

$ns^{D}E = 1.$

In analogy with Euclidean objects, the fractal dimension D for self similar objects can be obtained from

$ns^D = 1$.

Solving this expression for *D*, the fractal similarity dimension we have,

$D = \ln n/(\ln(1/s))$

Topological Covering Object Method that Approximates Object Subparts

For objects having a general object, we can use topological covering methods that have approximate object subparts with simple shapes.

A subdivided curve can be approximated with straight line sections and a subdivided polygon with small squares or rectangles. Other covering shapes such as circles, spheres and cylinders, can also be used to approximate the features of an object divided into a number of smaller parts. Covering methods are normally used in mathematics to determine geometric properties such as length, area or volume, of an object by summing the properties of a set of smaller covering objects. We can also use covering methods to determine the fractal dimension D of some objects.

Topological covering concepts were originally used to extend the meaning of geometric properties to non standard shapes. An extension of covering methods using circles led to the notion of *Hausdorff-Besicovitch* dimension or *fractal dimensions.*

Box Covering Methods

More commonly, the fractal dimension of an object is estimated with box covering methods using rectangles or parallelepipeds as in the following figure.

The figure illustrates the notion of box covering. Here the area inside the larger irregular boundary can be approximated by the sum of the areas of the small covering rectangles.

We apply box covering methods by:

1. Determining the coordinate extents of an object.
2. Subdividing the object into a number of small boxes using the given scaling factors.

The number of boxes *n* that it takes to cover an object is called the box dimension, and *n* is related to the fractal dimension *D* of the object.

For statistically self similar objects with a single scaling factor s we can cover the object with squares or cubes. We then count the number n of covering boxes and use an equation to estimate the fractal dimension.

For Self Affine fractals, we cover the object with rectangle boxes, since different directions are scaled differently. In this case, the number of boxes n is used with the affine transformation parameters to estimate the fractal dimension.

Geometric Construction of Self Similar Fractals

One of the unique things about fractals is that they have non-integer dimensions. Fractals can have a dimension of 1.8, or 4.12. Although fractals may not be in integer dimensions, they always have a smaller dimension than what they are displayed on. If you make a fractal by drawing lines that obey a certain rule, like Koch's Curve, that fractal cannot have a dimension higher than the paper it is drawn on, which would be 2.

It is a little difficult to calculate how many dimensions a fractal has. First you must realize that in mathematics, a dimension means much more than whether it is a point, or if it is flat, or if it has length, width, and height. This can be simplified with logarithms. If, for instance, you take a cube and multiply its edge length by 2, then you can fit 8 of the old cubes into the new cube. Taking these two numbers, you find that log 8/log 2 = 3, (it is not necessary to go into the mathematics that leads to this simple equation). So, a cube has a dimension of 3, which we already knew. Eight is also 2 raised to the 3rd power. It can be assumed that for any fractal object (of size P, made up of smaller units of size p), the number of units (N) that fit into the larger object is equal to the size ratio (P/p) raised to the power of d, which is called the Hausdorff dimension.

$$\mathrm{N} = \left(\frac{P}{p}\right)^d \quad \text{- or - } \quad \mathrm{d} = \frac{\log N}{\log(P/p)}$$

Let us apply this to Koch's Curve. Using only line segments that are 3 centimetres long (P), you make a simple Koch's Curve, which is just a Star of David, with 12 segments, of 3 centimetres per segment. Taking this to the next level and using line segments which are 1 centimetre long (p), you use 48 line segments. By cutting the length of the line segments by one third ($P = 3$, $p = 1$, $P/p = 3$), the number of line segments used (N) goes up four times (48 segments for p divided by 12 segments for P equals 4). That means $N = 4$, $P/p = 3$, so $d = \log 4/\log 3$ and we find that Koch's Curve has a dimension of 1.2618595071429.

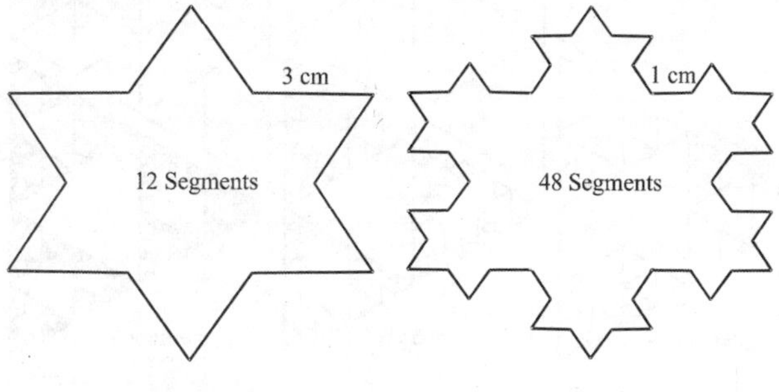

3 cm

12 Segments

1 cm

48 Segments

7.6 FRACTAL GENERATION PROCEDURES

A fractal object is generated by repeatedly applying a specified transformation function to points within a region of space. If $p_0 = (x_0, y_0, z_0)$ is the selected initial point, each iteration of a transformation function F, generates successive levels of detail with the calculations:

$P_1 = f(p_0), \quad p_2 = f(p_1), \quad p_3 = f(p_2), \ldots$

In general, the transformation function can be applied to a specified point set or we could apply the transformation function to an initial set of primitives, such as straight lines, curves, colour areas, surfaces and solid objects. Also we can use either deterministic or random generation procedures at each iteration. The transformation function may be defined in terms of geometric transformations or it can be set up with non linear coordinate transformations and decision parameters.

Although fractal objects, by definition, contain infinite detail, we apply the transformation function a finite number of times. Therefore, the objects we display actually have a finite number of times. A procedural representation approaches a "true" fractal as the number of transformations is increased to produce more and more detail. The amount of detail included in the final graphical display of an object depends on the number of iterations performed and the resolution of the display system. We cannot display detailed variations that are smaller than the size of a pixel. To see more of the object detail we zoom in on selected sections and repeat the transformation function iterations.

Fractals Construction Methods

Methods of Successive Approximations

To become familiar with this method consider the example of Sierpinski Gasket construction.

The Sierpinski Gasket can be formed as follows:

1. Begin with an equilateral triangle (although, we can begin with any figure as we will see later).
2. Divide the triangle into four equal-sized triangles.
3. Remove the middle triangle.
4. Go to Step #2.

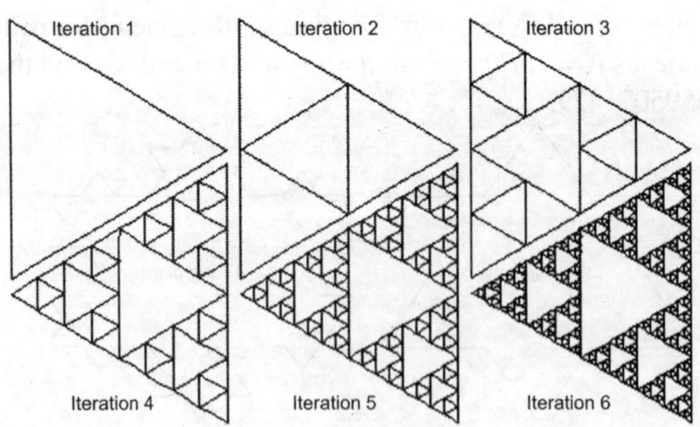

The above method will form a Sierpinski Gasket. However, it is not an Iterated Function System yet. Let us express this as an Iterated Function System.

1. Begin with an equilateral triangle (again, this is arbitrary)
2. Reduce the image by one-half.
3. Make three copies of the reduced image.
4. Align them in the shape of an equilateral triangle.
5. Translate the top copy to the left above the lower-left copy.
6. Go to step #2.

Before iteration

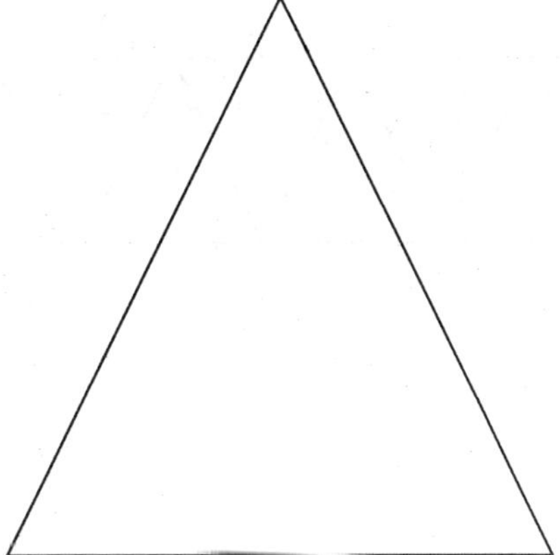

Iteration 1

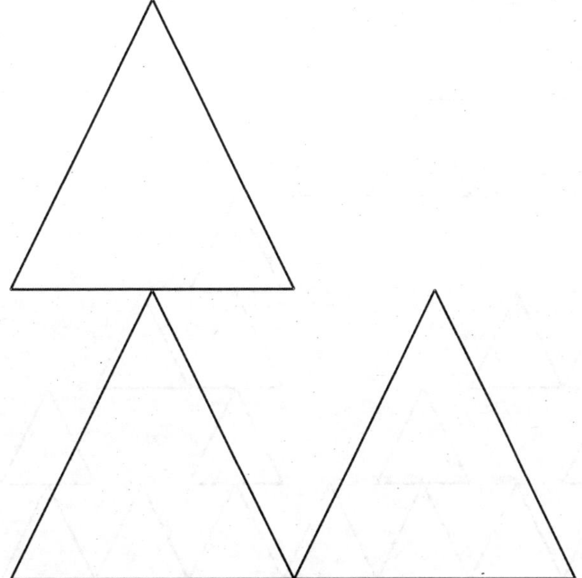

Iteration 2

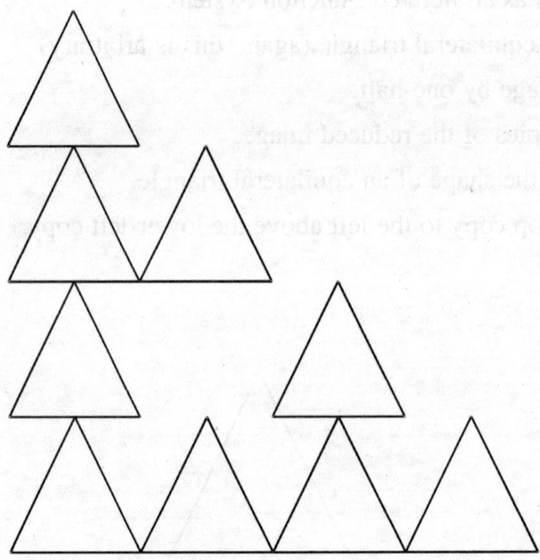

Iteration 3

Iteration 4

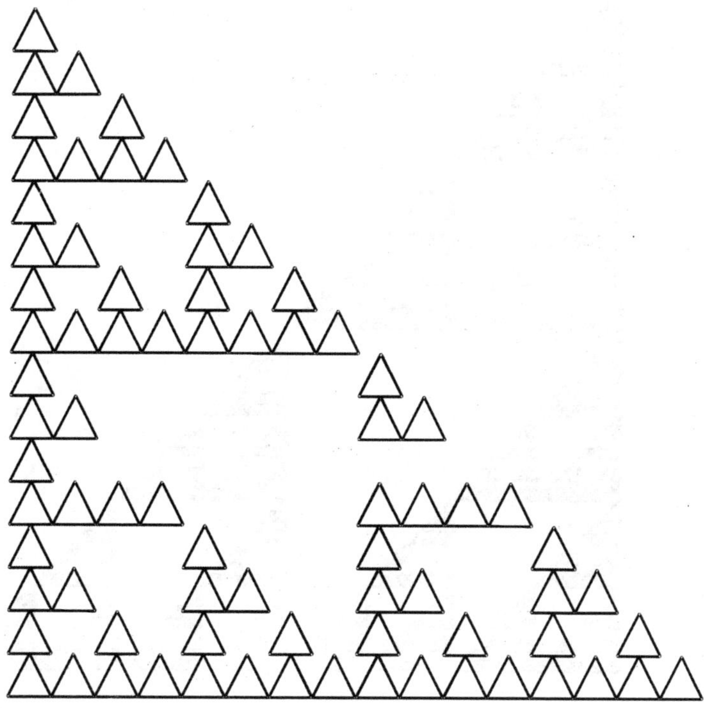

Iteration 5

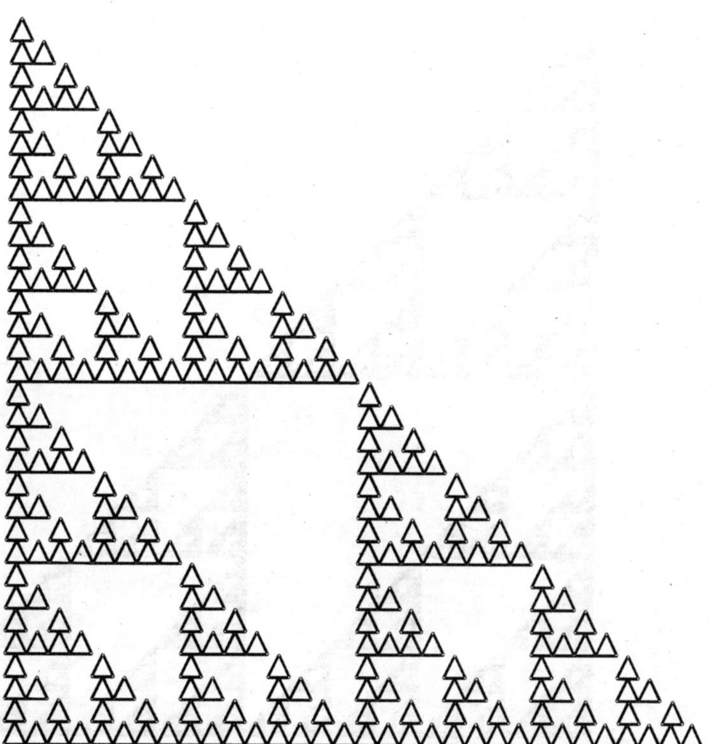

Iteration 6

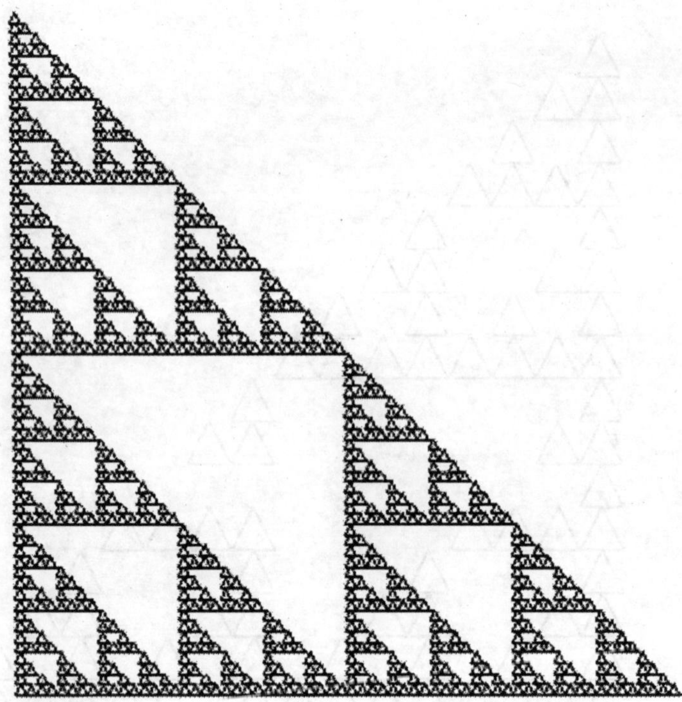

Iteration 7

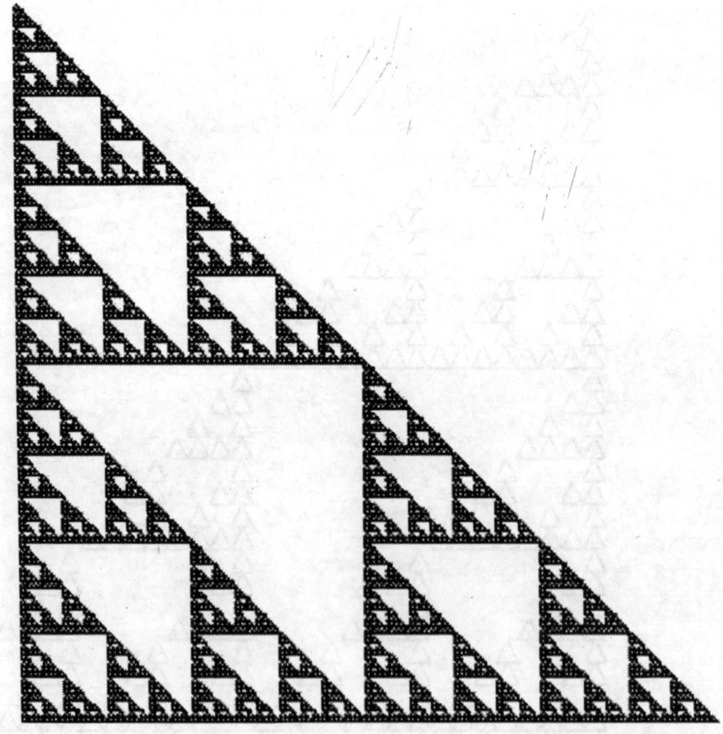

Construction by Points or Probabilistic Method

This is the easiest method to implement on a computer. For simplicity consider the case of the plain self-affine set. Let $\{S_1,..,S_m\}$ be some system of affine contractive maps. Maps S_i can be represented as: $S_i(x) = A_i(x - o_i) + o_i$, where A_i is a 2 x 2 matrix and o_i is a vector.

1. As the starting point we will take the fixed point of the first map S_1: $x := o_1$;

   Here we assume that all fixed points of contractions $S_1,..,S_m$ belong to the fractal. As the starting point we can choose any point. The generated sequence of points will converge to the fractal, but some wrong points will appear on the screen.

2. Draw the current point $x = (x_1, x_2)$ on the screen:

   putpixel(x_1, x_2, 15);

3. Select a number j from 1 to m randomly and recalculate coordinates of the x point: j: = Random(m)+1;

   x: = $S_j(x)$;

4. Go to step 2, or stop if a sufficient number of iterations have been carried out.

Remark: If the contraction coefficients of maps S_i are different, then the fractal will be filled irregularly with points. In the case, when S_i are similar, this can be avoided by a small modification of the algorithm. On the 3rd step of the algorithm, the number j from 1 to m should be selected by probabilities $p_1 = r_1^s,..,p_m = r_m^s$, where r_i denotes the similarity coefficient of the map S_i, and the number s (known as similarity dimension) is found from the equation $r_1^s + ... + r_m^s = 1$. One of the ways of solving this equation is to use Newton's method.

7.7 SUMMARY

- The dynamics of any situation refer to how the situation changes over the course of time. A dynamical system is a physical setting together with rules for how the setting changes or evolves from one moment of time to the next.
- One basic goal of the mathematical theory of dynamical systems is to determine or characterize the long-term behavior of the system. Dynamical systems are only one way to produce fractals.
- Highly irregular geometric objects are commonly called fractals.
- Fractals have come up as an important question twice before the invention of computers. The first time was when British map makers discovered the problem with measuring the length of Britain's coastline.
- One of the biggest problems of geometry is to describe the shape of a cloud, a tree or a mountain. The reason is that the shapes of these objects are irregular and cannot be analysed in standard forms. This means that a cloud cannot be represented as a sphere or ellipsoid or a mountain as a cone. Therefore, we can say that in nature many patterns (actually most of them) are irregular and fragmented.

- One way to describe these patterns was introduced in 1975-1977 by Benoit B. Mandelbrot. He used self-similar forms generated from the iteration of simple analytic forms.
- These self-similar forms were defined as fractals, which do not change in appearance when they are magnified. In association with chaos, fractals were proved to be very helpful in describing a variety of phenomena in Chemistry, Biology, Physics, Astrophysics, Material Sciences etc, because of their ability to represent irregular shapes and the random procedure introduced from the nonlinearity of the equations involved.
- The advances in computers facilitated the study of fractals and their applications on various topics, such as the development of realistic forms of physical objects in a random way.
- The word fractal comes from the Latin adjective *fractus* which means broken. A more scientific approach of the term fractal is that it is a fragmented mathematical geometric shape which can be subdivided into smaller pieces that represent a reduced-size copy of the whole. Some examples of known mathematical structures known as fractals are the 'Sierpinski triangle', the 'Koch snowflake', the 'Peanï curve', the 'Mandelbrot set' and the 'Lorenz attractor'
- Identifying chaos in experimental data usually includes searching for a strange attractor in the state space dynamics, identified by its fractal structure. Having found such an attractor, you can try to estimate its dimension, which is a measure of the number of active variables and hence the complexity of the equations required to model the dynamics.
- Fractals are to chaos what geometry is to algebra. The are a geometric manifestation of the chaotic dynamics. They have been called fingerprints of chaos. Many natural objects in real three dimensional space have fractal qualities.
- The basic concept of fractals is that they contain a large degree of self similarity. This means that they usually contain little copies of themselves buried deep within the original. They also have infinite detail. Like the coastal problem, the more you zoom in on a fractal, the more detail (coastline) you get.

7.8 REVIEW QUESTIONS

1. Write a routine to interactively select different colour combinations for displaying the Mandelbrot set.
2. Write a program to interactively select any rectangular region of the Mandelbrot set and to zoom in on the selected region.
3. Write a routine to implement point inversion, and any given point position.
4. Devise a set of geometric-substitution rules for altering the shape of an equilateral triangle.
5. Write a program to display the stages in the conversion of an equilateral triangle into another shape, given a set of geometric-substitution rules.
6. Write a program to model an exploding firecracker in the xy plane using a particle system.
7. Devise an algorithm for modelling a rectangle as a non-rigid body, using identical springs for the four sides of the rectangle.

8. Write a routine to visualise a two-dimensional, scalar set using pseudo-colour methods.
9. Write a routine to visualise two dimensional, scalar data using contour lines.
10. Write a routine to visualise a two-dimensional, vector data set using an arrow representation for the vector values. Make all arrows the same length, but display the arrows with different colours to represent the different vector magnitudes.

CHAPTER 8

Projection

8.1 INTRODUCTION

When a 3D object is represented in a drawing in a two-dimensional plane – it is said to be its projection. Or in other words, we can say that a projection is a transformation, which maps 3D objects onto a 2D screen.

In engineering drawing, when we represent any three-dimensional object, we draw three figures, namely plan, elevation and side view to represent all its possible dimensions. An example of such a drawing of a hexagonal prism is given in fig. 8.1.

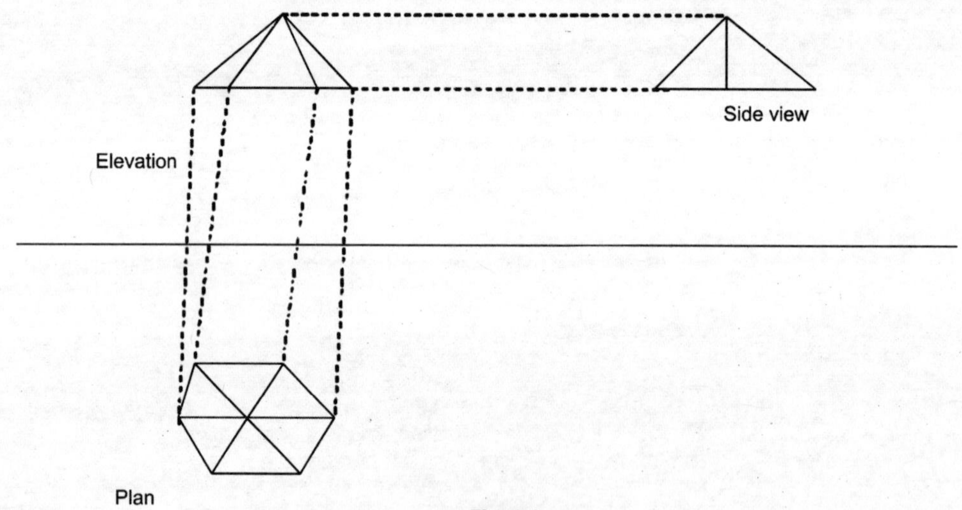

Fig. 8.1

In these figures the dotted lines are used to represent any hidden surface which is present but cannot be seen in that particular view. This type of drawing is mainly used in case of engineering drawings and may not be understood by lay persons, especially if the figure is a complicated one.

A better method used for viewing is the isometric view, which is basically drawn and can be understood by people who are not familiar with engineering drawings. An isometric view of a hexagonal prism is shown in fig. 8.2.

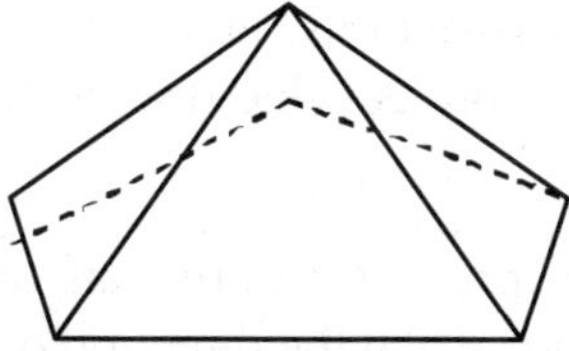

Fig. 8.2

Basically what we do is draw different types of projectional views of a three-dimensional object. Beside the ones already mentioned there are many more projectional views that are frequently used to represent any three-dimensional object in a two-dimensional plane. A list of all the different types of projections is given below.

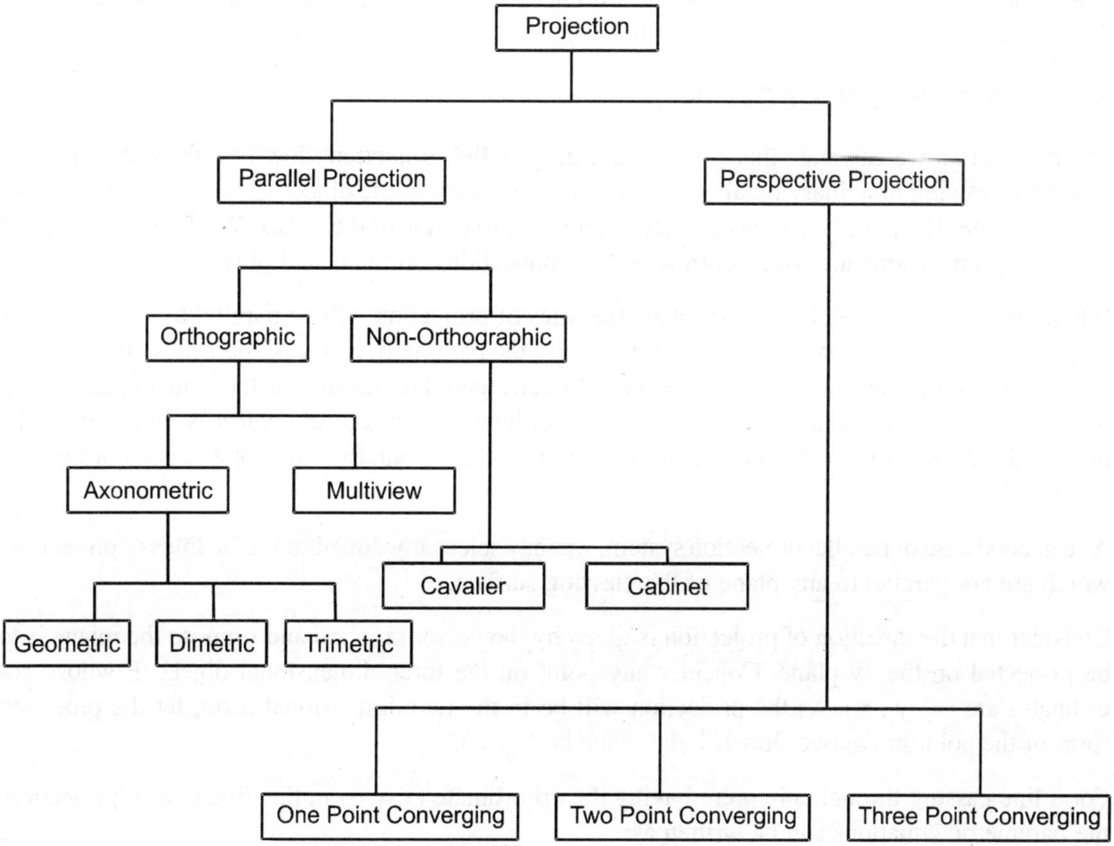

- Projection
  - Parallel Projection
    - Orthographic
      - Axonometric
        - Geometric
        - Dimetric
        - Trimetric
      - Multiview
    - Non-Orthographic
      - Cavalier
      - Cabinet
  - Perspective Projection
    - One Point Converging
    - Two Point Converging
    - Three Point Converging

Perspective types of drawing are used mainly by artists to develop the artistic views of three-dimensional objects and scenes. In the one-point converging type, what is seen by an artist from a particular point is drawn. In this type of perspective drawing normally no scale is maintained to represent proper dimensions. Thus, lines that are actually parallel, such as rail lines or parallel roads are seen to converge or diverge in different situations. The points of convergence are also known as vanishing points. What we see in an artistic picture is an example of this type of drawing.

Parallel projections are mainly used by engineers and draftsman to draw three dimensional objects in engineering drawings. In parallel projections, image points of the object are obtained by the intersection of the view plane and the project line drawn from the object points having a fixed direction.

The characteristics of orthographic projection are that the direction of projection must be perpendicular to the plane of view. Thus when the direction of projection is parallel to the x axis, it will give the plan, when it is parallel to the y axis, it will give the elevation and if it is parallel to the z axis, it will be the side view of the object.

Non-orthographic parallel projections are called oblique parallel projections. Oblique projections may be of the cavalier type, where, the direction of projection is chosen in such a way that there is no fore shortening of lines that are perpendicular to the xy plane. In contrast to this, in the cabinet type of projection the direction of projection is chosen in such a way that the lines perpendicular to the xy planes are fore shortened by half their lengths.

8.2 PARALLEL PROJECTION

In simple terms we can state that – we obtain the parallel projection view of a three dimensional object by drawing imaginary parallel lines from each vertex of the object so that they intersect the viewing plane. The point of intersection represents the projection of the vertex. We draw the projected vertices by line segments, which correspond to connections on the actual object.

When the object is parallel to the xy plane the lines of projection will be parallel to the z axis. So, when we move along these lines of projection, only the parametric value of the z axis changes. The values in the directions of the x and y axes remain unchanged. This means that the point of intersection with the viewing surface has the same x and y co-ordinates as the objects' vertices. In this case, the projected image is formed from the x and y coordinate values and the value of z axis co-ordinate is discarded.

As a general case of parallel projection system, we may select any direction for the lines of projection, which are not parallel to any plane of the viewing surface.

Consider that the direction of projection is given by the vector $[x_p\ y_p\ z_p]$ and suppose the image is to be projected on the xy plane. Consider any point on the three dimensional object, P whose co-ordinates are (x_1, y_1, z_1). As the projection will be in the two-dimensional form, let the projected form of the point in the two-dimensional plane be (x_2, y_2).

For a line passing through any point having the co-ordinate (x, y, z) in the direction of projection, the parametric equations can be written as:

$$x = x_1 + x_p.u \qquad (8.1)$$

$$y = y_1 + y_p.u \qquad (8.2)$$

and, $$z = z_1 + z_p.u \qquad (8.3)$$

As the value of z will be equal to 0 (because the projected image will appear on the xy plane), in equation (8.3), it can be written as:

$$0 = z_1 + z_p.u$$

Or, $$u = -z_1/z_p \qquad (8.4)$$

Substituting the parametric quantity, 'u' in the other two equations we obtain:

$$x = x_1 - (z_1/z_p).x_p \qquad (8.5)$$

$$y = y_1 - (z_1/z_p).y_p \qquad (8.6)$$

The projected co-ordinate (x_2, y_2) can be written as:

$$x_2 = x_1 - (x_p/z_p).z_1 \qquad (8.7)$$

$$y = y - (y/z_p).z_1 \qquad (8.8)$$

Rearranging these two equations we can write:

$$x_2 = x_1 + 0 - (x_p/z_p).z_1 \qquad (8.9)$$

$$y_2 = 0 + y_1 - (y_p/z_p).z_1 \qquad (8.10)$$

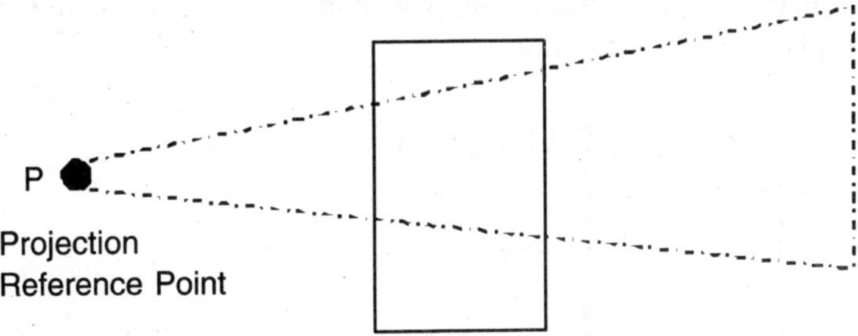

8.3 PERSPECTIVE PROJECTION

As already stated, perspective projection is the artistic way of projection and here the object appears smaller in size as we move away from it. Using this principle of projection we can indicate the depth of a figure. The part of the figure which is closer to the viewer will appear in larger size than the portion which is far away from the viewer.

In a perspective projection, the lines of projection are not parallel, instead the lines converge at a single point, which is called the centre of the projection. The projected image is developed at the intersections of this converging line with the viewing plane.

The centre of the projection signifies the position of the viewer's eye from where the object will be seen. The lines of the projection correspond to the paths of the light rays coming from the object to the viewer's eye. Thus the perspective projection has the closest resemblance to real world objects.

A view of perspective projection is shown in the figure below:

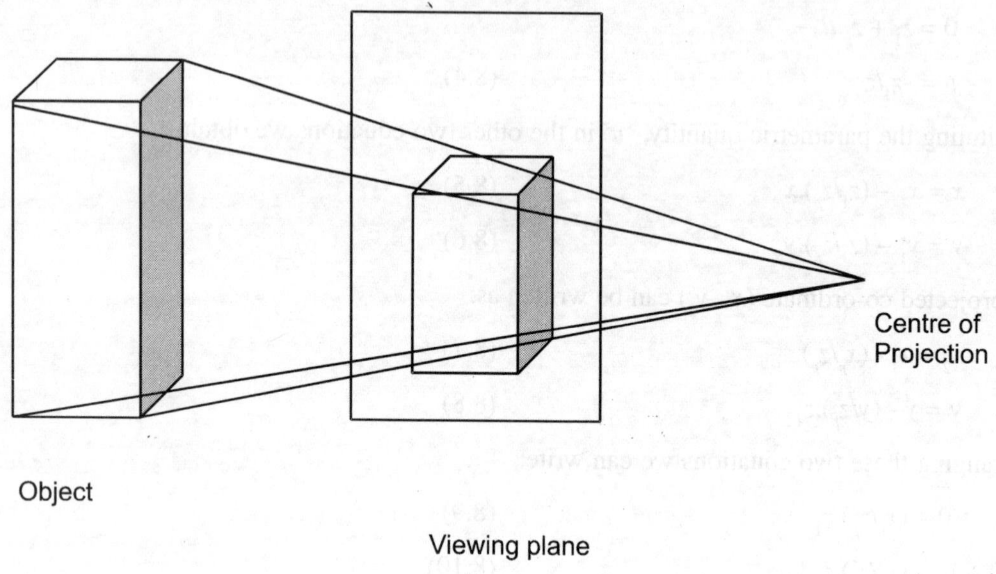

To develop the mathematical expressions, we draw a simplified diagram of this type of projection in a two-dimensional plane, as shown below.

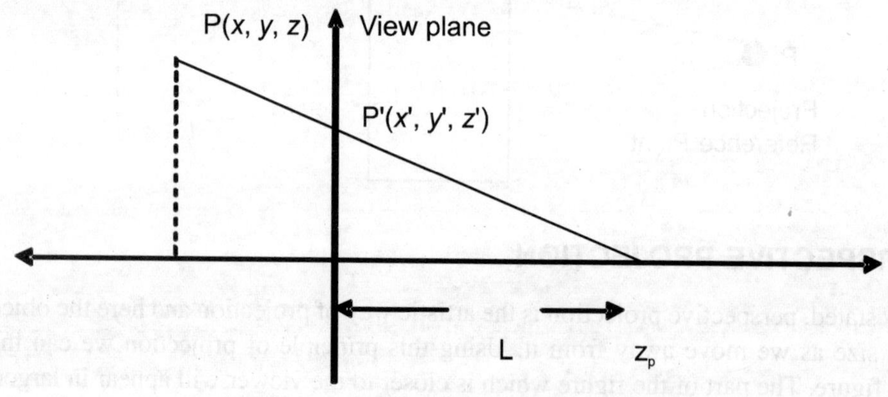

The equations in parametric form of co-ordinate positions on this perspective projection line can be developed as:

$x' = x - xu$ (8.11)

$y' = y - yu$ (8.12)

$z' = z - (z - z_p).u$ (8.13)

where (x', y', z') is the co-ordinate of any arbitrary point on the projection depth. The value of the parameter 'u' varies from 0 to 1. When u is equal to 0, the (x', y', z') co-ordinate will coincide with the co-ordinate (x, y, z). Similarly, when 'u' is equal to 1, the value of the co-ordinate (x', y', z') will be $(0, 0, z_p)$.

But, in the view plane z' will be equal to z'', so, from equation (8.12) we can write:

$u = (z'' - z)/(z_p - z)$

Substituting the value of u in equations (8.12) and (8.13) we obtain:

$$x' = x - xu$$

$$= x(1 - (z'' - z)/(z_p - z))$$

$$= x(z_p - z''/z_p - z)$$

But, $z_p - z'' = L$

= Distance of the view plane from the perspective reference point.

$x' = x.L/(z_p - z)$ (8.14)

These two equations can be written in a three-dimensional homogeneous co-ordinate representation as:

$$\begin{vmatrix} xh \\ yh \\ zh \\ h \end{vmatrix} = \begin{vmatrix} 1 & 0 & 0 & 0 \\ 0 & 1 & 0 & 0 \\ 0 & 0 & -z''/L & z''(zp/L) \\ 0 & 0 & -1/L & zp/L \end{vmatrix} \bullet \begin{vmatrix} X \\ y \\ z \\ 1 \end{vmatrix}$$

Where h is a factor, known as the homogeneous factor and which can be computed as:

$$h = (z_p - z)/L$$

The projection co-ordinates on the view plane can be calculated from the homogeneous factor as:

$x' = xh/h$ (8.15)

and $y' = yh/h$ (8.16)

From the expressions obtained we understand that as we are viewing along the z axis, the original z co-ordinate values will remain unchanged whereas the values for the other co-ordinate axes will be reduced depth wise.

8.4 SUMMARY

- When a 3D object is represented in a drawing in a two-dimensional plane – it is said to be its projection. Or in other words, we can say that a projection is a transformation, which maps 3D objects onto a 2D screen.
- In engineering drawing, when we represent any three-dimensional object, we draw three figures, namely plan, elevation and side view to represent all its possible dimensions.
- A better method used for viewing is the isometric view, which is basically drawn and can be understood by people who are not familiar with engineering drawings.
- The perspective types of drawing are used mainly by artists to develop the artiste views of three-dimensional objects and scenes. In one-point converging type, the eye of the artist is placed at a particular point and what is seen by the artist from that point is drawn.
- Parallel projections are mainly used by engineers and draftsman to draw the three dimensional object in engineering drawing form.
- In parallel projections, image points of the object are obtained by the intersection of the view plane and the project line drawn from the object points having a fixed direction.
- In a perspective projection, the lines of projection are not parallel. Instead they converge at a single point which is called the centre of the projection. The projected image is developed at the intersections of this converging line with the viewing plane.

8.5 REVIEW QUESTIONS

1. Write a procedure to obtain different parallel-projection views of a polyhedron by first applying a specified rotation.
2. Write a procedure to perform a one-point perspective projection of an object.
3. Write a procedure to perform a two-point perspective projection of an object.
4. Develop a routine to perform a three-point perspective projection of an object.
5. Write a routine to convert a perspective projection frustum to a regular parallelepiped.

CHAPTER 9

Multimedia

9.1 HISTORY OF MULTIMEDIA SYSTEMS

Newspapers were perhaps the first mass communication medium to employ multimedia – they used mostly text, graphics, and images.

In 1895, Gugliemo Marconi sent his first wireless radio transmission at Pontecchio, Italy. A few years later (in 1901) he detected radio waves beamed across the Atlantic. Initially invented for telegraph, radio is now a major medium for audio broadcasting.

Television was the new media of the 20th century. It brought about the video and has since changed the world of mass communications.

Some of the important events in relation to multimedia in Computing include:

- 1945 - Bush wrote about Memex
- 1967 - Negroponte formed the Architecture Machine Group at MIT
- 1969 - Nelson & Van Dam hypertext editor at Brown
- Birth of the Internet
- 1971 - Email
- 1976 - Architecture Machine Group proposal to DARPA: Multiple Media
- 1980 - Lippman & Mohl: Aspen Movie Map
- 1983 - Backer: Electronic Book
- 1985 - Negroponte, Wiesner: Opened MIT Media Lab
- 1989 - Tim Berners-Lee proposed the World Wide Web to CERN (European Council for Nuclear Research)

- 1990 - K. Hooper Woolsey, Apple Multimedia Lab, 100 people, educ.
- 1991 - Apple Multimedia Lab: Visual Almanac, Classroom MM Kiosk
- 1992 - the first M-bone audio multicast on the Net
- 1993 - U. Illinois National Center for Supercomputing Applications: NCSA Mosaic
- 1994 - Jim Clark and Marc Andreesen: Netscape
- 1995 - JAVA for platform-independent application development. Duke is the first applet.
- 1996 - Microsoft, Internet Explorer.

9.2 THE CONCEPT OF MULTIMEDIA

Multimedia can have many definitions. These include:

Multimedia means that computer information can be represented through audio, video, and animation in addition to traditional media (i.e., text, graphics drawings and images).

A good general definition is:

Multimedia is the field concerned with the computer-controlled integration of text, graphics, drawings, still and moving images (video), animation, audio, and any other media where every type of information can be represented, stored, transmitted and processed digitally.

A *multimedia application* is an application, which uses a collection of multiple media sources e.g. text, graphics, images, sound/audio, animation and/or video.

Hypermedia can be considered as one of the applications of multimedia.

9.3 HYPERTEXT AND HYPERMEDIA

Hypertext is text that contains links to other texts. The term was coined by Ted Nelson around 1965.

Hypertext is therefore usually non-linear (as indicated below).

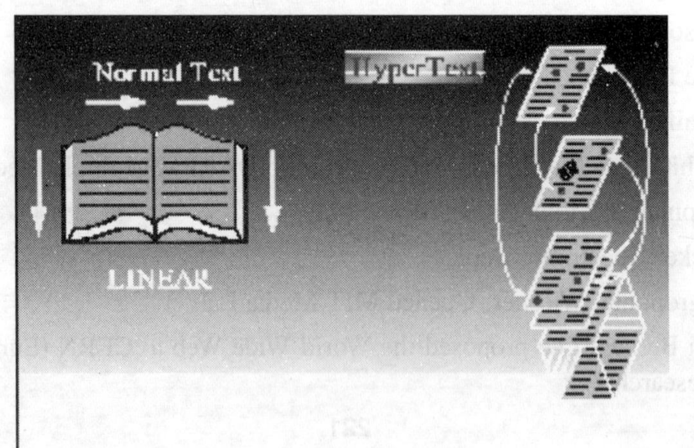

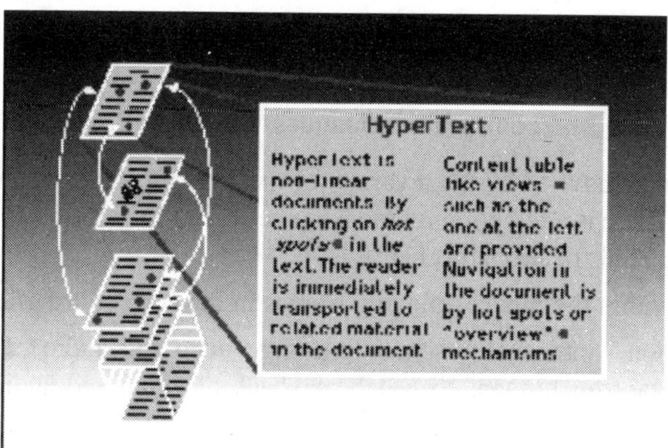

Definition of Hypertext

HyperMedia is not constrained to be text-based. It can include other media, e.g., graphics, images and especially the continuous media - sound and video. Apparently, Ted Nelson was also the first person to use this term.

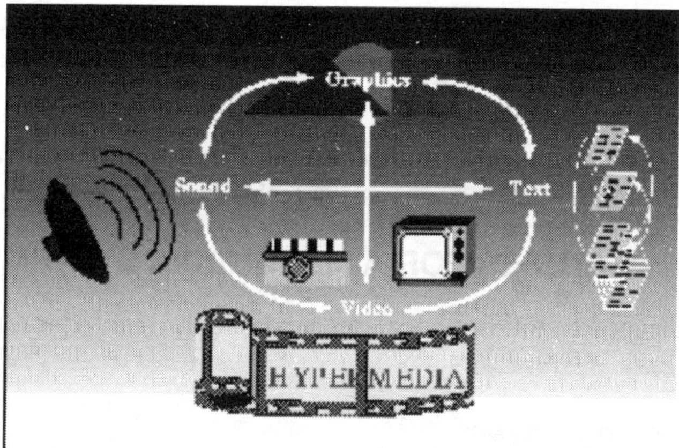

Definition of HyperMedia

The World Wide Web (WWW) is the best example of hypermedia applications.

9.4 CHARACTERISTICS OF A MULTIMEDIA SYSTEM

A multimedia system has four basic characteristics:

- Multimedia systems must be *computer controlled.*
- Multimedia systems are *integrated.*
- The information they handle must be represented *digitally.*
- The interface to the final presentation of media is usually *interactive.*

9.5 CHALLENGES FOR MULTIMEDIA SYSTEMS

Supporting multimedia applications over a computer network renders the application *distributed.* This will involve many special computing techniques, which are discussed later.

Multimedia systems may have to render a variety of media at the same instant - a distinction from normal applications. There is a temporal relationship between many forms of media (*e.g.* video and audio.) There are two kinds of problems here.

- Sequencing within the media - playing frames in the correct order/time frame in video.
- Synchronisation - inter-media scheduling (e.g. video and audio). Lip synchronisation is clearly important for humans to watch playback of video and audio and even animation and audio.

The key issues multimedia systems need to deal with here are:

- How to represent and store temporal information.
- How to strictly maintain the temporal relationships on play back/retrieval
- What processes are involved in the above.

Data have to be represented *digitally* so many initial sources of data need to be *digitised,* i.e. translated from an analog source to digital representation. This involves scanning (graphics, still images) and sampling (audio/video), although digital cameras now exist for direct scene to digital capture of images and video.

The data are large - several Mb for audio and video - therefore storage, transfer (bandwidth) and processing overheads are high. Data compression techniques are very common.

9.6 DESIRABLE FEATURES FOR A MULTIMEDIA SYSTEM

Given the above challenges the following features are desirable (if not a prerequisite) for a multimedia system:

Very High Processing Power

This is needed to deal with large data processing and real time delivery of media. Special hardware is common.

Multimedia Capable File System

These are needed to deliver real-time media, e.g. video/audio streaming. Special hardware/software needed e.g. RAID technology.

Data Representations/File Formats that Support Multimedia

Data representations/file formats should be easy to handle yet allow for compression/decompression in real-time.

Efficient and High I/O

Input and output to the file subsystem needs to be efficient and fast and needs to allow for real-time recording as well as playback of data, e.g. direct to disk recording systems.

Special Operating System

This is necessary to allow access to file system and process data efficiently and quickly. It needs to support direct transfers to disk, real-time scheduling, fast interrupt processing, I/O streaming etc.

Storage and Memory

Large storage units (of the order of 50 -100 Gb or more) and large memory (50 -100 Mb or more) are necessary. Large caches are also required and frequently of Level 2 and 3 hierarchy for efficient management.

Network Support

Client-server systems and distributed systems are common.

Software Tools

User friendly tools are needed to handle media, design and develop applications and deliver media.

9.7 COMPONENTS OF A MULTIMEDIA SYSTEM

The components (hardware and software) required for a multimedia system are as follows:

Capture devices

Video camera, video recorder, audio microphone, keyboards, mice, graphics tablets, 3D input devices, tactile sensors, VR devices, digitising/sampling hardware.

Storage devices

Hard disks, CD-ROMs, Jaz/Zip drives, DVDs, etc.

Communication networks

Ethernet, Token Ring, FDDI, ATM, Intranets, Internets.

Computer systems

Multimedia desktop machines, workstations, MPEG/VIDEO/DSP hardware.

Display devices

CD-quality speakers, HDTV, SVGA, Hi-Res monitors, colour printers, etc.

9.8 APPLICATIONS

Examples of multimedia applications include:

- World Wide Web
- Hypermedia courseware
- Video conferencing
- Video-on-demand
- Interactive TV
- Groupware
- Home shopping
- Games
- Virtual reality
- Digital video editing and production systems
- Multimedia Database systems

Trends in Multimedia

The current major application areas in multimedia include:

World Wide Web

Hypermedia systems - these embrace nearly all multimedia technologies and application areas. They are ever increasing in popularity.

MBone

Multicast backbone: Equivalent of conventional TV and radio on the Internet.

Enabling technologies

These are developing at a rapid rate to support the ever increasing needs of multimedia. Carrier, switching, protocol, application, coding/compression, database, processing and system integration technologies are at the forefront of enabling technologies.

9.9 MULTIMEDIA DATABASE SYSTEMS (MMDBS)

Searching for Multimedia Data

Multimedia database systems can be defined as collections of media elements like text, images, audio and video that can be stored, manipulated and retrieved. The definition implies that the database is not simply a repository for the media components but has an organized structure for efficient retrieval. The architecture however is much more complicated than for a normal text database. The main reason for this is that text that has been stored in a database may easily be retrieved by comparing it with other text strings and producing a resulting list of text strings that match the query strings. Things however become complicated when we try to apply the same technique for retrieving multimedia data, because we cannot directly compare one media element with another. A picture of a car can only be retrieved when it has previously been associated with the text term 'car'. This may lead to ambiguities as different persons may search for the same item using different keywords e.g. 'car', 'vehicle' and 'automobile' refer to the same object.

9.9.1 Storage and Retrieval of Multimedia Data

Textual annotations

The inclusion of a MMDB means that the database needs to be populated before it can be utilized. This is typically done off-line by a system administrator before it can handle on-line user queries. A multimedia database can be defined as a data structure which enables searching and retrieval of textual as well as non-textual media, such as images both audio and video. Traditionally, relational databases have functioned by using pattern matching algorithms in textual strings to find query results. Media components like images or audio essentially consist of raw data bytes with very little inherent meaning or useful information within them, which may be used for query matching.

Low-level features

In order to overcome the limitations due to textual annotations, feature extraction algorithms were developed which could extract low level features like colour, shape, loudness, pitch, etc. from media components in an unsupervised or semi-supervised manner. Apart from the fact that these required minimal human intervention and so were much faster than manual methods, they also overcame the limitations of subjective manual descriptions and so were much more reliable. They also overcame the limitation that queries need to be expressed in textual terms.

Semantic features

In the context of CBSR systems, humans tend to pose queries using the semantic nature of media contents. Systems based on low-level features would not be very effective in these situations because of the gap between how the media content is interpreted by the humans and the machines. To be truly effective a CBSR system would need to understand the semantic nature of media content and tune its retrieval engines according to the interpretation of these features.

Knowledge based interpretation

Extraction and representation of low-level features and semantic objects is not sufficient to appropriately handle user queries because the system still cannot interpret what the features or objects mean. Humans are most likely to post queries mentioning semantic concepts like people, trees, road, car and events like running, laughing, explosion, etc. For example, 'display a list of all images containing trees on the right side of a road'. The gap between recognizing a pattern of features and knowing what it means is bridged by feeding knowledge to the system. Based on this knowledge, the system should not only be able to interpret the meaning of the objects but also to learn and deduce about related matters. Usually this is done by the inclusion of a knowledge base into the architecture to accomplish these tasks. Only in very recent times have researchers begun looking into the task of automatic semantic interpretation. In most cases these involve use of statistical methods to analyze and deduce unknown parameters of a system, and to use a previously trained knowledge-base into interpreting them for resolving a query.

Queries and searching

Once the media objects have been analyzed and interpreted at various levels, the system would need to handle queries from the users and search for relevant information within the database. The queries can contain low level features pertaining to different features like colour, shape, location, etc. e.g 'display all images containing the colour red', or 'display all images showing the sun over the mountains', or 'display all audio files containing a laugh or scream'. Queries can also be based on physical file parameters, e.g. 'retrieve all GIF images', or 'retrieve all audio files having a duration of less than 30 seconds and created within the current month'. Lastly, queries may be based on semantic information which has been added manually during the database population phase, e.g. 'display all images of the third Indian prime minister', or 'display all songs sung together by father and son'.

9.10 GENERAL ARCHITECTURE OF A MMDBS

In a multimedia database how we retrieve media elements will be determined by how we store them in the first place. When a query is issued to a multimedia database, media objects are retrieved based on similarity matching between the query and the stored objects. However unlike a text database where the objects (alphanumeric data) themselves are compared with each other to determine a match, for a multimedia database, the media objects themselves are not compared directly but rather some characteristics of objects are compared to determine a match, e.g. dimensions or colour of an image. Thus, a multimedia database consists of two levels of abstractions – the physical level consisting of the media objects themselves and the logical level consisting of the features characterizing the media objects. In effect a multimedia database consists of two separate databases – a 'Media-DB' and a 'Feature-DB' with a link between them for associating the physical objects to their descriptions.

While the Media-DB may simply be a folder populated by media files, a feature-DB is to be designed based on the type of information it contains. If the features can be expressed as alphanumeric strings then a conventional relational database would suffice. Such information can be specified in two different ways. The first is by manually attaching the information with the media files. It has already been seen that this would be an ambiguous way of characterizing media however there is certain information that could be specified only in this way, which includes semantic descriptions of objects, e.g. name and date of birth of a person in a photograph. The second way of attaching textural information is by using software to read file attributes directly from file headers. These include image dimensions. Other feature information cannot be expressed simply as textual strings but needs to be expressed as mathematical vectors. Specialized algorithms are required to analyze the media content structure and extract the feature set as multidimensional vectors. For example, the colour content of an entire image may be expressed as a summation of a series of histograms calculated over all the pixels; the loudness of an audio clip may be indicated by the average energy levels calculated over all the audio samples; displacements of objects within a video clip may be described by motion vectors, etc. Storage of these values might not be possible using relational databases as in most cases these represent multi-dimensional vector quantities while relational tables only support atomic attributes. Hence, object-oriented (O-O) databases are preferred for storing multimedia content because O-O terminology supports properties or attributes of objects which are themselves complex objects, e.g. an audio track of a video clip. Another reason why O-O concepts are preferred relates to the dynamic time-varying properties of multimedia objects that may be conveniently represented by object methods, which is not possible in a relational framework.

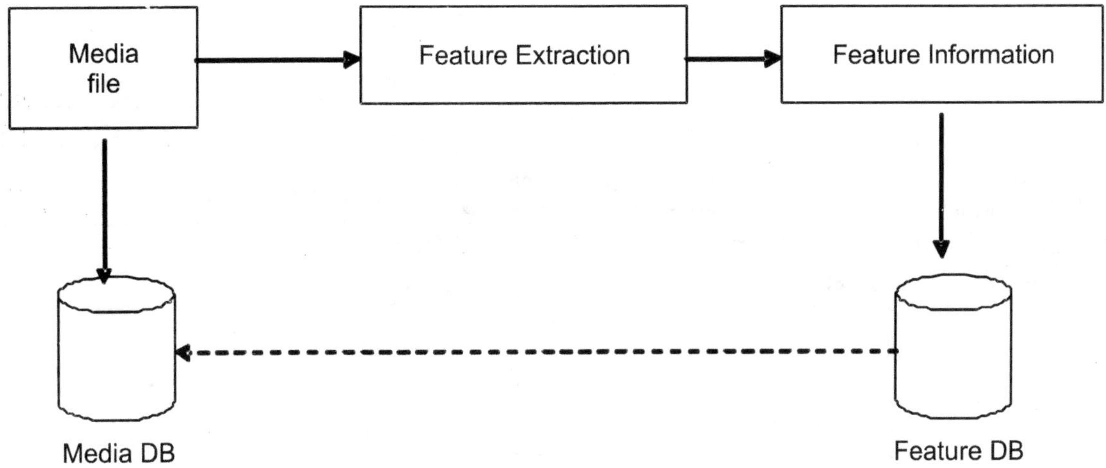

Fig. 9.1 : Basic Overview of an MMDBS

During a database querying session the user performs a query to retrieve the desired media object from the DB. Typically the user works in an iterative way. Queries may be direct or by example. Direct queries are typically based on keywords associated with the media components or properties like colour values which can be expressed through textual parameters. A better interaction is allowed by querying by example, where the user inserts a media object as a query and asks the system to return a specified number of similar objects. For example, to specify a query-by-sketch the user makes a freehand drawing of the dominant lines and edges in the desired image. The ideal query would be where both textual and non-textual modes could be combined to form a composite query object.

Based on the above ideas we can extend the model of a MMDBS to an object as shown in the figure below.

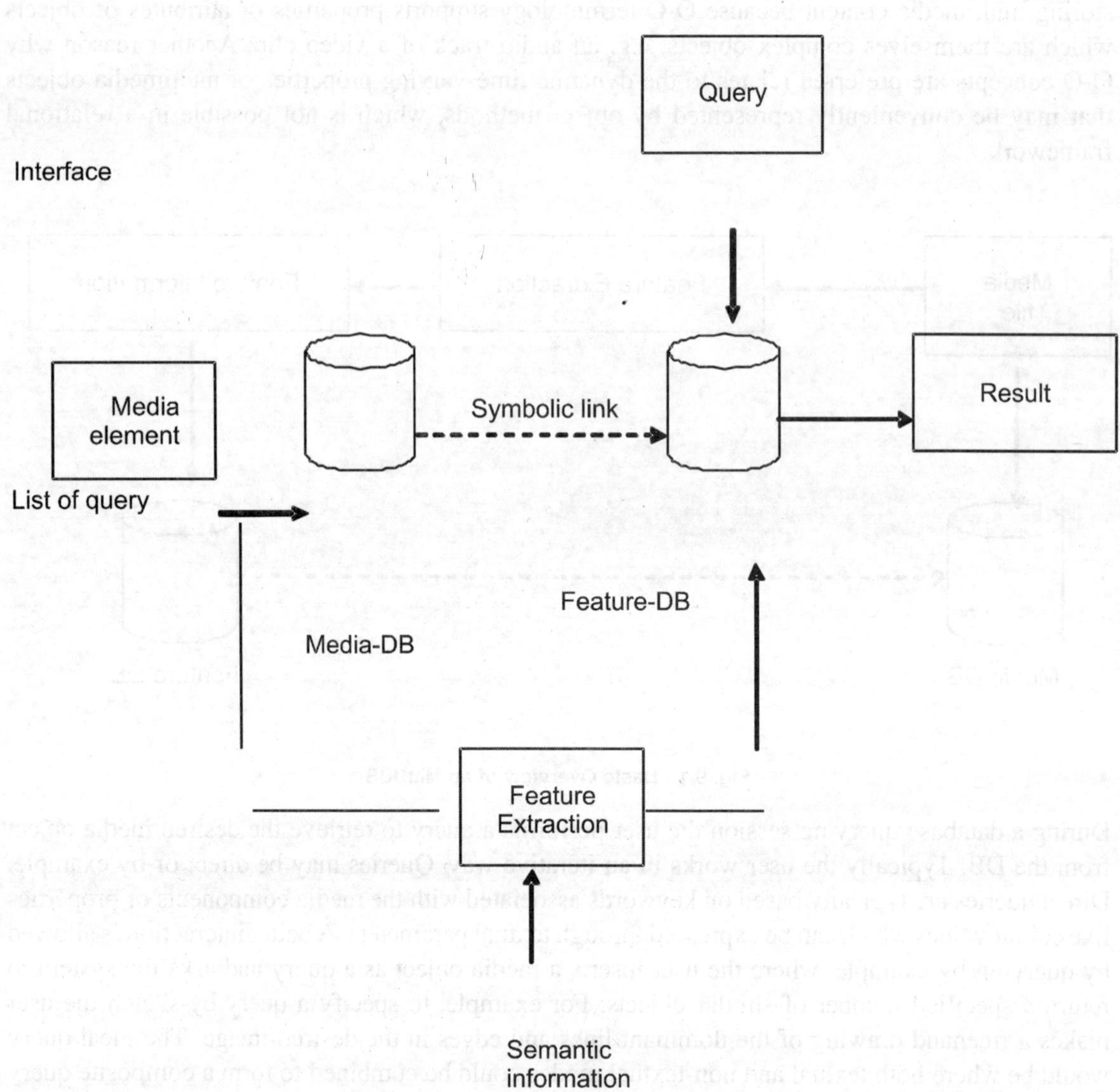

Fig. 9.2 : Extended View of an MMDBS

9.11 CHARACTERISTICS OF MULTIMEDIA DATABASES

Multimedia database systems should provide the functionality found in traditional database systems, i.e. query processing, concurrency control, recovery mechanisms, etc. In order to provide such functionality for multimedia data two problems appear fundamental; the first is the multimedia data modelling or how to structure and organize multimedia data, and the second is the nature of the interface provided to clients of a multimedia database system. Basically there are four general characteristics which differentiate multimedia database systems from other forms of data base systems.

Specialized Hardware

The production, consumption and processing of multimedia values often requires special hardware such as A/D and D/A converters, digital signal processors, CODECs, A/V capture cards. It should be possible to place some of these hardware elements under the control of the database. The reasons are: first, the devices are quite expensive and it would be more cost effective if they could be shared among different clients; second, placing the devices at the server may reduce data traffic significantly.

Scheduling Activities

Traditional database performs various scheduling activities. For instance read and write operations are scheduled by concurrency control sub-system and disk accesses are scheduled by storage sub-systems. However these schedule activities are hidden from the client. With multimedia databases certain forms of scheduling activities should be under the control of clients. The need for this arises from three observations: first, multimedia values often have long durations (e.g. in hours); second, it may not be possible to allow concurrent use of special purpose hardware, third, system resources like processing power bandwidth, etc. are limited. Thus, client requests can tie up resources for significant periods of time. Consequently concurrent access to multimedia data may require explicit scheduling by clients.

Client Interface

With conventional database systems the interaction between the client and the system resembles a call-by-value procedural interface. The client issues a request and then receives a reply. The requests and replies contain all the data exchanged by the client and the database system. With multimedia data this type of interaction is not suitable. For example, consider that a client requests an audio value. In many cases the client will not be interested in handling the reply stream sample-by-sample but rather simply directing the stream to a suitable sink, e.g. multimedia presentation. Again, certain audio-video media require significant lengths of time for transfer. The client does not want to stay blocked during the interval; rather he wants to initiate the transfer and then move on to other tasks. Thus, the client should be based on multiple asynchronous mode rather than issue-request/receive-reply protocol.

Quality Factors

Multimedia database systems introduce a new concept called the quality of result to a query. This is due to the necessity of approximate retrieval for multimedia data. This is especially important in the context of the queries in imprecise data collections and assumes an even more important role when the queries are also imprecise. Quality was never an issue in database engines developed for OLTP (On-Line Transaction Processing) applications. They simply returned an answer that satisfied the conditionals in the query or returned a null. Hence, the quality dimension was completely ignored. Given the prevalence of the imprecise nature of both data and queries in multimedia databases, quality takes on a greater role than speed given that an incorrect response however fast it is, will be of little value.

9.12 DISTRIBUTED MULTIMEDIA APPLICATIONS

Distributed computing refers to a computing paradigm in which the various computing tasks being carried out are distributed to multiple geographically dispersed processors. Similar to client-server computing, distributed computing relies heavily on data networks for communication between distributed resources. One of the main motivations in moving from single-site computing to distributed computing is to avoid the possibility of a single failure which would bring the entire system to a halt. In true distribution systems not only the hardware but the software also remains dispersed. For example a database application may be subdivided into geographical dispersed components, but this should be transparent to the user to whom it should seem like a single entity.

The requirements for distribution of multimedia objects are those of traditional data processing objects plus some new ones. The reasons for distribution have been: moving and sharing, i.e. moving data to the point of use and sharing of data and resources. With multimedia there is a new reason for distribution and interaction. A geographically dispersed group of people can interact. An enterprise might have a corporate wide multimedia application. A group at one location is responsible for the creation of new objects as well as maintenance of existing objects, clips, graphics, etc., groups at other locations must incorporate these objects into presentations – courses, product descriptions, reference documents, etc.

For example an architectural blueprint can be worked upon by different groups of construction engineers, dispersed geographically. A copy of the blueprint is displayed on each participant's workstation. Each person can edit his/her copy and these changes are viewed by all the others. The supervisor can then choose which changes will become part of the new design.

Some other examples of distributed multimedia applications are:

- Companies can communicate product information to customers in the format and location they prefer.
- In advertising, creative designers can share ideas for video commercials with colleagues and customers through audio/video enhanced multimedia documents.
- Medical professionals can collaborate by sharing diagnostic images or video-taped procedures across the world.
- Education, through distance learning saves on travel costs and increases productivity by allowing office workers to gain immediate access to material rather than wait for scheduled classes.

9.12.1 Video-on-Demand (VoD)

Video on Demand (VoD) covers a range of application whereby users can request access to video servers of still and moving pictures on an individual basis. The definition does not specify where the video server should be located, so VoD can be a service offered within an organization as well as a public service. The definition also does not specify the level of interaction that the users are expected to perform with the video server. VoD usually does not imply any special kind of video. Sometimes specific applications like distribution of movies is explicitly called Movie on Demand (MoD). Another point in the definition says that the users may request at any time, which does not imply that the users would be able to see the video at any time. True VoD are very demanding in terms of processing power, access to storage media and bandwidth requirements. Thus, there may be several requests of identical material shifted by seconds or minutes. To reduce resource requirements a concept called Near Video-on-Demand (N-VoD) groups identical requests and serves them at regular intervals.

9.12.2 Movie-on-Demand (MoD)

Movie-on-Demand (MoD) is a public VoD service where the accessed object is a stored movie. The objective of the MoD is to replace and improve on two earlier services by combining them into one:

- Pay-Per-View (PPV) by offering a much wider choice of movies.
- Videotape rental service by eliminating the fetch/return cycle and manipulation of physical tapes.

However one drawback of MoD systems might be a lack of interaction options. Earlier systems offered either no interaction or coarse controls like pause and play. Ideally all VCR like functions should be available during the movie delivery, called a fully interactive MoD. A quality equivalent to VHS videocassette requires a transmission bit rate of the order of 1.5 Mbps. Existing implementations of the MPEG 2 standard operate at 6 Mbps with a quality slightly superior to a broadcast TV. A quality lower than PAL/NTSC may not be acceptable to customers. Available connection options include satellite transmission, CATV cables, copper telephone wires, optical fibres and microwave transmission. A technology called ADSL (Asymmetric Digital Subscriber Loop) can support digital transmission over the regular two-wire copper telephone loop. It supports two VCR quality channels, i.e. a bit rate of about 3 Mbps over 3-5 kms. An associated problem is to interpret the request from the users of what they actually want when it cannot be specified explicitly as a movie name. This is an area of active research referred to as Content Based Information Retrieval (CBIR) or Content Based Storage and Retrieval (CBSR) or Multimedia Database (MMDB).

9.12.3 Interactive Television (ITV)

Interactive Television (ITV) is another class of services offered to residential customers. The principle is to give access from home to a range of servers supporting a variety of interactive services. The information is intended to be displayed on regular TV sets but is not necessarily of motion video type: it may be text, graphics, images or animation. ITV services include information servers for providing information like TV guides, transport service schedules, sport scores or may be financially/corporate/business oriented. Additionally it may also include transaction services like teleshopping, telebanking, etc as well as electronic mail and computer games. The services may be free of cost or pay per view type.

9.12.4 Voice Over IP (VoIP)

Voice Over IP (VoIP) applications have originated from the concept of Internet telephony which makes it possible to have a telephone conversion over the Internet or dedicated network where the voice data is carried via IP packets instead of voice transmission lines. This incorporates packet switching instead of circuit switching for conventional telephone lines. Its advantages include lower cost per call and lower infrastructural costs. The protocols used to carry voice data over IP networks are called VoIP protocols. One of the most widely used protocols is the H.323 which is an ITU-T recommendation. It is currently implemented in Microsoft NetMeeting and Voxilla (for Linux). VoIP is used by large companies to eliminate call charges between their offices by using their data network to carry inter-office calls.

9.13 REAL TIME PROTOCOLS

The most dominant characteristic of multimedia applications is to preserve the temporal requirement at presentation time. Therefore multimedia data are handled in a Real-time Environment (RTE), i.e. its processing is scheduled according to the inherent timing requirements of multimedia data. On a multimedia computer RTE deals with all data that have timing relationships and requirements, e.g. a video frame is passed from the RTE to the display.

9.13.1 Real-time Transport Protocol (RTP)

Real-time Transport Protocol (RTP) is a protocol providing network transport functions suitable for applications transmitting real time data such as audio, video and animation. It was developed by the Audio Video Transport Working Group of the IETF and published in 1996. RTP defines a standardized packet format for delivering audio and video over the Internet in real time. It was originally designed as a multicast protocol (multicast is the delivery of information to multiple destinations simultaneously), but has since been applied in many unicast (point to point delivery) applications. It can be used for media-on–demand, as well as interactive services such as Internet telephony. RTP consists of a data part and a control part. The latter is called RTCP (Real Time Control Protocol).The data part of RTP is thin protocol providing support for application with real-time properties such as continuous media (e.g. audio and video), including timing reconstruction, loss detection, security and content identification. RTCP provides supports for real time conferencing of groups of any size within an Internet. This support includes source identification and support for gateways like audio and video bridges as well as multicast–to-unicast translators. It offers quality service feedback from receivers to the multicast group as well as support for synchronization of different media streams. RTP does not guarantee quality for real-time services, nor does it guarantee delivery or prevent out-of-order delivery but assumes that the underlying network is reliable and delivers packets in sequence. Efforts are being made to make RTP transport independent so that it can be used over other transport protocols like IPX. Because of its real time delivery properties, RTP is used extensively for Voice-over-IP (VoIP) applications.

9.13.2 Resource ReserVation Protocol (RSVP)

Resource Reservation Protocol (RSVP) is a protocol that transfers reservations and keeps a state at the intermediate nodes. It is a part of a larger effort to handle Qos (Quality of service) issues. The RSVP protocol is used by a host to request specific qualities of service from the network for particular application data streams or flows. RSVP requests will generally result in resources being reserved in each node along the data path. It does not have a data transfer component. RSVP messages are sent as IP datagrams and the router keeps a 'soft copy' of the resource, which is refreshed by periodic reservation messages. A reservation specifies the amount of resources to be reserved for all or some subset of the packets in a particular session. In the absence of the refresh messages the routers delete the reservation after a certain timeout.

9.13.3 Real Time Streaming Protocol (RTSP)

Real Time streaming Protocol (RTSP) is a client server multimedia presentation control protocol designed to address the needs for efficient delivery of streamed multimedia over IP networks. Jointly developed by Real Networks, Netscape communication and Columbia University, it was published as a standard in 1998, by the IETF (Internet Engineering Task Force). Streaming of data involves a number of components. Multimedia content must be stored in specific file formats that support streaming like Apple QuickTime or Microsoft Active Streaming Format (ASF), usually on a dedicated server. The servers in turn stream the contents using protocols like RTSP to the clients. For the client the streamed content is played back using compatible players like Apple's QuickTime Movie Player or RealNetwork's RealPlayer. RTSP and H.323, a teleconferencing framework standardized by ITU (International Telecommunications Union) have similar functionalities. While H.323 is used for setting up moderately sized A/V conferences, RTSP is useful for large scale broadcasts. RTSP provides VCR–like control functionalities like pause, fast forward, reverse, which are not supported by H.323. Both H.323 and RTSP use RTP as their standard means of actually delivering multimedia data. (RTCP is a part of RTP and helps in management of issues like lip synchronization and quality of service).

9.14 SUMMARY

- *Multimedia* means that computer information can be represented through audio, video and animation in addition to traditional media (i.e., text, graphics drawings and images).
- *Multimedia* is the field concerned with the computer-controlled integration of text, graphics, drawings, still and moving images (video), animation, audio, and any other media where every type of information can be represented, stored, transmitted and processed digitally.
- *Hypermedia* is not constrained to be text-based. It can include other media, e.g., graphics, images and especially the continuous media - sound and video. Apparently, Ted Nelson was the first to use this term.
- Supporting multimedia applications over a computer network renders the application *distributed*. This involves many special computing techniques.
- Multimedia systems may have to render a variety of media at the same instant - a distinction from normal applications. There is a temporal relationship between many forms of media, e.g. video and audio.

- Multimedia database systems can be defined as collections of media elements like text, images, audio and video that can be stored, manipulated and retrieved. The definition implies that the database would not simply be a repository for the media components but must have an organized structure for efficient retrieval.
- The architecture however is much more complicated than for a normal text database. The main reason for this is that text that has been stored in a database may easily be retrieved by comparing it with other text strings and producing a resulting list of text strings that match the query strings.
- Things however become complicated when we try to apply the same technique for retrieving multimedia data, because we cannot directly compare one media element with another.
- Multimedia database systems should provide the functionality found in traditional database systems, i.e. query processing, concurrency control, recovery mechanisms, etc.
- Distributed computing refers to a computing paradigm in which the various computing tasks being carried out are distributed to multiple geographically dispersed processors. Similar to client-server computing, distributed computing relies heavily on data networks for communication between distributed resources.

9.15 REVIEW QUESTIONS

1. Discuss the data storage and retrieval process for multimedia applications.
2. Why is data compression needed for multimedia?
3. What is computer audio? Give a few examples to explain its use in multimedia applications.
4. What is meant by the terms multimedia and hypermedia? Distinguish between these two concepts.

CHAPTER 10

Animation

10.1 INTRODUCTION

'Animate' means 'to give life to'. Animations are created from a sequence of still images. Each image is slightly changed from the previous one with respect to one or more objects in the image. The images are then displayed rapidly in succession so that the eye perceives continuous motion due to persistence of vision, which is discussed in detail later in this chapter. For example, a sequence of images, of a bird with its wings in slightly different positions, when displayed rapidly one after another, gives the illusion that the bird is flapping its wings. In this respect animation uses the same principles as motion video. However animation generally deals with graphics drawn by individuals, either by hand or by using software, in contrast to motion video, which deals with actual photographs of real world objects taken through a camera. Animation can also involve a model, which is changed by small amounts at a time and then repeatedly photographed. This type of animation is referred to as stop motion animation. Traditionally animation sequences are created by animators who draw those frames where major changes take place within the sequence, called key-frames, while the frames in between the key-frames are drawn by software, a process called tweening. Animation file formats like animated-GIF and Flash-SWF allow us to view animations on a computer.

10.2 USES OF ANIMATION

Since animation involves the movements of still pictures, something that does not seem to occur naturally, it increases the interest of the viewer and can create a lasting impression. By adding the appearance of movement to an inanimate object, the resulting image stimulates emotions and builds excitement. Animation is therefore widely used in the entertainment industry. It is also the heart of most computer games, making the graphics more realistic, exciting or engaging.

Nowadays animation is increasingly used in education as it provides an excellent way to explain dynamic processes which cannot easily be captured on video, e.g. movement of the pistons of an IC engine, movement of sub-atomic particles, movement of planetary bodies, etc. A major use of animation in industrial and scientific applications is to visualize simulation of scientific phenomena, e.g. flight simulations for aircraft and guided missiles, fluid-flow simulations for studying viscous resistance, chemical simulations for studying positions and orientations of atoms in chemical reactions to mention only a few.

10.2.1 Key Frames and Tweening

In traditional animation lead animators draw the most important frames or key frames, which define the frames where the course of action changes. The intermediate frames between the key frames are drawn by the assistant animators. This process is called Tweening, derived from the word 'in-between'. For example, to depict the motion of the rectangle moving from the lower left corner to the upper right corner of the frame, the initial and final positions provide the key frames, while the middle frames are the intermediate frames.

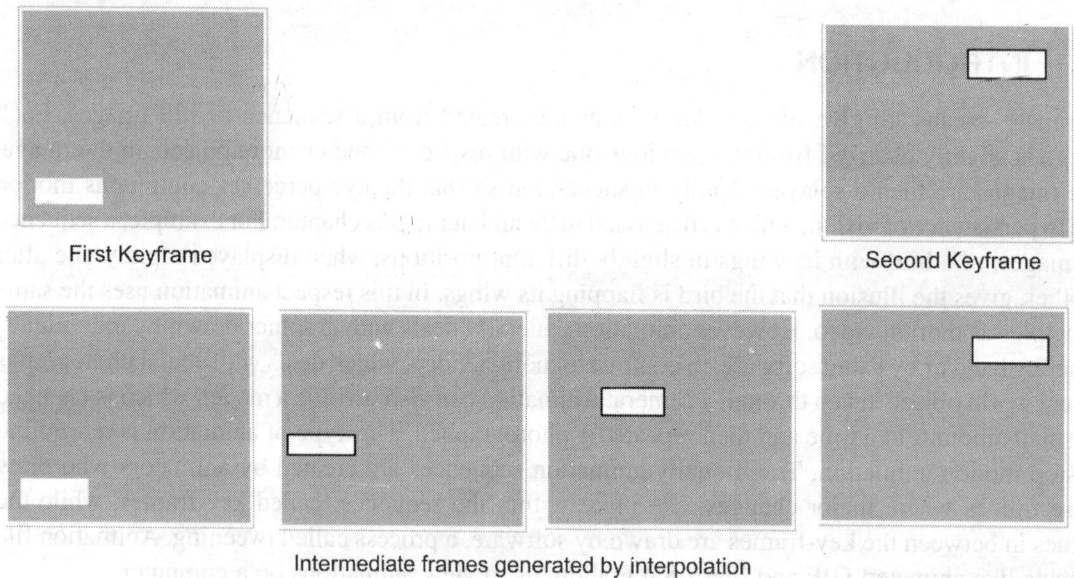

Intermediate frames generated by interpolation (tweening)

10.3 TYPES OF ANIMATION

10.3.1 Cell Animation

Cell animation is a term from traditional animation. Cel comes from the word celluloid the material that made up early motion picture film, and refers to the transparent piece of film that is used in hand-drawn animation. Animation cels are generally layered, one on top of the other, to produce a single animation frame. Layering enables the animator to isolate and redraw only the parts of the image that change between successive frames. A frame consists of the background cel and the overlying cels and is like a snapshot of the action at one instant of time. To depict movement only a portion, typically the foreground cel, can be changed between frames without changing the background cel.

10.3.2 Path Animation

With the advent of computers for creating animation, we have another class of animation that differs from the traditional cel-based animation. Here the animation does not exist as a collection of frames but rather as mathematical entities, called vectors, stored by the animation program. It involves an image or a collection of images together, called a sprite, that moves as an independent object, like a flying bird, a rotating planet, a bouncing ball or a spinning logo. The sprite moves along a motion path, typically curved, called a spline. The vectors define how the movement of the sprite takes place, i.e. they represent a spline as a set of equations. The spline passes through a series of anchor points which the user can control to change the shape of the curve. During playback of the animation, vectors are used to generate the curved path on the screen and the sprite is made to move along the path, using other parameters like speed and duration to control its motion. Path animation is also therefore known as sprite animation. Usually path animation takes up less disk space to store compared to cel animation because of the compact vector representations, however they are dependent on a particular software program for execution, which can interpret the mathematical relations defining the movement and render the images on screen.

10.3.3 2D vs 3D Animation

2D animation programs do not take into consideration the depth of objects and typically depict animated objects on flat surfaces. These are drawn taking into account two coordinate axes along the x and y directions. 3D animation monitors objects by considering space coordinates and usually involves modelling, rendering and adding surface properties, lighting and camera motions. These are usually more complex than 2D animations and have to take into account three axes along the x, y and z directions to define locations of objects in space.

10.3.4 Computer Assisted Animation

Computer assisted animation is also based on the key frame concept. The great advantage of computer assisted animation is that in-between frames are created by the animation program itself. Computer animation software typically simulates the process of traditional cel based animation, by placing the animated object on a timeline to depict the flow of time. A playback head moves across the timeline to display each of the frames one after the other. You create a key frame by picking a point on the timeline and then choosing a value for a time-varying parameter such as position or colour at this point of time. The computer generates or tweens intermediate frame between key frames interpolating the values for the parameters. Because key frames mark transitions between properties it is important to make these transitions appear smooth. Linear motion paths contain sharp angle bends at the key frames. Many programs will automatically smoothen the sharp corners for you. To ensure smooth transitions between frames, each frame must be carefully aligned or registered with other frames. A registration point is a point on each cel that lines up with the same point on every other cel. Computer animation programs usually have grid and alignment commands to help animators to correctly register drawings.

It is to be noted that a computer cannot create animation all by itself. The key frames have to be drawn by human artists using appropriate software, and placed on the timeline at specific locations. Once the key frames are in place, the computer can interpolate between successive key frames to produce a smooth transition between one key frame and the next. Hence the computer essentially assists in the tweening process, although it is true that key frame generation might also be faster and more accurate using software.

10.4 SOME TECHNIQUES OF ANIMATION

10.4.1 Onion Skinning

Onion Skinning is a technique of drawing borrowed from traditional cel animation that helps the animator create the illusion of smooth motion rather than working on each frame in isolation, animators lay these transparent cels one on top of the other. This enables them to see the previous and following frames while they are drawing the current frame. Onion skinning is an easy way to complete a sequence of frames at a glance and to see how each frame flows into the frames before and after.

10.4.2 Motion Cycling

Human and animal motion such as walking, running and flying, is mainly a repetitive action that is best represented by a cycle. A walk cycle requires from 8 to 12 frames. The sequence usually falls into two halves. The first half begins at an extreme when the feet are farthest apart, with the back toe and front heel touching the ground. In the remainder of the first half the legs trade position. So do the arms – but when the left leg is forward, the right arm is forward, and vice versa. The second half of the cycle is simply a variation of the first half, but with arms and legs reversed. The finished walking character can be used as a moving cel, i.e. a sprite.

10.4.3 Masking

Artists often use cutouts of a red plastic called rubylith to protect parts of their work from the application of paint. A mask in a computer program is in a sense a model of the plastic masks – it protects parts of a frame from effects of other editing tools. This technique can be used to make an animated object move "behind" the protected area.

10.4.4 Adding Sound

Sound is an important enhancement to moving images. Background music can evoke emotions. Sounds that arise from the actions being viewed can clarify what is happening and create an effect of realism.

10.4.5 Flip-book Animation

A flip book is a book with a series of pictures varying gradually from one page to the next, so that when the pages are turned rapidly, the pictures appear to animate, simulating motion or some other change. Flip books are often illustrated books for children, but may also be geared towards adults and employ a series of photographs. Flip books are not always separate books, but may appear as an added feature in ordinary books or magazines, often in the page corners. Flip books are essentially a primitive form of animation.

10.4.6 Rotoscoping and Bluescreening

Rotoscoping was an early animation technique which enabled animators and video editors to trace the contour of objects on each frame of an animation and video sequence to create a silhouette called a matte. Rotoscoping has been used as a tool for special effects in action movies. Nowadays this technique has largely been superseded by the bluescreen technique, however it can still be used in special cases where bluescreening will not be accurate enough. Bluescreening is a technique for shooting live action against an even coloured blue background and then replacing the background by another image. This is nowadays extensively used as chroma-keying using digital editing tools whereby the background colour is selected by a selection tool and replaced by pasting over with some other background. Blue is normally used for people because human skin has very little blue colour in it. Sometimes when the scene itself contains objects with a blue colour, other colours like green and orange can be used instead.

10.4.7 Colour Cycling

Colour cycling allows you to change the colour of objects by cycling through a range of colours. The software provides smooth colour transitions from one colour to another. The sequence of colours is usually chosen by mentioning a colour model and specifying in what order and how fast the colours should change. In an RGB colour wheel this can be done by specifying an initial colour, a clockwise or anti-clockwise direction for changing colours and the total time duration for a complete rotation over the wheel.

10.4.8 Morphing

Morphing is the process of smoothly interpolating between two different images. When played back it appears that the first image gradually and seamlessly changes into the second image. Examples include an individual's face gradually transforming into the face of another person or even an animal. In the early days of films a morph would be achieved by cross-fading techniques however nowadays this is achieved more realistically using computer software.

10.5 ANIMATION ON THE WEB

The World Wide Web supports animated files included in Web pages. The biggest obstacles in the use of animations on the Web are bandwidth limitations, the differences in platforms and browser support. Typically Web based animations involve computer files that must be completely downloaded to the client machines before playback. This can take a long time depending on the file size, which is usually large as it contains a series of images. A way around this problem is streaming, which is the capability of specially formatted animation files to begin playback before the entire file has been completely downloaded. As the animation plays the rest of the file is downloaded in the background. Another problem with Web animation is that once the animation has been delivered to the user, the user must have the proper helper application or plug-in to display the animation. Several formats exist today like GIF animation, based on extensions to GIF specifications, QuickTime animation, based on QuickTime movie format, Java animation based on Java programming language, shockwave animation based on Macromedia Director/Flash file format, etc.

The Shockwave Format

Macromedia Director Macromedia's Shockwave technology for Director was one of the first animation plug-ins for browsers. Shockwave enables Director Authors to publish interactive, multimedia content on the Web. Director is a popular 2D animation and interactive multimedia authoring tool, which is used in CD-ROM publishing, broadcast video and film, interactive advertisements, kiosks, presentations, games courseware, etc. To create Shockwave animations for the Web you will need the Director authoring program for Windows. Shockwave animations created on either Windows Macromedia Flash animation sequences can be saved in the Shockwave format which uses the SWF extension and played back on a Shockwave player. The Shockwave player can either be a stand alone player program or integrated into the browser as a plug-in.

Client-Pull Animation

In Client-Pull animation an HTML page gives the browser instructions to request and load another document automatically which contains the next frame of the animation. This feature is like a slideshow – Web pages are displayed one after the other with a specified time delay in between.

Server-Push Animation

Server-Push animation requires a CGI (Common Gateway Interface) script that tells the server when to automatically serve a new document or image.

10.6 3D ANIMATION

Creation of 3D animation involves a number of steps:

1. Modelling
2. Surface texture
3. Lighting camera
4. Animating
5. Rendering

Modelling involves creation of 3D objects from 2D shapes. Two of the most common methods are lofting and lathing. Lofting is a process of changing a 2D shape into a 3D object by moving the shape along a specific direction. For example, a circle may be moved perpendicular to its plane to create a cylinder. Lathing involves rotation of a 2D shape about an axis to create a 3D object. For example, a circle may be rotated about an axis passing through its centre to create a sphere.

Surface texture involves imparting realistic appearances to the 3D models by applying textures over the object surface, e.g. a wood texture applied to a flat surface to show a table.

Lighting involves placing the lights in the scene by specifying their intensities, direction and colour. The directions of shadows are also considered. Camera placements determine how the scene should look. Movement of the camera can be used to produce zooming and panning effects.

Animating the objects involves creation of key-frames and tweening to produce intermediate frames.

Rendering produces the final output file and needs specifications of the file type, frame size, frame rate, etc.

10.7 CAMERA

10.7.1 Camera Location and COI

When you create a computer rendering of a three-dimensional scene, you first define the point of view from which the scene is to be observed. A point of view consists of two factors: where you are standing and what you are looking at. If you stand in front of a house and look at the chimney, you see one image however if you stand behind the house and look at the same chimney you see a different image. This example is an illustration of changing the 'where you are standing' factor while keeping the 'what you are looking at' factor the same. Now reverse the situation and keep the 'where are you standing' factor constant, but change the 'what you are looking at' factor. In the first instant you might stand in front of the house and look at the chimney and in the second instance you might stand at the same spot but look at the window instead. In computer graphics the point of view is called the camera. The first factor – where you are standing – is called the camera location. The second factor – what you are looking at – is called the COI (centre of interest).

10.7.2 Camera Movements

There are a number of standard camera movements in 3D animation scenarios. Keeping the camera location constant and moving the COI is called a pan. If you stand in one spot and turn your head to the left or to the right, it is equivalent to a pan. The opposite of a pan is called an orbit which keeps the centre of interest stationary while moving the camera location.

Another standard camera move is called a track, which involves changing the camera location and the centre of interest at the same time, as a unit, e.g. moving the camera parallel to an object while looking towards the object.

If both the camera location and the centre of interest are moved, in or out, the movement is called a dolly, e.g. moving the camera perpendicular to an object while looking towards the object. In most cases camera movements are specified in terms of xyz triplets, however an alternative way to define movements is to use the rotational approach. Here the moves are specified in terms of rotations of the camera. A pan is a rotation of the camera about an origin located at the camera location. An orbit is a rotation of the camera about an origin located at the centre of interest. Pitch is the rotation of the camera around the x-axis, yaw is the rotation of the camera around the y-axis, and roll is a rotation around the z axis. Zooming magnifies the image and makes objects appear closer or farther away.

10.7.3 Zones of Vision

The human field of view can be thought of as a cone shaped area called the cone of vision. Objects that lie within the cone of vision are visible, objects that lie outside the cone are not visible. In computer graphics the cone of vision becomes a pyramid of vision in order to conform to the rectangular shape of the computer monitor. The shape of the pyramid is the angle from top to bottom of the pyramid, referred to as the field-of-view angle or FOV measured in angles. When you view a scene some objects appear in focus and some appear out of focus. Some rendering programs reproduce this effect through a parameter called depth of field. Depth of field is specified by two numbers: the first represents the nearest distance at which objects will be in focus, and the second represents the farthest distance at which they will be in focus.

10.8 CREATING & RENDERING ANIMATION

Animation involves the production of a series of still images that when played back in quick succession, appear as continuously moving. This illusion is produced by a physiological characteristic of our eyes known as persistence of vision. When the human eyes are stimulated, for example by a still image, the impression of the image is left on the retina for a small interval of time even after the stimulus is removed. As a sequence of still images or frames plays back, each eye retains the impression for each frame for a brief moment and this fills in the minute gap between the frame just past and the frame yet to come. As a result adjacent frames seem to flow together smoothly. If the time between frames is too long, the afterimage does not persist long enough to fill in the gap between the frames and you see a jerky playback of the individual images. In film a playback rate of twenty-four frames per second works well. In video the standard rate of playback is thirty frames per second. Thus, for producing a one-hour animation on video 108000 frames would be required.

10.9 RENDERING ALGORITHMS

10.9.1 Ray Casting Algorithm

The word algorithm means a well-thought-out, logical procedure for doing something. A rendering algorithm therefore is the procedure that a particular program uses to calculate a picture. Most rendering algorithms in software packages use a general approach called scan-line rendering. Here the program looks at each pixel one after the other and calculates the colour that pixel should be rendered in. It allows you to see the pixels filling in one by one and line by line. To determine what colour a given pixel should be, one common approach is a process called ray casting.

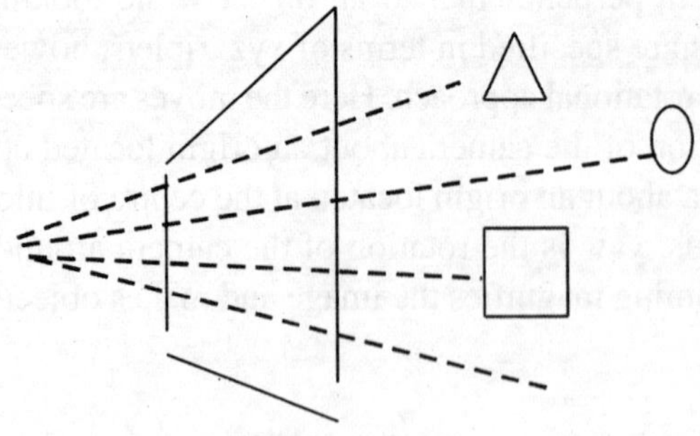

10.9.2 Shading Algorithm

To actually calculate the colour at a point, another algorithm called a shading algorithm is used to calculate the shading of a surface. One simplifying assumption made by a shading algorithm is that any flat surface is the same colour at every point on the surface. Rendering each flat surface with only one colour gives objects a faceted look and therefore is called faceted shading. Faceted shading results in very fast renderings and so appears in many 3D packages. In order to calculate the colour of a given surface any shading algorithm must know whether the surface faces towards or away from light. Accordingly the surface will appear lighter or darker. In order to determine the direction in which the surface faces, computer graphics programs employ the surface normal. A surface normal is a line perpendicular to a surface at a given point on that surface and is represented by an arrow coming off the surface. For a flat surface a single surface normal suffices to indicate the orientation of the entire surface. Using the surface normal a rendering program can calculate the exact angle at which a surface is oriented towards the light. The surfaces which directly face the light appear lighter and those facing away from the light are darker.

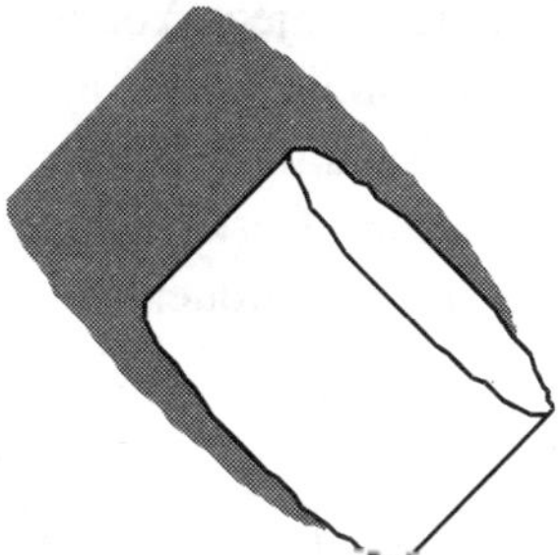

10.9.3 Z-buffer Algorithm

In general most scenes consist of several objects, in which case the rendering algorithm also needs to decide which objects should be rendered in front of other objects. For rendering of scenes with multiple objects, one approach is to sort all the objects by depth so that the rendering program can start rendering those objects that are farthest away. Once rendered each new object covers up distant objects that have already been rendered. This procedure resembles the way a painter might complete the background of a scene before painting objects in the foreground and as such it is called the painter's algorithm. To presort objects by depth can be very time-consuming particularly with a scene involving a large number of objects because each polygon of each object has to be sorted by depth. An alternative solution to this problem is known as the Z-buffer algorithm. The Z-buffer is an area of memory which stores the distance of each pixel from the observer (i.e. along the Z-axis which comes out of the screen). If a point on the surface is far away the Z-buffer stores a large number. When a ray is cast through a pixel, the ray might hit any of the several objects that lie in its path. When the ray hits a pixel, its Z-value is looked up from the Z-buffer and stored. As the ray hits another pixel, its Z-value is only looked up and compared with that of the earlier one. If the second value is less, the second pixel is rendered in front of the first one. This process is continued for all pixels in the image.

10.9.4 Ray Tracing Algorithm

Ray casting algorithms can produce very sophisticated renderings, but they have one fundamental limitation: they deal with the shading of each object as if it existed in isolation, i.e. as if the other objects do not have any effect on the object being rendered. As a result creating effects that involve interaction of multiple objects becomes a problem like, reflections, shadows and transparency. A different category of rendering algorithm called ray tracing addresses this problem by dealing with all the objects in a scene simultaneously. When you look at a specific point on a surface, the colour at that point is affected not only by the light falling from the light source, but also by the light bouncing onto it from nearby surfaces. As with the ray-casting technique, a ray is projected from the eye through the pixel and into the scene and hits the first surface. If the surface has been defined as somewhat reflective, the ray bounces off it and hits the second object which might have been defined as partially reflective and partially transparent. This contact generates two ray paths: one bounces off it and the other passes through it and hits the third object. In order to calculate the colour of the pixel at the point where the ray first hit it, you begin by calculating the colour of the first object at the point indicated, which in turn is affected by the colour of the second object, which in turn is influenced by the colour of the third object. You also need to know the colour of the space around the objects since rays from the surrounding space also hit the object. Because the calculation of each surface point takes into consideration all the different surfaces in the scene the effects of all those surfaces show up in the final rendering. Cast shadows, reflections, and transparency are all automatically calculated by the ray-tracing technique.

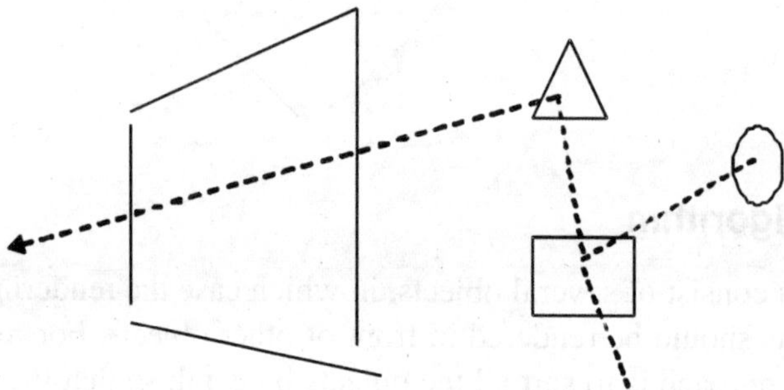

In a complex scene with a great many objects ray tracing can become immensely complex. If you continue tracing the path of a ray in such a scene the ray can go on bouncing off and through hundreds of objects, creating paths so complex that they can be impractical to render. Consequently most ray-tracing programs ask you to define the maximum number of bounces that each ray should follow. This is called the depth of the ray tracing. The larger the depth, the more accurate but also the more time-consuming is the rendering. If the depth is zero – that is, if no bounces are followed – the ray traces becomes effectively the same as a ray caster.

10.9.5 Polygon Subdivision

The process of converting curved surfaces to polygonal approximations prior to rendering is known as polygon subdivision or sometimes rendering subdivision. Most systems allow you to control the number of polygons used to approximate the patches. Some systems also offer another more sophisticated way of determining the number of polygons. This approach takes advantage of the fact that some sections of a patch need far fewer polygons than do other sections. In relatively flat areas of the patch, only a few polygons are necessary to produce a good approximation. However where the curvature of a patch changes abruptly, a lot of polygons are required to make the rendering look smoothly curved. Specifying the minimum and maximum number of polygons to be used in any given region addresses this problem. If the region is relatively flat, the minimum will be used, if the region is relatively curved, the maximum will be used. Because the number of polygons adapts to the curvature of the surface, this technique is called adaptive subdivision.

10.9.6 Aliasing

When rendering final frames you must also consider the staircasing effect inherent to computer images. Because any digital image is composed of a grid of tiny rectangular pixels, a curved or slanted edge of an object tends to appear as a stepped pattern. This effect is called aliasing, meaning that something appears to be other than it really is. For example, a truly curved surface may appear to be a jagged line. The technique developed to handle this problem, anti-aliasing, consists of selectively blurring certain pixels along the aliased edge of a rendered surface. Because the colour patterns of the pixels change very gradually, rather than abruptly, the eye perceives the edges as smooth. Calculating the blurred pixels of an anti-aliased image requires additional time on the part of a rendering program. Because of this you can usually turn anti-aliasing on or off. Some high-end systems provide you with parameters for controlling the quality of the anti-aliasing. However higher the quality, the longer is the time required for rendering. Temporal aliasing is a problem that occurs when objects are moving very quickly. Sometimes the placement of an object within the frame changes drastically from frame to frame, and this produces a jerky effect when you play the animation back. One of the two ways of handling temporal aliasing takes place at the recording stage and involves a technique for creating and recording frames at smaller intervals. The other approach, motion blur, involves rendering fast-moving objects with a slight blurring at each frame. This causes the eye to fuse the frames so that they appear smooth.

10.10 ANIMATION SOFTWARE

Various types of software are available to create different grades of animation. Elementary animation can be created by software such as Microsoft PowerPoint and GIF Animator. More sophisticated 2D animation can be done using Autodesk Animator Studio, Macromedia Director and Macromedia Flash. For 3D animation, one can use tools like 3D studio Max and Maya.

The facilities offered by a typical animation software package, whether 2D or 3D can be categorized into two broad classes: creation of objects and specifying how they should animate. For creation of objects drawing and painting tools are usually used in 2D animation software like Flash, while in 3D animation packages like Studio MAX techniques for converting 2D surfaces into 3D objects as well as ready made 3D primitives are available for modelling 3D object structures.

Creating Content

Various drawing and painting tools are generally provided to draw figures of various shapes and paint them in flat colours or gradients. For example Flash, in which drawing and painting facilities and tools are available.

Creating Object Instances

To create multiple instances or copies of the same object, a library or similar repository can be specified from which copies of the object can be dragged out and placed on a stage. If necessary each copy of the object can be given different characteristics like colour, size, etc.

Provisions for Interactivity

Interactivity elements like buttons can be defined with provisions for specifying what the appearance of the button would be when the pointer rolls over it or is clicked on it.

Provisions for Aligning and Grouping

To align or group objects on the screen with respect to each other or with respect to the stage, dialogue boxes are generally available with a variety of options.

Transforming Objects

Tools like rotate, scale, skew, flip, etc. are generally provided for transforming objects

Changing Content

A popular way of changing content is to arrange objects on a timeline structure and specify where the key frames should be located. The content of each key frame can be specified and the software can be instructed to tween between the key frames. A layered scheme is also followed to specify the vertical layering of various content overlapping each other. Both the shape as well as the position of the object can be changed between key frames.

Path Animation

In addition to tweening object properties, guide paths can be associated with objects to provide for path animation.

Masking

Masking allows certain selected portions of graphical objects to be protected from editing changes allowing them to appear in front of other objects.

Scripting Language

High-end animation packages allow the developer to perform sophisticated tasks through the use of an embedded scripting language. A major portion of the commands are designed for event handling which may be either user initiated or system generated.

For example the developer might want to instruct the application to perform a particular task, say jump to a different scene within the file when the user clicks on a button (user initiated) or stop the playback head from proceeding when it enters a specific frame (system generated).

10.11 FILE FORMATS

Animation files are usually rendered as AVI or QuickTime movies which can be played back just like video clips. Web animation today mostly uses the Shockwave (SWF) format, although animated-GIF is also a popular format. Internally most animation software uses a separate file format to store the editable version which requires the corresponding packages to open.

Animated GIF

The animated-GIF format has provisions for carrying multiple images in a single file. This can be used to create animated displays. The GIF format is a block-oriented file format – it consists of a stream of functional blocks.

FLIC (Autodesk Format)

The FLIC format is a proprietary Autodesk format for animation. It is supported by the Autodesk Animator Studio and Autodesk 3D Studio programs. There are two versions of the FLIC format, designated by the filenames .FLI and .FLC.

FLA and SWF (Flash Format)

SWF (Shockwave Format) is one of the file formats used by Macromedia Flash to save animation sequences. It is essentially a vector based format but can also support bitmap images. The latest versions also allow audio, video and a number of interaction mechanisms.

MAX (3D Studio MAX Format)

3D studio MAX is a three dimensional vector graphics and animation software developed by Autodesk Media & Entertainment, formerly known as Discrete and Kinetix. It is one of the most popular 3D software packages on Windows platform. It provides powerful editing capabilities for specifying modelling structures, surface characteristics, lights camera and animation utilities. The MAX file format is the internal editable vector format for 3D MAX scenes and requires the application software to open.

10.12 SUMMARY

'Animate' means 'to give life to'. Animations are created from a sequence of still images. Each image is slightly changed from the previous one with respect to one or more objects in the image.

The images are then displayed rapidly in succession so that the eye perceives continuous motion due to persistence of vision.

- Persistence of vision is the tendency of the eye and brain to continue to perceive an image even after it has disappeared.

- Animation involves the movements of still pictures, something that does not seem to occur naturally, it increases the interest of the viewer and can create a lasting impression.
- By adding the appearance of movement to an inanimate object, the resulting image stimulates emotions and builds excitement.
- Animation is therefore widely used in the entertainment industry. It is also the heart of most computer games, making the graphics more realistic, exciting or engaging.
- Cel animation is a term from traditional animation. Cel comes from the word celluloid the material that made up early motion picture film, and refers to the transparent piece of film that is used in hand-drawn animation.
- Animation cels are generally layered, one on top of the other, to produce a single animation frame.
- Layering enables the animator to isolate and redraw only the parts of the image that change between successive frames.
- 2D animation programs do not take into consideration the depth of objects and typically depict animated objects on flat surfaces.
- Computer assisted animation is also based on the key frame concept. The great advantage of computer-assisted animation is that in-between frames are created by the animation program itself. Computer animation software typically simulates the process of traditional cel based animation, by placing the animated object on a timeline to depict the flow of time.
- The World Wide Web gives support for animated files included in Web pages. The biggest obstacles in the use of animations on the Web are bandwidth limitations, the differences in platforms and browser support.
- Modelling involves creation of 3D objects from 2D shapes. Two of the most common methods are lofting and lathing. Lofting is a process of changing a 2D shape into a 3D object by moving the shape along a specific direction.
- Lighting involves placing lights in the scene by specifying their intensities, direction and colour. The directions of shadows are also considered. Camera placements determine how the scene should look. Movement of the camera can be used to produce zooming and panning effects.
- Animating the objects involves creation of key frames and tweening to produce intermediate frames.
- Animation involves the production of a series of still images that when played back in quick succession, appear as continuously moving. This illusion is produced by a physiological characteristic of our eyes known as persistence of vision.
- When rendering final frames you must also consider the staircasing effect inherent to computer images. Because any digital image is composed of a grid of tiny rectangular pixels, a curved or slanted edge of an object tends to appear as a stepped pattern.
- Various types of software are available to create different grades of animation. Elementary animation can be created by software such as Microsoft PowerPoint and GIF Animator.

- More sophisticated 2D animation can be done using Autodesk Animator Studio, Macromedia Director and Macromedia Flash. For 3D animation, one can use tools like 3D studio Max and Maya.

10.13 REVIEW QUESTIONS

1. Design a storyboard layout and accompanying key frames for an animation of a single polyhedron.
2. Write a morphing program to transform a sphere into a specified polyhedron.
3. Set up an animation specification involving accelerations.
4. Set up an animation specification involving both accelerations and decelerations and implement the between spacing calculations.
5 Set up an animation specification implementing the acceleration-deceleration calculation.
6. Write a program to simulate the linear, two-dimensional motion of a filled circle inside a given rectangular area. The circle is to be given an initial velocity, and the circle is to rebound from the walls with the angle of reflection equal to the angle of incidence.
8. Differentiate between traditional animation and computer-generated animations.
9. Discuss the hardware tools that are used for animations.
10. Discuss any four software tools that are used for animations.
11. Discuss the GIF Animator in detail.
12. Explain the purpose of animation and discuss its advantages and disadvantages in detail.

CHAPTER 11

Compression, Streaming, Synchronization and Playback Architecture

11.1 INTRODUCTION TO COMPRESSION

Compared to text files other media files like images, audio and video take up a huge amount of disk space. A typical five page document file occupies 75KB of space, whereas a single image can take up about 1.4 MB, a 1 minute audio clip can take up over 10 MB and 1 minute video clip can take up 2GB of disk space. It is extremely difficult working with such huge files mainly because of two reasons:

- Due to their huge sizes, storage requirements increase rapidly with multiple such media files thereby increasing the cost. During multimedia development work, one can quickly run out of disk space.
- Even if there is adequate storage space, such files require a large data transfer rate that may be beyond the capabilities of both the processor and hard disk. For example, to play back an audio file, the disk and processor have to process about 1.4 million bits of data per second.

Due to these facts it is customary to subject the media files to a process called compression. Compression reduces the file sizes using mathematical algorithms, after which it becomes much easier to manipulate these files. The amount of compression which can be achieved depends both on the original media data as well as the compression technique applied. There are various compression methods available and the compression factors can vary from two to over ten times.

CODEC

After an analogue quantity has been digitized, it is stored on the disk as a digital file. Such files are referred to as raw or uncompressed media data. To compress the file and reduce its size, it needs to be filtered through specialized software called a CODEC, which is short for Compression/ Decompression or Coder/Decoder. The software reads the media data and applies mathematical algorithms to reduce its size. The algorithms work by trying to find redundant information within the media files. Redundant information is that which can either be discarded without affecting the media quality by appreciable measures, or data that can be expressed in a more compact form. In either case this leads to a reduction in file size, but the actual amount of reduction depends on a large number of factors involving both the media data and the CODEC used. The compressed media is then again stored on the disk or other storage media, frequently as a different type of file with another extension. When the media needs to be played back either as stand-alone or as part of a presentation, the same CODEC is again used to decompress the data which was previously compressed. Hence, the compression process needs to be essentially reversible. However depending on the type of CODEC used, the decompressed data may or may not be exactly identical to the original uncompressed data. The decompression process is necessary because the playback devices like the monitor or speakers cannot directly handle compressed data. The decompression process usually takes place in the memory or buffer so that the original compressed file stays intact. After decompression, the raw digital data is usually converted to analogue form before being played back.

11.2 TYPES OF COMPRESSION

11.2.1 Lossless vs. Lossy Compression

Based on the methodologies, compression can broadly be classified into two types: lossless and lossy.

Lossless compression implies the original data is not changed permanently during compression. After decompression therefore the original data can be retrieved back exactly. CODECs used for lossless compression are called lossless CODECs. The algorithms within these CODECs attempt to represent the existing information in a more compact form without actually discarding any data. The advantage of lossless compression is that the original data stays intact without degradation of quality and can be reused. The disadvantage is that the compression achieved is not very high and may be typically of the order of two to five times. Lossless compression is used where media quality is of utmost importance and the larger space requirements may be justified. For example, quality might play an important part in diagnosing faults from digitally stored medical images like X-ray plates and ultra-sonography.

While lossless compression is always desirable images with very little redundancy do not produce acceptable compression results with this technique. In lossy compression techniques, parts of the original data are discarded permanently to reduce file size. After decompression the original data cannot be recovered which leads to a degradation of media quality. However if done correctly the quality loss may not be immediately apparent because of the limitations of the human eye and ears, and also because of the tendency of the human senses to bridge the gaps in information. An important consideration is how much information can be lost before the human eye can tell the difference. Compression ratios of the order of 10 to 50 times may be achieved by this method. Lossy compression is usually used where media quality may be sacrificed to a certain extent for reducing space requirements, like in multimedia presentations and Web page content.

CODEC Working System

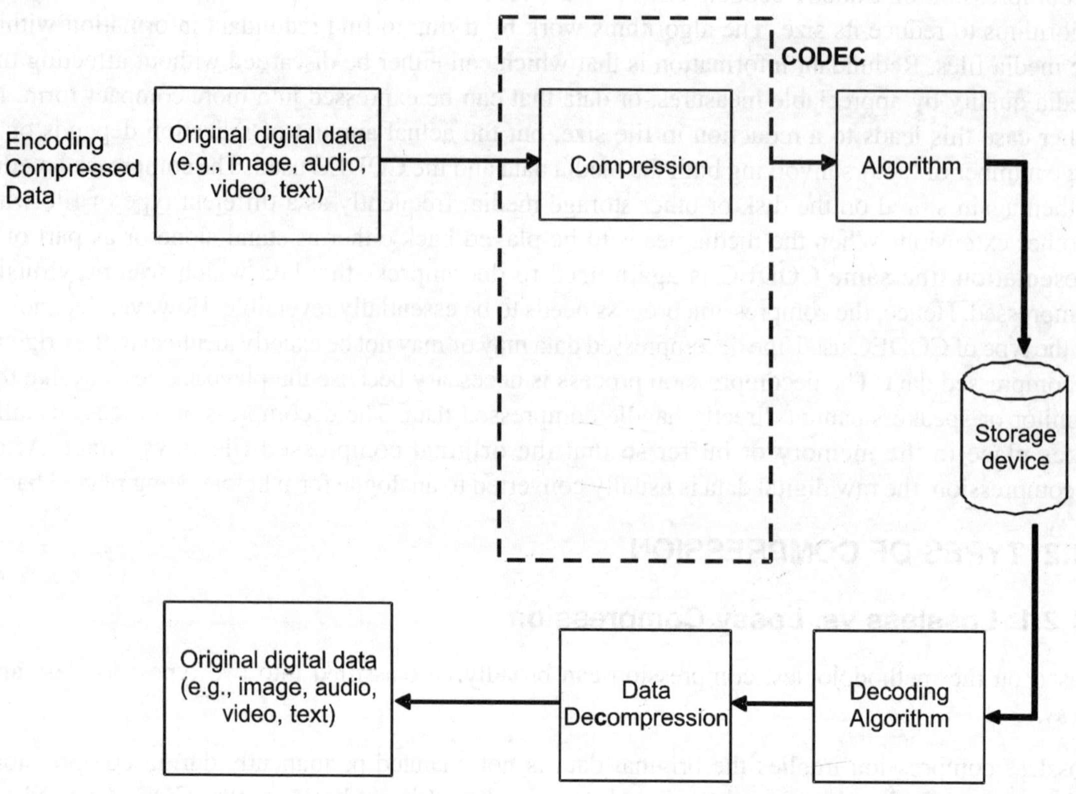

11.2.2 Intraframe vs. Interframe Compression

Based on the kind of redundancies exploited, compression can be divided into two categories: Intraframe and interframe.

Intraframe compression is applicable within a still image or a single video frame. In this technique, spatial redundancies are detected and exploited to reduce the file size. Such redundancies occur when different portions of an image are identical or similar to each other, e.g. an area of flat colour in an image has pixels of identical values. A video CODEC can also implement another type of compression called interframe compression when it exploits the redundancies between adjacent frames in a video sequence, referred to as temporal redundancy. Such redundancies occur when subsequent frames in a video sequence are also identical or very similar, e.g. in a video of a news reader, most of the information between adjacent frames remain unchanged with minor variations in lip movement and facial expressions of the reader.

11.2.3 GIF Image Coding Standard

The Graphics Interchange Format (GIF) is used extensively to compress images for use on the Internet. It is an 8-bit format which means that it can represent a maximum of 256 colours. When images of higher colour depth are converted to GIF, the algorithm chooses those 256 colours from the original set which most closely represents the colours of the image. The GIF format uses a Colour Lookup Table (CLUT) to store the colour values of pixels. The table consists of 256 rows and three columns. When an image is converted to the GIF format, the algorithm selects the 256 most representative colours from the image and stores all these values in the 256 row table.

11.2.4 JPEG Image Coding Standard

The JPEG (Joint Photographers Expert Group) is the ISO/IEC international standard 10918-1, developed in collaboration with the International Telecommunication Union (ITU). It became an international standard in 1992. The essential characteristics of JPEG are: JPEG is a compression standard for continuous-tone grey-scale or colour images. It uses a combination of discrete cosine transform, quantization, run length encoding and Huffman encoding techniques, and supports several modes of operation including lossless and various types of lossy modes. Its performance depends on the complexity of the image. Normally image compression ratio is around 20:1. JPEG will not perform well on bitonal images or line drawings.

MPEG Standards Overview

The Motion Picture Expert Group (MPEG) is a working group under ISO/IEC set up to formulate a set of standard relating to a range of multimedia applications, primarily involving audio and video.

- **MPEG–1**

MPEG first devised the ISO/IEC international standard 11172 for the reduced data rate coding of video and audio signals. The standard was finalized in 1992 and is known as MPEG-1.

- **MPEG–2**

MPEG – 2 is used for video and audio storage and transmission standards for broadcast quality television. Used for digital TV transmission, digital satellite TV services, digital cable TV signals and for DVD applications. It is defined in a series of documents which are all subsets of ISO recommendations 13818. The standard currently has nine parts, the first three have reached international standard status while the other are at different levels of completion, one has been withdrawn.

- **MPEG-3**

Originally designed for HDTV but abandoned when it became apparent that MPEG-2 was sufficient for the purpose.

- **MPEG-4**

It was introduced in late 1998, and is a designation for a group of audio and video coding standards and related technology agreed upon by the ISO/IEC Moving Picture Experts Group (MPEG). The primary uses for the MPEG-4 standard are Web (streaming media) and CD distribution, conversational (videophone), and broadcast television. MPEG-4 absorbs many of the features of MPEG-1 and MPEG-2 and other related standards, adding new features such as (extended) VRML support for 3D rendering, object-oriented composite files (including audio, video and VRML (Virtual Reality Modelling Language) objects), support for externally-specified Digital Rights Management and various types of interactivity. Most of the features included in MPEG-4 are left to individual developers to decide whether to implement them.

- **MPEG–7**

The ISO subcommittee SC29, WG11, MPEG (Moving Picture Experts Group), published in February 2002 another standard called "Multimedia Content Description Interface" (also known as MPEG-7), which provides a set of Descriptors (D) i.e. quantitative measure of audio-visual features and Description Schemes (DS), i.e. structures of descriptors and their relationship. A language called the Description Definition Language (DDL) can be used to specify the scheme. Audio-Visual (A/V) material that has MPEG–7 data associated with it can be indexed and searched for. This 'material' may include: Images, graphics, 3D models, audio, video, and information about how these elements are combined in a multimedia presentation. It is currently the most complete description standard of multimedia.

11.3 STREAMING TECHNOLOGIES

Streaming media is media that is consumed (read, heard, viewed) while it is being delivered. Streaming is more a property of the delivery system than the media itself. The distinction is usually applied to media that is distributed over computer networks; most other delivery systems are either inherently streaming (radio, television) or inherently non streaming (books, video cassettes, audio CDs).

A streaming media system is made of many interacting technologies. Video cameras and audio recorders create raw media. Editors use composition tools to combine raw media into a finished work. Servers store media and make it available to many people. Clients retrieve media from servers and display it to the user. Servers and clients store media in various file formats; they send and receive it in various stream formats. Servers and clients communicate over computer networks, using agreed upon network protocols. Servers encode media into a stream for transmission; clients receive the stream and decode it for display. CODECs perform the encoding and decoding. Under current technology, media storage and transmission costs are still significant; therefore, media is often compressed for storage or streaming. A media stream can be on demand or live. On demand streams are stored on a server for a long period of time, and are available to be transmitted at a user's request. Live streams are only available at one particular time, as in a video stream of a live sporting event.

11.3.1 Web Radio

Web radio (or Internet radio) is a broadcasting service transmitted via the Internet. Many Web radio stations are completely independent from traditional radio stations and broadcast only on the Internet. Broadcasting on the Internet is usually referred to as Web casting. Because the radio signal is relayed over the Internet through the World Wide Web, it is possible to access the stations from anywhere in the world for example, to listen to an Australian radio station from Europe or America. Some of the Web radio services available via the Internet offer news, sports, talkback, and various genres of music – everything that is on the radio station being re-broadcast. One of the most common ways to distribute Web radio is via streaming MP3 technology, which uses the well-known MP3 Music format. The bits are 'streamed' over a TCP/IP connection, then reassembled and played within about two seconds. Therefore, streaming MP3 radio has a lag time of about two seconds.

11.3.2 Internet Television

This refers to traditional television content, accessible freely and legally over the Internet. This comes in four basic forms:

- TV channels which exist only on the Internet
- Traditional stations that simulcast live on the Internet
- Traditional stations making select content available on demand at their Web site
- Traditional TV stations making extra content exclusively for their website

One of the main barriers to wider adoption of streaming technology is both the quality and the cost, but it appears that the Direct project at the BBC will be able to create a scalable, high-quality and more importantly free-for-all codec for streaming video content over the net. Parallel to this trend are attempts to more easily transmit existing pay-TV channels over the net, to a regular TV set, while retaining control over how the media is used. This is in order to protect the subscription and pay-per-view business models.

Initiatives to use P2P technology to distribute live TV are just starting to emerge. The main advantage of this approach over the traditional distribution model is that it provides a way of sharing data delivery workloads across connected client systems as well as the distributor's own server infrastructure, which drastically decreases the operational costs for a stream provider. Costs do not rise with rising user numbers. Popular TV streams do not need to suffer from server overloads anymore, because not every user needs to access the source server. The developments in P2P TV are likely to give Internet television a boost, but the industry is already fearing a new Napster scenario, i.e. real-time TV sharing. With the arrival of P2P TV and the ever growing number of people with a broadband connection, this year we might see Internet television break through to a mainstream audience. Some initiatives for P2P TV are already working, others are being tested.

11.3.3 Web TV

A Web TV is a specially-adapted television set designed to allow internet connection, or more commonly, a set-top box (i.e. cable decoder) which connects to a standard TV for the same purpose. The setup includes a web browser, cord or wireless (i.e. bluetooth) keyboard and connection to the Internet (i.e. using a modem, cable etc.) While Web TV does not allow as much functionality as a computer-based browser (e.g. they cannot run JavaScript or multi-task, and they do not have nearly as much versatility, power or memory as an actual computer), it is nonetheless a popular and low-cost alternative in some countries. A recent alternative to Web TV are game consoles with a built-in Internet connection.

The first Web TV device featured a proprietary operating system, file system and Web browser in just two megabytes of Flash RAM. No hard drives were present in these Web TV Classic boxes. The software comprised a TCP/IP stack, HTML rendering engine, JavaScript interpreter, audio engine (Mp3, MIDI, Realaudio, and WAV), and video engine (Flash and MPEG). Video rendering for the television was done by a proprietary chip.

11.4 TEMPORAL RELATIONSHIPS

Multimedia systems are characterized by storage, manipulation and presentation of time dependent and time-independent media. The key issue which provides integration is the synchronization of and between various kinds of media and data. The word synchronization refers to time. Synchronization in a multimedia system refers to the temporal relations between media objects in the multimedia system. Synchronization can occur both between time-dependent media as well as time-independent media. Synchronization between an audio clip and a video clip is an example of the former, while an example of the latter is the synchronization between a set of images and corresponding set of text captions.

11.4.1 Delay Factor

The delay factor is used to measure the end-to-end time delay encountered in distributed or networked applications. The delay encountered depends on the type of the applications. In a streamed application the delay refers to the total time taken for the objects to travel from the source to the destination, while in an interactive application it also includes the user response to travel from the destination to source. The delay is actually a combination of various delays occurring at various points in the system, which include processing delays by the processor, seek delays for object retrieval from storage, capturing delays for real-time media capture for capture device, compression/decompression delays by the CODEC and networking delays for the transmission of the network.

11.4.2 Jitter

Due to variation in delay factors, the temporal relationships between media components can deviate from their desired values. This is referred to as jitter. For example, two media streams which are supposed to be displayed at the same time on the screen may get displaced slightly and one stream may lag behind the other by a couple of seconds. Quantitatively, jitter is expressed as the instantaneous difference between the desired presentation times and actual presentation times. While delay only wastes time in waiting for the response, jitter leads to unacceptable presentation quality. Acceptable values range from 10ms for TV-quality presentation to 1ms for higher quality.

11.5 SYNCHRONIZATION

Need for Synchronization

Synchronization can be of two types. Intra-object synchronization refers to the time relation between various presentation units of a single time-dependent media object. An example is the time relation between the single frames of a video sequence. Inter-object synchronization refers to the synchronization between media objects. An example is the time relation between an audio/video sequence, followed by several images and an animation commented by an audio sequence. Time dependent media objects usually consist of a sequence of information units. Such information units are called Logical Data Units (LDU), for example each frame of a video clip. LDUs can be classified as closed and open. Closed LDUs have a predictable duration. The duration of open LDUs is not predictable before the execution of the presentation. Open LDUs typically represent input from a live source like a camera or microphone.

For delivering multimedia data correctly at the user interface, synchronization is essential. This means that the application should decide how to handle synchronization if resources are not available or sufficient for maintaining proper relationships between the media elements. One option is to use an alternative presentation. For example, if there is a loss of synchronization between the video and audio streams, alternative single pictures, a sequence of pictures or audio signals can be presented, or simply previously used presentation units can be repeated. The other possibility is the re-sampling of a stream. The basic idea of re-sampling is to speed up or slow down streams for the purpose of synchronization. For video samples, re-sampling involves re-defining the playback rate, duplicating, interpolating or skipping samples. Audio streams are more complex. A user will be annoyed by duplicated or deleted blocks of audio. Also changes occur in the playback because the frequency is changing. Algorithms exist that can stretch or widen an audio sequence without changing the pitch of sound.

11.6 AUDIO CLASSIFICATION

Audio Classification Characteristics

In the following we summarize the main characteristics of speech and music. They are the basis for audio classification.

Speech

The bandwidth of a speech signal is generally low compared to that for music. It is normally within the range 100 to 7000 Hz. Because speech mainly has low frequency components, the spectral centroids (also called brightness) of speech signals are usually lower than those of music. There are frequent pauses in speech, occurring between words and sentences. Therefore, speech signals normally have a higher silence ratio than music. The characteristic structure of speech is a succession of syllables composed of short periods for vowels. Compared to music, speech has higher variability in ZCR.

Music

Music normally has a high frequency range, from 0 to 20000 Hz. Thus, its spectral centroid is higher than that of speech. Compared to speech, music has a lower silence ratio. One exception may be music produced by a solo instrument or singing without accompanying music. Compared to speech, music has lower variability in ZCR. Music often has regular beats which can be extracted to differentiate it from speech. The following table summarizes the major characteristics of speech and music, but the list is not exhaustive. There are other characteristics derived from specific characteristics of speech and music.

Features	Speech	Music
Bandwidth	0-7 kHz	0-20 kHz
Spectral centroid	Low	High
Silence ratio	High	Low
Zero-crossing rate	More variable	Less variable
Regular beat	Do not exist	Often existing

Audio Classification Framework

All classification methods are based on calculated feature values, but they differ in how these features are used. In the first group of methods, each feature is used individually in different classification steps, while in the second group a set of features is used together as a vector to calculate the closeness of the input to the training sets. These two types of classification frameworks are discussed below. It should be noted that although most techniques calculate features from raw audio samples (uncompressed audio data), there have been proposals to calculate some features directly from compressed audio files.

Step by step classification

In this approach to audio classification, each audio feature is used separately to determine if an audio piece is music or speech. Each feature can be seen as a filtering or selection criterion. At each filtering step, an audio piece is determined as one type or another. In a possible filtering process, first the centroid of all input audio pieces is calculated. If an input has a centroid higher than a preset threshold, it is deemed to be music. Otherwise, the input is speech or music because not all music has a high centroid. Secondly, the silence ratio is calculated, if the input has a low silence ratio, it is deemed to be music. Otherwise, the input is speech or solo music because solo music may have a very high silence ratio. Finally, the ZCR is calculated. If the input has very high ZR variability, it is speech, otherwise, it is solo music.

Audio Segmentation

A long sound track normally consists of a mixture of speech, music and other types of sound. An entire audio clip is usually segmented into small intervals before applying the above methods. The basic idea is to divide the audio piece into a number of small windows and then apply one of the above audio classification methods to determine if the window is speech or music. Consecutive windows are then grouped into the speech or music interval if they are of the same type.

11.7 SPEECH RECOGNITION AND RETRIEVAL

The basic approach to speech indexing and retrieval is to apply speech recognition techniques to convert speech signals into text and then to apply IR techniques for indexing and retrieval. In addition to actual spoken words, other information contained in speech, such as the speaker's identity and the mood of the speaker can be used to enhance speech indexing and retrieval. In the following, the basic speech recognition and speaker identification techniques are described.

Basic Concepts of Automatic Speech Recognition

In general, the Automatic Speech Recognition (ASR0) problem is a pattern matching problem. An ASR system is populated with models or feature vectors for all possible speech units. The smallest unit is a phoneme. Other possible units are words and phrases. During the recognition process, the feature vector of an input speech unit is extracted and compared with each of the feature vectors previously stored during the population phase. The speech unit whose feature vector is closest to that of the input speech unit is deemed to be the unit spoken.

An ASR system operates in two stages: Population and query. During the population stage, features of each speech unit are extracted and stored in the system. In the query phase, features of an input speech unit are extracted and compared with each of the stored features and the speech unit with the best matching features is taken as the recognized unit. If each phoneme can be uniquely identified by a feature vector independent of speakers, environment and context, speech recognition would be simple. In practice, however, speech recognition is complicated by the following factors. Firstly, a phoneme spoken by different speakers or by the same speaker at different times produces different features in terms of duration, amplitude and frequency components. That is, a phoneme cannot be uniquely identified with 100% certainty. Secondly, the above differences are exaggerated by the background or environmental noise. Thirdly, normal speech is continuous and it is difficult to separate it into individual phonemes because different phonemes have different durations. Fourthly, phonemes vary with their location in a word. The frequency components of a vowel's pronunciation are heavily influenced by the surrounding consonants.

Due to the above factors, the earlier ASR systems were speaker dependent, required a pause between words, and could only recognize a small number of words. The above factors also illustrate that speech recognition is a statistical process in which ordered sound sequences are matched against the likelihood that they represent a particular string of phonemes and words. Speech recognition should also make use of knowledge of the language including a dictionary of the vocabulary and a grammar of allowable word sequences.

11.8 PLAYBACK ARCHITECTURE

Windows Media Framework

Windows media is a framework for media creation and distribution for Microsoft Windows. It consists of a software development kit with several application programming interfaces and a number of prebuilt technologies. The following are part of Windows Media Framework:

Windows Media Players

Advanced Streaming Format (ASF)

Windows Media Audio (WMA)

Windows Media Video (WMV)

QuickTime Architecture

Quick time framework developed by Apple Computer, is capable of handling audio, video, text, animation with support for VR. It consists of 3 components: The File Format, which is openly documented and royalty free, a media player which is freely downloadable from Apple's website and SDKs available for Macintosh and Windows platforms enabling users to develop their own software for manipulating QuickTime files.

File Format: The standard data type of QuickTime is a movie (extension .MOV). The QuickTime File Format functions as a multimedia container file that contains one or more tracks, each of which store a particular type of data, such as audio, video, effects, or text (for subtitles for example). A track represents a stream of information (audio or video data) that flows in parallel to every other track.

Background: Apple released the first version of QuickTime in 1991, as an add-on for their Macintosh System 7 OS which included the CODECs video, animation and graphics. Microsoft's competing technology video for Windows appeared the next year in 1992.

QuickTime Architecture: The QuickTime architecture comprises 3 major components: the Movie Toolbox, the Image Compression Manager and the Component Manager. The **Movie Toolbox** offers a set of services (API) to the user that allows the user to incorporate movies into applications. These applications may directly manipulate the characteristics of audio and video data of a movie. Movie data can be imported and exported with the system clipboard and a movie can be edited. The second component known as the Image Compression Manager provides a common interface for compression and decompression of the data to and from the hard disk, CD-ROM, floppy disc, etc. It offers a directory service to select compression component. The compression techniques are proprietary image compression scheme, a JPEG implementation and a proprietary video compressor for digitized video data (leading to a compression ratio of 8:1, and if temporal redundancies are also removed, to a ratio of 25:1). The Component Manager provides a directory service related to the components. It is the interface between the application and the various system components. It shields developers from having to deal with the details of interfacing with specific hardware. The components managed by the component manager include the image compressor and de-compressor, the movie controller, the sequence grabber, etc.

11.9 SUMMARY

- Compared to text files other media files like images, audio and video take up a huge amount of disk space.
- A typical five page document file occupies 75KB of space, whereas a single image can take up about 1.4 MB, a 1 minute audio clip can take up over 10 MB and 1 minute video clip can take up 2GB of disk space.
- Due to their huge sizes, storage requirements increase rapidly with multiple such media files thereby increasing the cost. During multimedia development work, one can quickly run out of disk space.
- Even if there is adequate storage space, such files require a large data transfer rate that may be beyond the capabilities of both the processor and the hard disk. For example, to play

back an audio file, the disk and processor have to process about 1.4 million bits of data per second.

- After an analogue quantity has been digitized, it is stored on the disk as a digital file. Such files are referred to as raw or uncompressed media data.
- To compress the file and reduce its size, it needs to be filtered through specialized software called a CODEC, which is short for Compression/Decompression or Coder/Decoder.
- Lossless compression implies the original data is not changed permanently during compression. After decompression therefore the original data can be retrieved back exactly. CODECs used for lossless compression are called lossless CODECs.
- Streaming media is media that is consumed (read, heard, viewed) while it is being delivered. Streaming is more a property of the delivery system than the media itself.
- Multimedia systems are characterized by storage, manipulation and presentation of time dependent and time-independent media. The key issue which provides integration is the synchronization of and between various kinds of media and data.
- The basic approach to speech indexing and retrieval is to apply speech recognition techniques to convert speech signals into text and then to apply IR techniques for indexing and retrieval.
- Windows media is a framework for media creation and distribution for Microsoft Windows. It consists of a software development kit with several application programming interfaces and a number of prebuilt technologies.

11.10 REVIEW QUESTIONS

1. What is a "Hypertext"? Explain how it helps in presentation and use of information.
2. Describe the JPEG compression scheme.
3. What is meant by "text importing" and "text exporting"? Explain how these features help in the creation of a document.
4. Describe the JPEG compression scheme.
5. JPEG uses transform domain coding. Is this statement true? Discuss.
6. Comment on the error tolerance of compressed media data, as compared to uncompressed ones.
7. Which part of the JPEG algorithm introduces losses and why? What type of JPEG can be used in medical imaging?
8. In a decompressed JPEG image some compression artefacts were found. Explain what has possibly happened to the image.

CHAPTER 12

Virtual Reality & VRML

12.1 INTRODUCTION TO VIRTUAL REALITY – VIRTUAL ENVIRONMENT

An artificial environment created by computers, in which people can immerse themselves and feel that this artificial reality really does exist. Virtual Reality (VR) creates a 'Cyber Space' where it is possible to interact with anything and anyone on a virtual level.

Definitions

Virtual: Something which is a representation rather than the real thing.

Virtual Reality: A generic term associated with computer systems that create a real time Visual/Audio/Haptic experience.

Virtual Reality: A 3D data set describing an environment based upon real world or abstract objects and data.

Virtual means a space which should not be Actual. A space created in one's mind with the purpose of:

- Innovation
- Intuition
- Experiment
- Entertainment
- Presentation
- Myths
- Real world landscape to a computer screen
- Expressing feelings towards a specific subject

- Education
- Entertainment
- Training
- Product demonstration
- Simulator
- Product analysis etc.

For the above mentioned purposes, a Virtual Environment needs to be created, which gives the user the feeling of a Real Environment. In Virtual Reality many factors affect the objects and environment, such as:

- The new position of the object
- Changing light levels
- Transformation of object and environment
- Animation exploring shadows and other effects that make objects look real.

As a computer screen presents data in two dimensions, data should be in the form of documents, charts, reports, Web pages, images or animation. However, this has the limitation that the entities shown do not appear real. To give the user the appearance of reality, Virtual Reality – Virtual Environment were initiated. The aim of a Virtual Environment is to provide an interface to user so that the entity appears the same as in the real world.

For example, consider a box, which can easily be presented on a computer screen in 2D. But a Virtual Environment requires that the box should be presented in 3D, along the x, y and z coordinate axes, as well as being able to undergo the real time operations like rotation, scaling, transformation, change of location, change in size, as well as user interface especially in video games, where it is necessary to control the movement of an object.

History of Virtual Reality

Virtual Reality – Virtual Environment came into being in the mid 1950s. Digital computers were used for various applications. Morton Heiligs invented the "Sensorama" a device that allowed the user to take an imaginary journey through the Manhattan traffic. The user experienced a 3D view of the journey, along with the associated effects of vibrating handlebars and seats, and changes in wind speed and humidity as the user's speed changed in traffic.

12.2 SOFTWARE FOR CREATING 3D VIRTUAL REALITY

1. Virtual Reality Modelling Language (VRML) – Open Source
2. Virtool – Virtual Scripting Language (VSC)
3. Wavefront
4. Alisas, Multigen
5. Avtaar

6. 3D Game Studio (C Script)
7. Unity 3D

VRML

Definition

VRML is a powerful, text-based language to build 'virtual worlds', which include 3D objects, light sources and animations. It is possible for the user to interact with an apparently 3-D scene, where objects can be moved or rotated.

Language

VRML is an open standard for 3D multimedia and shared virtual worlds on the Internet. It is a Scene Description Language.

Purpose

The Virtual Reality Modelling Language is a file format for describing interactive 3D objects and worlds. VRML is designed to be used on the Internet, intranets, and local client systems. VRML is also intended to be a universal interchange format for integrated 3D graphics and multimedia.

Use

VRML may be used in a variety of areas such as engineering and scientific visualization, multimedia presentations, entertainment and educational titles, web pages, and shared virtual worlds.

Basic idea of VRML

- A website may want to use lots of 3D graphics for certain purposes, but sending 3D geometry, textures, animation etc. over the Web is time and space intensive.
- Display systems at the client's end vary and so sufficient memory and processing space may not be affordable.
- The developed web site is sent to the client with the markup description of the scene and render being sent to access it locally on client.
- Incorporate the rendering software in the local browser works as a plug-in for received codes and display the 3D graphics, animation generated from Codes.
- VRML works on DirectX, OpenGL and inbuilt software technology.
- VRML 97 works on 32-bit colours.

History of VRML

In 1989 Rikk Carey & Paul Strauss at Silicon Graphics Inc., implemented a project named "Open Inventor Project."

VRML 1.0:

Mark Pesce & Tony Parisi presented a 3D User Interface Prototype named "Labyrinth" in 1994. This was the first step in exploring the possibility of sending a 3D object over the Internet.

This Open Inventor Project + 3D User Interface Prototype (Labyrinth) was called VRML 1.0. Along with the prototype, a parallel VRML email list was also established. Open Inventor was selected as the basis for VRML, and the released version was called VRML 1.0.

VRML 2.0:

By 1995 SGI released WebSpace Navigator, the first VRML browser. A VRML Architecture Group (VAG) was established and a Request-For-Proposals (RFP) for VRML 2.0 was also initiated. Silicon Graphics' "Moving Worlds" proposal became VRML 2.0 and a VRML Consortium was formed for the expansion of 3D graphics and animation activities called VRML.

VRML 97:

After forming the consortium VRML 2.0 became an International Standard in 1997, and was called VRML97 (ISO/IEC DIS 14772-1). This ISO VRML Consortium became the Web 3D Consortium in 1998. The Working groups targeted the next generation VRML called x3D. In 1999 VRML Browser code went open source for research and development of VRML.

VRML file

- **File Format:** VRML is a plain file, built up with UTF-8 or ASCII text file format.
- **Extension:** VRML text files use a .wrl extension
- **Editor for VRML:** VRML file can be created using
  - A text editor e.g., Notepad
  - A world builder application e.g., CosmoWorlds
  - A 3D modeller and format translator
  - A shape generator (like a Perl script)

VRML viewers

VRML files can be viewed in a VRML viewer as well as an HTML browser. A VRML Plug-in to a Web Browser supports loading of VRML files.

If VRML Plug-ins are not installed in an HTML browser, VRML data cannot be viewed. VRML files can be seen from a local hard disk as well as from the Internet.

- **VRML viewer for Windows platforms**
  - Blaxxun's Cortona Pro
  - Platinum's Cosmo Player
  - WebFX
  - WorldView
  - Fountain
- **VRML viewer for Mac platforms**
  - Whurlwind
  - Voyager

Features of VRML

- **Composability:** This provides the ability to use and combine dynamic 3D objects within a VRML world and thus allow reusability. (Object orientated approach).
- **Extensibility:** Provides the ability to add new object types not explicitly defined in VRML, e.g. sound.
- **Performance:** Emphasizes scalable, interactive performance on a wide variety of computing platforms. (Platform independent).
- **Event:** VRML supports event-handling and parallel routing of objects to realize a 3D world on the screen.
- Built-in geometric primitives.
- Lighting, material, texture, movie control.
- Absolute time for animations.
- Scripting.
- Prototyping.

Characteristics of VRML

- VRML is capable of representing static and animated dynamic 3D and multimedia objects with hyperlinks to other media such as text, sounds, movies and images.
- VRML browsers, as well as authoring tools for the creation of VRML files, are widely available for many different platforms.
- Other formats: OpenGL, Inventor (not designed for WWW use).

Basics of VRML

- A VRML file is essentially a collection of objects called **Nodes** which can be divided into two categories.
- **Physically:**
  - Sphere
  - Cylinder
- **Non-Physically:**
  - Viewpoints
  - Hyperlinks
  - Transformations
  - Sound
- Each node contains **Fields** which hold the data of the node.
- Some nodes are **container nodes** or **grouping nodes**, which contain other nodes.
- Nodes are arranged in hierarchical structures called **scene graphs.** Scene graphs are more than just a collection of nodes; the scene graph defines an ordering for the nodes. The scene

graph has a notion of **state**, i.e. nodes earlier in the world can affect nodes that appear later in the world, a simple example is given below.

```
#VRML V2.0 utf8
Shape
{
appearance Appearance
{
material Material { }
}
geometry Sphere
{
radius 3.0
}
}
```

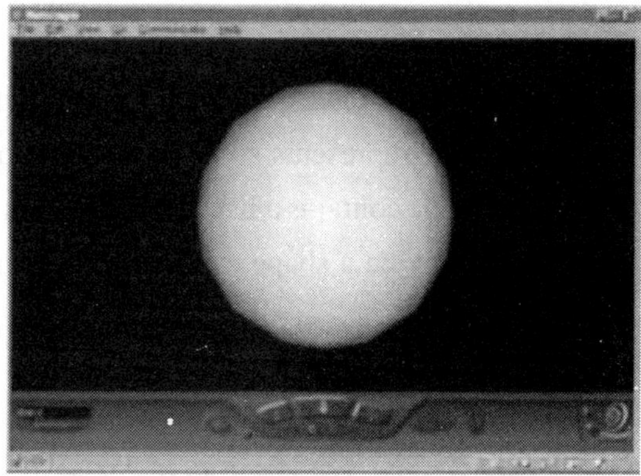

General information of VRML coding

- File Header
  - #VRML V2.0 utf8
    - **#VRML: File contains VRML text**
    - **V2.0 : Text conforms to version 2.0 syntax**
    - **utf8 : Text uses UCS (Universal Character Set) Transformation Format, 8-bit standard**
      - ASCII is a subset
- Comments
  - start with a number-sign (#) and extend to the end of the line

Basic concepts for VRML coding

1. Scene graph

- A scene graph in VRML is the structure of the world being created.
- A VRML scene graph comprises among other things, a group object. When rendered this object exists in 3D space.
- It represents graphics presenting a virtual world.

- The scene creates with two entities in an hierarchical data structure:
  1. nodes
  2. links connecting nodes

2. Nodes

- A node in VRML implements some functionality.
- The node represents some basic function like transform, cone etc.
- Each node contains a list of fields which hold values that define parameters for its functions.
- Node may be a shape, geometry, appearance, location etc.
- Every node has:
  - A node type (shape, cylinder, etc.)
  - A pair of curly-braces
- Zero or more fields inside the curly-braces
- Node type names are case sensitive

Types of nodes

- Grouping nodes
  - Shape
    - Geometry
    - Appearance
  - Group
  - Transform
  - Collision
  - Billboard
  - Anchor
  - Interpolators
- Bindable nodes
  - Viewpoint

- NavigationInfo
- Fog
- Background
- Lights
- Audio
- Sensors
- Scripts

Fields

- Each node is a list of fields
  - A field describes node attributes
- Every field has
  - A field name (height, radius, etc.)
  - A data type (float, integer, etc.)
  - A default value
- Field names are case sensitive

Shapes

- Primitive shapes are standard building blocks of VRML.
  - Box
  - Cone
  - Cylinder
  - Sphere
  - Text
- Each shape has a geometric field that contains a geometry node and an appearance field that contains an appearance node.

Syntax

- A shape node builds a shape
  - **appearance**: colour and texture
  - **geometry**: form, or structure

```
Shape
{
    appearance <some appearance>
    geometry <some geometry>
}
```

Geometry nodes

Box

- defined by its size field

```
Box
{
    size 2.0 2.0 2.0
}
```

Sphere

– defined by its radius field

```
Sphere
{
    radius 1.5
}
```

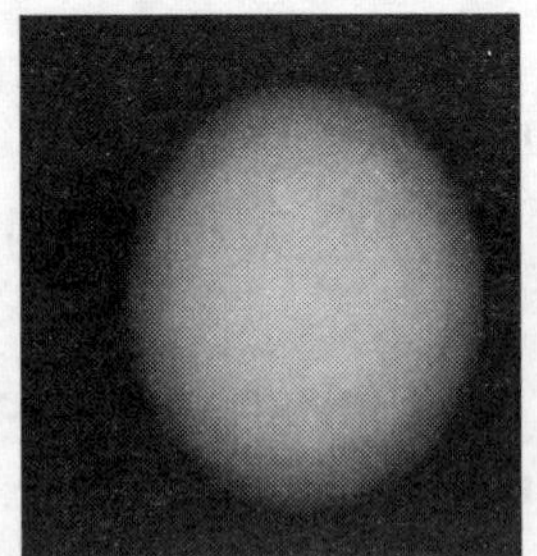

Cylinder

– defined by its height and radius fields

```
Cylinder
{
    height 2.0
    radius 1.0
}
```

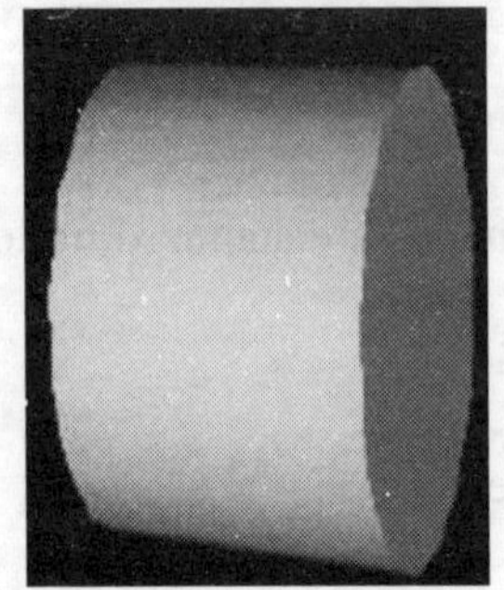

Cone

– defined by its height and radius fields

```
Cone
{
    radius 1.3
    height 1.8
}
```

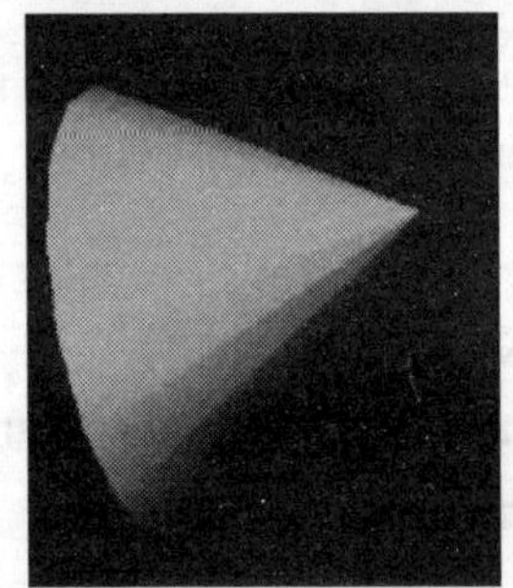

Text

– defined by the string and the font

```
geometry Text
{
    string ["Hi!"]
    fontStyle FontStyle
{
    family "TYPEWRITER"
    style "ITALIC"
}
}
```

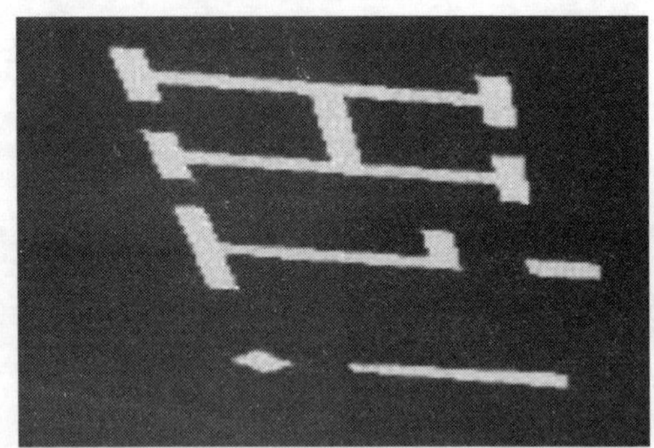

Appearance node

Defines the look of a geometrical shape

- Material
  - combination of
    - ambient colour
    - diffuse colour
    - emmisive colour
    - shininess
    - transparency
    - specular colour
- Texture
  - defines a picture to paste to the object
    - fetch from a URL
    - supports movies
- Texture transform
  - defines how the picture is applied to the object

Material examples

- Material
  - Shiny material

    ambientIntensity 0.3

    diffuseColor 0.1 0.7 0.2

    specularColor 0.6 0.8 0.6

    shininess 0.6
  - Dull material

    ambientIntensity 0.1

    diffuseColor 0.1 0.7 0.2

    shininess 0.0
  - Transparent material

    diffuseColor 0.1 0.7 0.2

    transparency 0.5

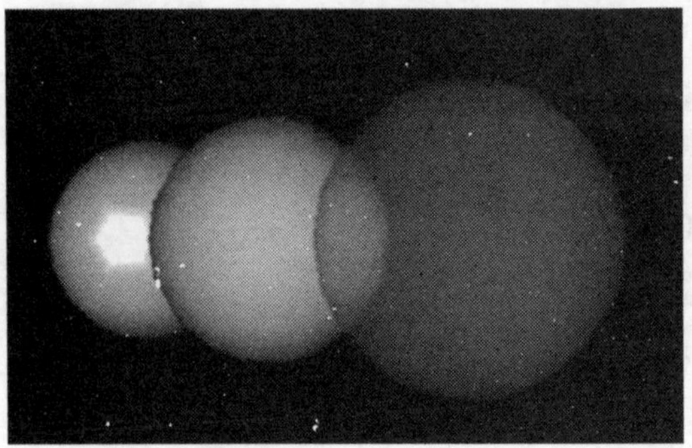

Texture Mapping

- **Original Image**

- **Applied to a Box**

Manipulating Textures

- **TextureTransform**
  - translation

    textureTransform TextureTransform {
    translation 0.5 0.5 }
  - rotation

    textureTransform TextureTransform {
    rotation 0.785 }
  - scale

    textureTransform TextureTransform {
    scale 3.0 3.0 }

Transformations

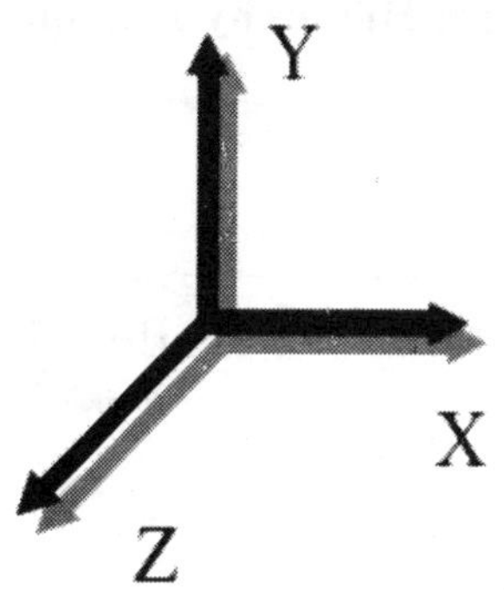

- **Define the positions of objects in 3D space**
- **XY are the plane of the screen**
- **Z is towards the Viewer**
- **Transformation basically contains**
  - rotation
  - scale
  - translation
  - a set of children nodes
- **Rotations follow "right-hand screw rule"**

Effects of Transformation

- **Translation**

```
Transform
{
    translation 1 1 -1
    children
    [
        ...
    ]
}
```

Rotation

translation 1 1 -1

rotation 0 1 0 0.785

Scale

translation 1 1 -1

rotation 0 1 0 0.785

scale 0.5 1.0 0.5

Transform Hierarchy Example

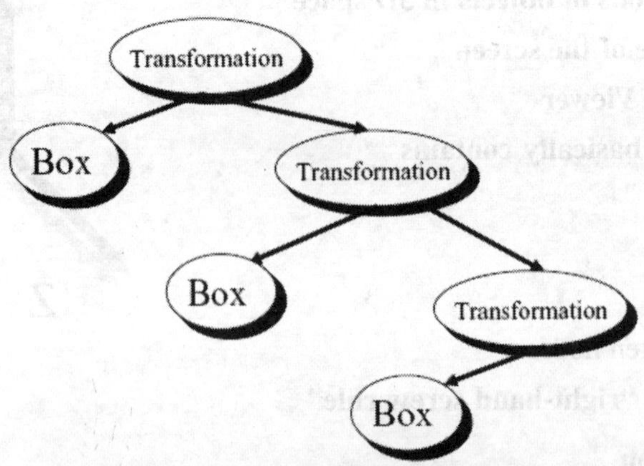

Example

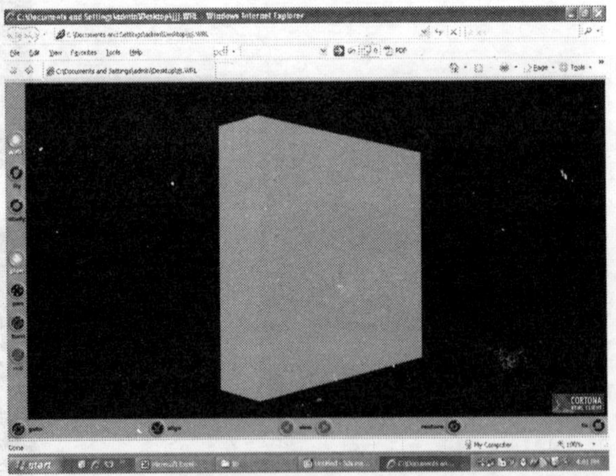

Screen Shot: 1

```
#VRML V2.0 utf8

# Produced by 3D Studio MAX VRML97 exporter, Version 7, Revision 0.65
# Date: Tue Apr 08 16:01:20 2008

DEF Camera01 Viewpoint {
  position 7.359 24.51 108.8
  orientation 0 -1 0 -0.1005
  fieldOfView 0.6024
  description "Camera01"
}
DEF Box01 Transform {
  translation 0 0 0
  children [
   DEF Box01-TIMER TimeSensor { loop TRUE cycleInterval 3.333 },
   DEF Box01-ROT-INTERP OrientationInterpolator {
    key [0, 0.03, 0.06, 0.09, 0.12, 0.15, 0.18, 0.21, 0.24, 0.27, 0.3,
       0.33, 0.36, 0.39, 0.42, 0.45, 0.48, 0.51, 0.54, 0.57, 0.6,
       0.63, 0.66, 0.69, 0.72, 0.75, 0.78, 0.81, 0.84, 0.87, 0.9,
       0.93, 0.96, 0.99, 1, ]
    keyValue [1 0 0 0, 0 1 0 -0.04729, 0 1 0 -0.181, 0 1 0 -0.3891,
     0 1 0 -0.6592, 0 1 0 -0.9793, 0 1 0 -1.337, 0 1 0 -1.721,
     0 -1 0 -4.166, 0 -1 0 -3.768, 0 -1 0 -3.381, 0 -1 0 -3.017,
     0 -1 0 -2.688, 0 -1 0 -2.407, 0 -1 0 -2.169, 0 -1 0 -1.925,
     0 -1 0 -1.675, 0 -1 0 -1.42, 0 -1 0 -1.163, 0 -1 0 -0.906,
     0 -1 0 -0.6508, 0 -1 0 -0.3999, 0 -1 0 -0.1554, 0 1 0 -0.08034,
     0 1 0 -0.3052, 0 1 0 -0.5169, 0 1 0 -0.7134, 0 1 0 -0.8923,
     0 1 0 -1.051, 0 1 0 -1.189, 0 1 0 -1.302, 0 1 0 -1.388,
```

```
    0 1 0 -1.446, 0 1 0 -1.474, 0 1 0 -1.475, ] },
    Transform {
     translation 0 23.19 0
     children [
      Shape {
        appearance Appearance {
         material Material {
          diffuseColor 0.6 0.8941 0.6
         }
        }
        geometry Box { size 10.96 46.39 48.68 }
      }
   ] }
  ]
ROUTE Box01-TIMER.fraction_changed TO Box01-ROT-INTERP.set_fraction
ROUTE Box01-ROT-INTERP.value_changed TO Box01.set_rotation
}
```

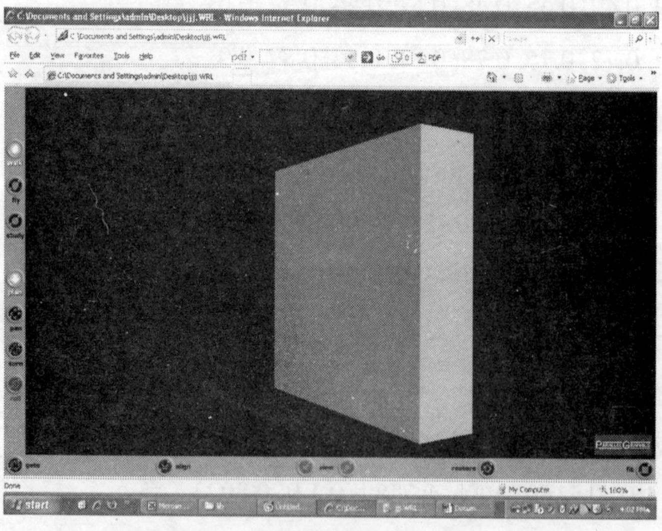

Screen Shot: 2

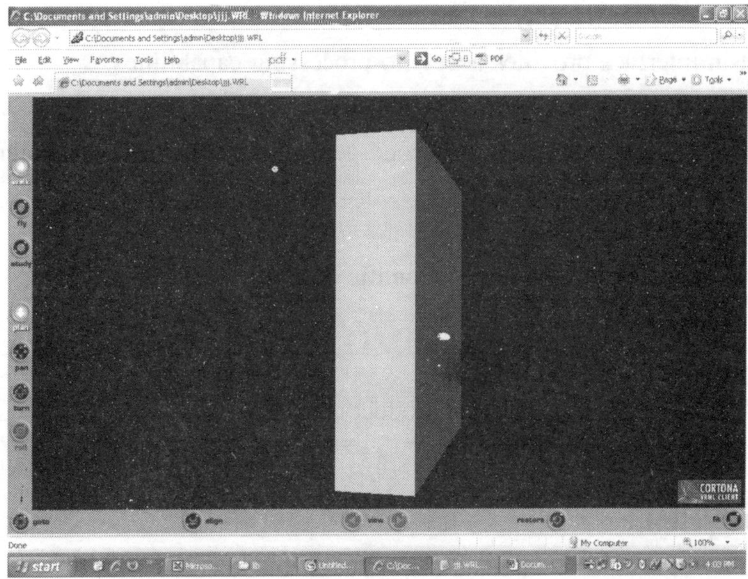

Screen Shot: 3

Application Areas of VRML

- Business
  - Data visualization
  - Product demonstration
  - Shopping
  - Virtual office
- Work
  - Simulation/Training
  - Collaborative design
  - Visualization
- Simulation
- Education
- Entertainment
  - Adventure
  - Gaming
- Others

Conclusion

- Virtual reality systems can enhance effectiveness & productivity at work, home, and play.
- Virtual space on the Internet can be easily modelled using VRML

  - VRML is a user-friendly language
  - Built-in interface provides access to processing capabilities:
    - VRMLScript, JavaScript, Java
- VRML provides the foundation for second-generation Web interfaces. Potential applications include:
  - Homespaces on the Web
  - Visualization of business and scientific data
  - Simulation and training
  - Multiuser online games
  - Collaborative projects such as product design
  - Educational programs

Drawbacks of VRML

- Low quality of shading (e.g. hand display with single colour)
- Low quality of shadow (e.g. book on a table)
- Anti-aliasing text processing power which consumes more memory and processing power (e.g. showing a smooth edge of an object like a book on a table).
- For smooth performance of the computer system a high speed processor like Dual Core is required.

12.3 APPLICATIONS OF VIRTUAL REALITY

The use of immersive Virtual Reality (VR) technology is a relatively recent trend enjoyed almost exclusively by the academic, military, and industrial research and development communities. However, as VR technologies mature, research is expanding from the realm of military and scientific visualization into more multidisciplinary areas, such as education, art, culture, and the humanities. As representative institutions involved in the research and presentation of these fields, museums, cultural centres, and entertainment venues may be in a better position to make use of advanced virtual reality technologies in order to investigate their educational potential while effectively shaping how they deliver public education and recreation.

Virtual Reality in a Museum

When used for cultural heritage purposes, a virtual reality exhibit may give scholars a completely new way of communicating the scientific results of archaeological investigation within the scientific community, also improving the way in which these results are communicated to the public. In addition to the fairly photorealistic representation of places, people and sites that do not exist, never existed, or may not be easily experienced, there are two basic advantages offered by virtual reality programs, namely the immersive experience and interactive capabilities that characterize this medium. Immersion is the illusion of being in the projected world, being surrounded by the image and sound in a way, which makes you believe that you are really there. It offers a "better than real life" or "better than being there" experience. Interaction refers to the fact that members of the audience are not merely a viewer of the realistic scenery, but can actively participate in the program and determine what their experience is.

Fig. 12.1 : A view of the Temple of Zeus at Olympia in virtual reality

By applying virtual reality many aspects, which may not actually survive at the present time, but of which there is some evidence, can be presented in the form in which they existed many centuries ago.

Fig. 12.2 : The famous statue of Zeus at Olympia as seen through the doors of the temple

Applications of Virtual Reality in War

The figures below help us to understand the application of virtual reality in war. How this project is creating an immersive virtual reality system for the treatment of war veterans diagnosed with combat. The treatment environment is based on a creative approach to recycling and adding to the virtual assets that were initially built for the combat tactical simulation and commercially available X-Box game, Full Spectrum Warrior.

City view

Desert view

Interior view

Helicopter view

Virtual Reality in Chemical Experiments

VR is a useful tool in the fields of engineering, science and education. Initially it was used in the areas of higher-dimensional scientific visualization and the development of virtual accident scenarios for the reduction of laboratory accidents.

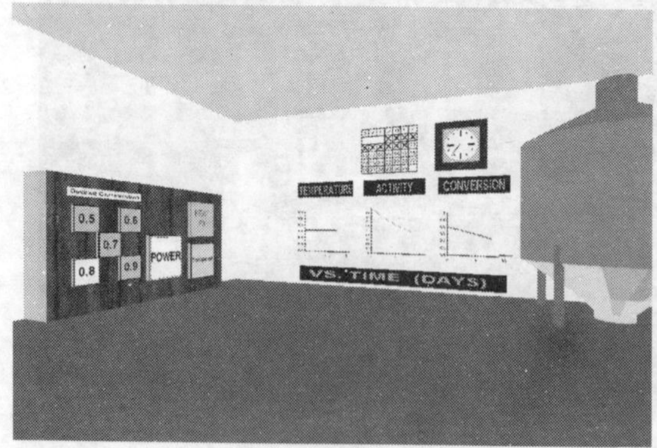

Reactor room

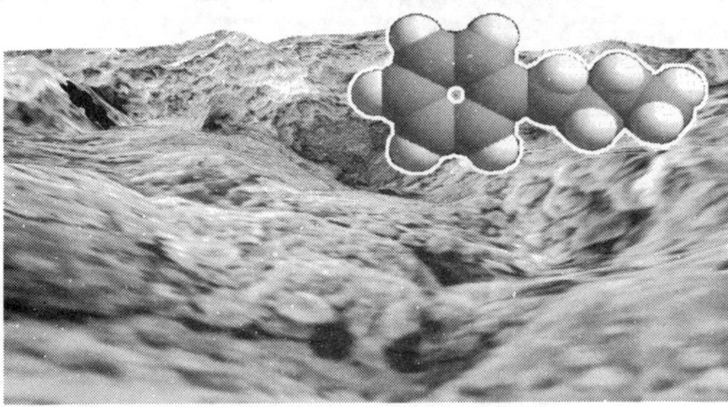

Close-up of the surface of a catalyst

Virtual Reality in Medical Diagnosis

Virtual Reality covers every aspect of human life. The human body is also a key sector to be worked on by Virtual Reality developers. This application is likely to be useful for medical science personnel, like doctors, researchers, students etc. It will also be useful for patients as it will give laypersons a better understanding of their ailments. For example it is difficult for a layperson to understand an x-ray film, but a view as shown below will be easy for him to comprehend.

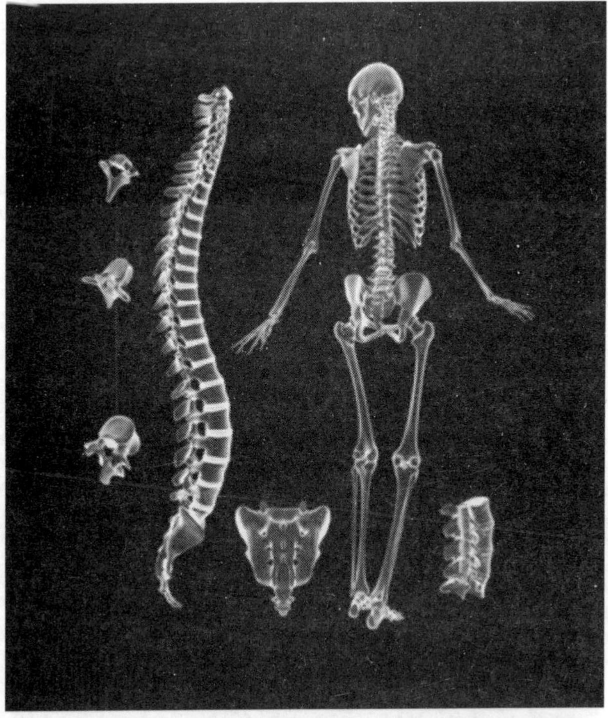

Fig. 12.3 : Skeleton layout of a man

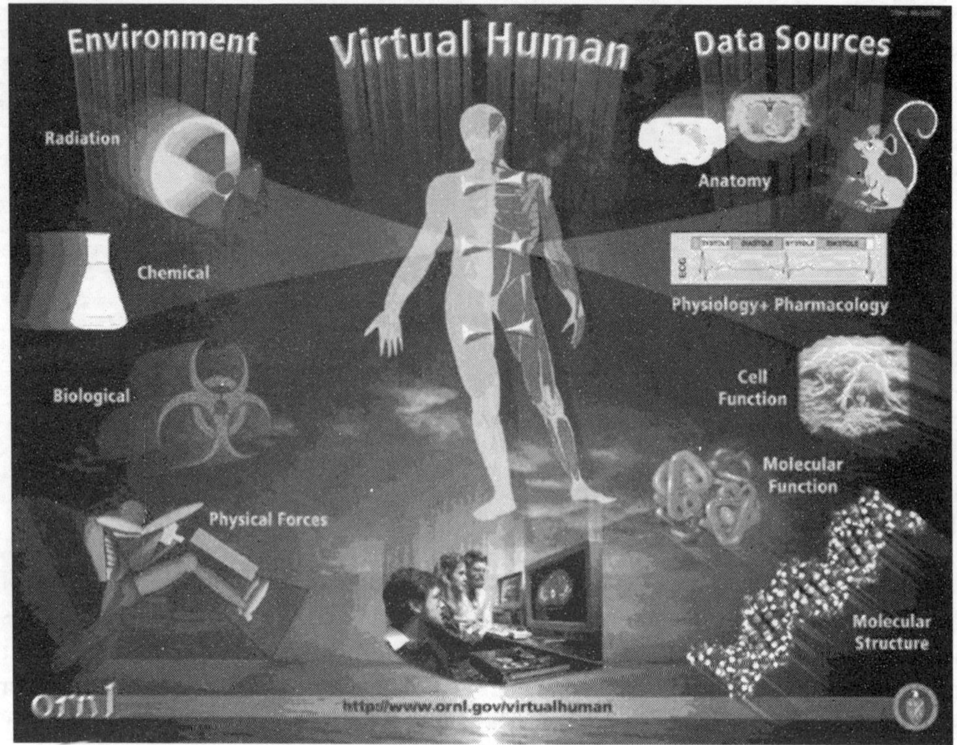

Fig. 12.4 : Muscle layout

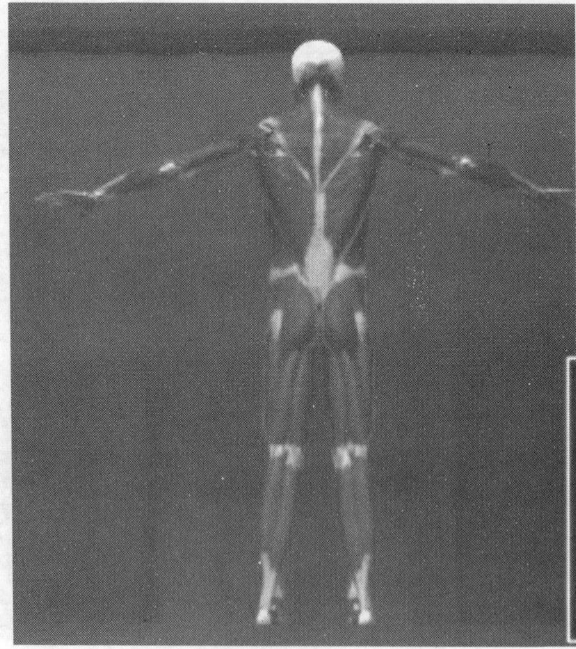

Muscle layout

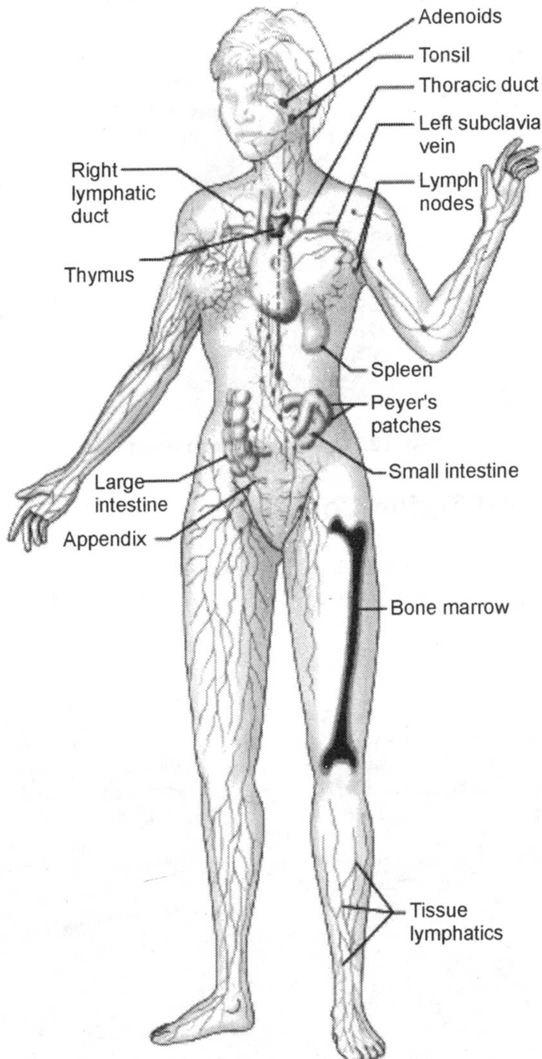

Fig. 12.5 : Virtual human representing body parts

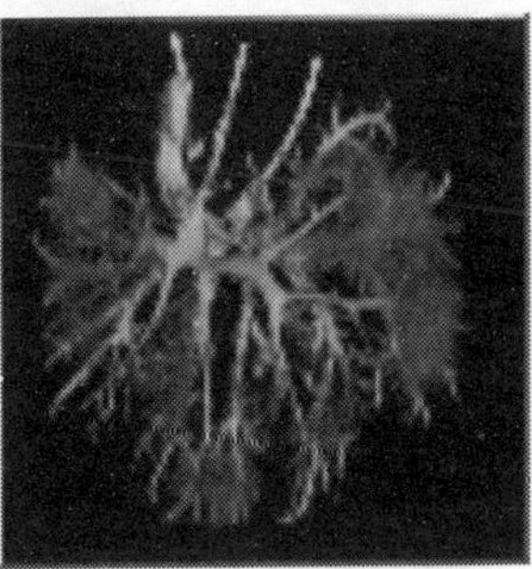

Fig. 12.6 : Visualization and interaction with the virtual liver

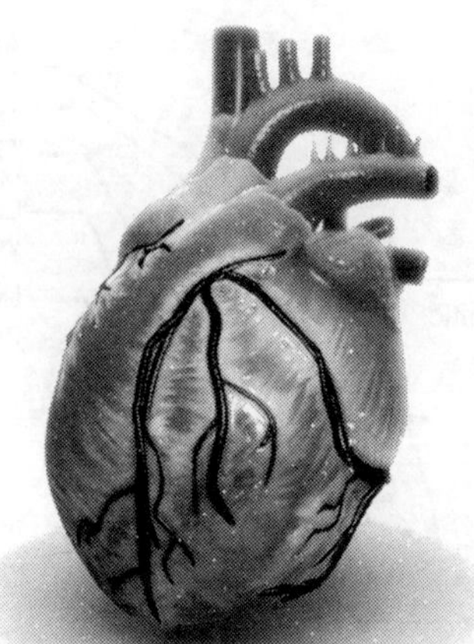

Fig. 12.7 : Virtual human heart

Virtual Reality for Airport Traffic Control

Airport authorities have to work on control and monitoring aeroplanes. Virtual reality will be very useful in helping the authorities to take decisions regarding the infrastructure and management of air ports, as well as training personnel.

Top view of an airport

Night scene at an airport

Virtual Reality for Disaster Training (Fire Fighting, Accidents)

Firemen face extremely difficult as well as hazardous situations, as they have to rescue persons, save lives and avert disasters. Virtual Reality is extremely useful in training personnel.

Virtual image of a disaster

Firefighter training process in Virtual Reality (Accident)

Firefighter training process in Virtual Reality

Virtual Reality for Home/Office Decoration

Arrangement of amenities and/or furniture in homes and offices always requires a lot of thought and usually involves a number of people. In addition the arrangements are often changed around before the final design is approved. This is an obvious use for Virtual Reality as it allows as many changes as one wants. It can also be used to decide the theme of a conference and its arrangement.

Conference planning

Virtual Reality for Intuition/Scientific Presentations

Some facts in nature cannot be seen with the naked eye, e.g. in the case of an iceberg only the portion above the water can be seen. Using the technique of Virtual Reality and applying the scientific method or intuition it is possible to present the whole iceberg within a frame.

Ice berg

Presentation of Scientific Data with Virtual Reality

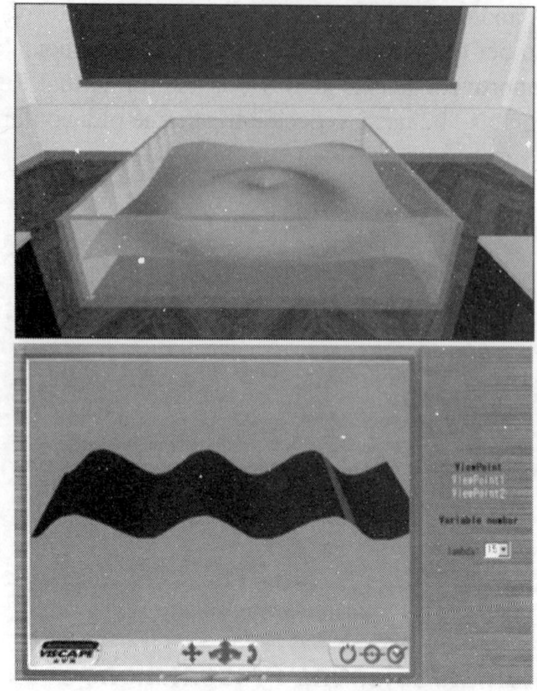

Water waves

Virtual Reality for Entertainment

There is a wide application of Virtual Reality in the entertainment sector. Almost all video games are designed using Virtual Reality. Some examples are shown below.

Golf

Man in hand

Virtual Reality for Maldives beach house

Virtual Reality for Training (Simulator)

A person stands in a virtual train station

A person driving a simulator for a virtual train track

Front view of a virtual cockpit

Complete view of a virtual cockpit

A trainee flying a virtual plane

A pilot working at a flight simulator

Virtual Reality for creating a City Environment

Virtual reality city environment (Road level view)

Virtual reality city environment (Building view)

Virtual reality city environment (Tunnel view)

Virtual reality city environment (Bridge view: Bottom)

Virtual reality city environment (Bridge view: Top)

VIRTUAL MAN

In future, many services may be offered with virtual humans, like reading the news, help desks at airports, railway stations, banking kiosks, entertainment, educational purposes etc. The user will be able to work easily following the instructions of the virtual human instructor.

It will also be possible in the fields of entertainment, games and education, where the user can interact with a virtual person. Learning from a virtual human may be an upcoming innovation in the sector of Virtual Reality.

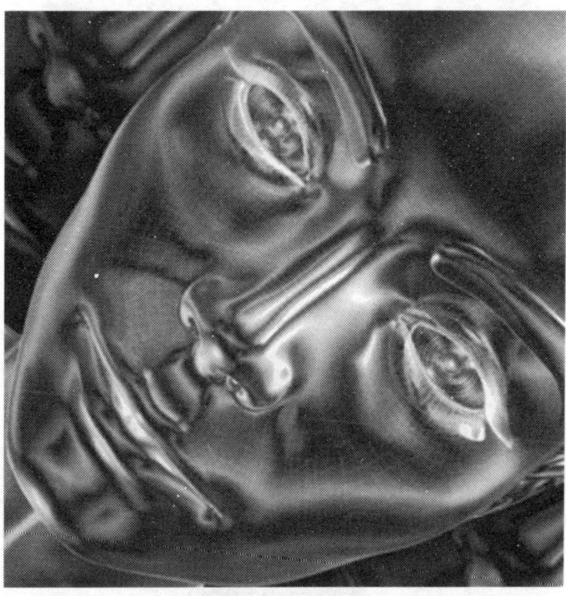

Virtual human (only a skeleton style layout)

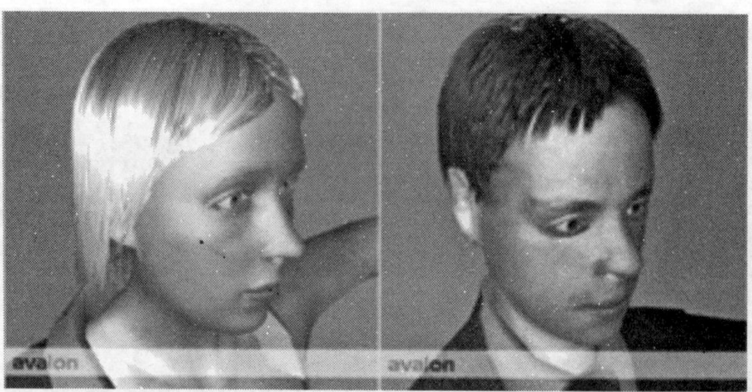

Virtual humans (exact human like design including clothes, hair, skin etc.)

Virtual human playing a game

Virtual human (instructor)

12.4 SUMMARY

- An artificial environment created by computers, in which people can immerse themselves and feel that this artificial reality really does exist. Virtual Reality (VR) creates a 'Cyber Space' where it is possible to interact with anything and anyone on a virtual level.
- As a computer screen presents data in two dimensions, data should be in the form of documents, charts, reports, Web pages, images or animation. However, this has the limitation that the entities shown do not appear real.
- To give the user the appearance of reality, Virtual Reality – Virtual Environment were initiated. The aim of a Virtual Environment is to provide an interface to user so that the entity appears the same as in the real world.
- Virtual Reality Modelling Language.
- VRML is a powerful text-based powerful language to build 'Virtual Worlds', which include 3D objects, light sources and animations. The user can interact with a 3D scene by viewing, moving, rotating and otherwise interacting with objects in the 3D scene.
- VRML is an open standard for 3D multimedia and shared virtual worlds on the Internet. It is a scene description language.
- The Virtual Reality Modelling Language is a file format for describing interactive 3D objects and worlds. VRML is designed to be used on the Internet, intranets, and local client systems. VRML is also intended to be a universal interchange format for integrated 3D graphics and multimedia.
- VRML may be used in a variety of areas such as engineering and scientific visualization, multimedia presentations, entertainment and educational titles, Web pages, and shared virtual world.
- VRML files can be viewed in a VRML viewer as well as in a HTML browser. A VRML Plug-in to a Web Browser supports loading of VRML files.
- If VRML Plug-ins are not installed in an HTML Browser, VRML data cannot be viewed. VRML files can be seen from a local hard disk as well as from the Internet.
- VRML is capable of representing static and animated dynamic 3D and multimedia objects with hyperlinks to other media such as text, sounds, movies and images.
- VRML browsers, as well as authoring tools for the creation of VRML files, are widely available for many different platforms.
- When used for cultural heritage purposes, a virtual reality exhibit may give scholars a completely new way of communicating the scientific results of archaeological investigation within the scientific community, also improving the way in which these results are communicated to the public.
- VR is a useful tool in engineering, science and education. Initially it was used in the areas of higher-dimensional scientific visualization and the development of virtual accident scenarios for the reduction of laboratory accidents.
- Virtual Reality covers every aspect of human life; the human body is a key sector for work by the Virtual Reality developer.

- Airport authorities have to work on control and monitoring aeroplanes. Virtual reality will be very useful in helping the authorities to take decisions regarding the infrastructure and management of air ports, as well as training personnel.
- Firemen face extremely difficult as well as hazardous situations, as they have to rescue persons, save lives and avert disasters. Virtual Reality is extremely useful in training personnel.
- Arrangement of amenities and/or furniture in homes and offices always requires a lot of thought and usually involves a number of people. In addition the arrangements are often changed around before the final design is approved. This is an obvious use for Virtual Reality as it allows as many changes as one wants.
- It can also be used to decide the theme of a conference and its arrangement.
- Some facts in nature cannot be seen with the naked eye, e.g. in the case of an iceberg only the portion above the water can be seen. Using the technique of Virtual Reality and applying the scientific method or intuition it is possible to present the whole iceberg within a frame.
- There is a wide application of Virtual Reality in the entertainment sector. Almost all video games are designed using Virtual Reality.

12.5 REVIEW QUESTIONS

1. Discuss the concept of virtual reality and virtual environments.
2. Discuss the history of virtual reality.
3. Explain in detail the features of VRML.
4. Discuss the application areas of the VRML.
5. Explain the drawback of VRML.
6. Discuss the applications of virtual reality.